Sir Arthur Helps

The Life of Las Casas

The Apostle of the Indies

Sir Arthur Helps

The Life of Las Casas
The Apostle of the Indies

ISBN/EAN: 9783337415075

Printed in Europe, USA, Canada, Australia, Japan

Cover: Foto ©Lupo / pixelio.de

More available books at **www.hansebooks.com**

PREFACE BY THE AUTHOR.

THE life of Las Casas appears to me one of the most interesting, indeed I may say the most interesting, of all those that I have ever studied; and I think it is more than the natural prejudice of a writer for his hero, that inclines me to look upon him as one of the most remarkable personages that has ever appeared in history. It is well known that he has ever been put in the foremost rank of philanthropists; but he had other qualifications which were also extraordinary. He was not a mere philanthropist, possessed only with one idea. He had one of those large minds which take an interest in everything. As an historian, a man of letters, a colonist, a missionary, a theologian, an active ruler in the Church, a man of business, and an observer of natural history and science, he holds a very high position amongst the notable men of his own age. The ways, the customs, the religion, the policy, the laws, of the new people whom he saw, the new animals, the new trees, the new herbs, were all observed and chronicled by him.

In an age eminently superstitious, he was entirely devoid of superstition. At a period when the most extravagant ideas as to the divine rights of kings prevailed, he took occasion to remind kings themselves to their faces, that they are only permitted to govern for the good of the people; and dared to upbraid Philip the Second for his neglect of Spanish and Indian affairs, through busying himself with Flemish, English, and French policy.

At a period when brute force was universally appealed to in all matters, but more especially in those that pertained to religion, he contended before Juntas and Royal Councils that missionary enterprise is a thing that should stand independent of all military support; that a missionary should go forth with his life in his hand, relying only on the protection that God will vouchsafe him, and depending neither upon civil nor military assistance. In fact his works would, even in the present day, form the best manual extant for missionaries.

He had certainly great advantages: he lived in most stirring times; he was associated with the greatest personages of his day; and he had the privilege of taking part in the discovery and colonization of a new world.

Eloquent, devoted, charitable, fervent, sometimes too fervent, yet very skilful in managing men, he will doubtless remind the reader of his prototype, Saint Paul; and it was very fitting that he should have been called, as he was, the " Apostle of the Indies."

Nothwithstanding our experience, largely confirmed by history, of the ingenuity often manifested in neglecting to confer honour upon those who most deserve it, one cannot help wondering that the Romish Church never thought of enrolling Las Casas as a saint, amongst such fellow-labourers as Saint Charles of Borromeo, or Saint Francis of Assisi.

His life is very interesting, if only from this circumstance, that, perhaps more than any man of his time, he rose to great heights of power and influence, and then, to use a phrase of his own, fell sheer down "into terrible abysses." His spirit, however, almost always rose indomitable: and the "abysses" did not long retain him as their captive.

Among his singular advantages must be mentioned his great physical powers, and tenacity of life. I do not remember that he ever mentions being ill. He exceeded in his journeyings his renowned master and friend, Charles the Fifth, and he lived fully as laborious a life as did that monarch.

When Charles, a youth of sixteen, came to the throne, Las Casas was a man of about forty, of great power and influence. He soon won the young king's attachment; during the whole of whose active life he worked vigorously with him at Indian affairs; and when, broken in health and in spirit, Charles retired to San Yuste, Las Casas was in full vigour, and had his way with Philip the Second, not, however, without the aid of the Imperial recluse. For almost the last business which Charles attended to was one in which the dying monarch gave his warm support to his friend Las Casas.

With Charles's grandfather, Ferdinand the Catholic, Las Casas had also worked at Indian affairs; and, with his usual sincerity, had not failed to inform that king of many truths which concerned his soul and the welfare of his kingdom.

Columbus, Cardinal Ximenes, Cortes, Pizarro, Vasco Nuñez, Gattinara the great Flemish statesman, were all known to Las Casas: in fact, he saw generations of notable men—statesmen, monarchs, inventors, discoverers, and conquerors—rise, flourish, and die; and he had continually to recommence his arduous conflict with new statesmen, new conquerors, and new kings. He survived Ferdinand fifty years, Charles the Fifth eight years, Columbus sixty years, Cortes nineteen years, Ximenes forty-nine years, Pizarro twenty-five years, and Gattinara thirty-seven years.

He was twenty-eight years old when he commenced his first voyage to the Indies; and he was still in full vigour, not failing in sight, hearing, or intellect, when, at ninety-two years of age, he contended before Philip the Second's ministers in favour of the Guatemalans having Courts of

Justice of their own. Having left the pleasant climate of Valladolid, doubtless excited by the cause he was urging, and denying himself the rest he required, he was unable to bear up against that treacherous air of Madrid, of which the proverb justly says, " though it will not blow out a candle, it will yet kill a man," and so, was cut off, prematurely, as I always feel, in the ninety-second year of his age.

His powers, like those of a great statesman of our own time, decidedly improved as he grew older. He became, I believe, a better writer, a more eloquent speaker, and a much wider and more tolerant thinker towards the end of his life. His best treatise* (in my judgment) was written when he was ninety years of age, and is even now, when its topics have been worn somewhat threadbare, a most interesting work.

To show that I have not exaggerated his great natural powers as well as his learning, I need only refer to his celebrated controversy with Sepulveda. This Sepulveda was then the greatest scholar in Spain, and was backed, more-

---

* On Peru.

over, by other learned men; but Las Casas was quite a match for them all. In argument he was decidedly superior. Texts, quotations, conclusions of Councils, opinions of fathers and schoolmen were showered down upon him. He met them all with weapons readily produced from the same armouries, and showed that he too had not in vain studied his Saint Thomas Aquinas and his Aristotle. His great opponent, Sepulveda, in a private letter describing the controversy, speaks of Las Casas as " most subtle, most vigilant, and most fluent, compared with whom the Ulysses of Homer was inert and stuttering." Las Casas, at the time of the controversy, was seventy-six years of age.

The reader of this introduction will perhaps think that if Las Casas is such a man as I have described, and his life is of such exceeding interest, it is strange that, comparatively speaking, so little has been heard about him. This, however, can be easily explained. His life can only be fully pourtrayed after reference to books, manuscripts, and official documents of the greatest rarity, not within the reach even of scholars, until recent years. The government of Spain has of late years thrown open to all students, in the most unreserved manner, its literary treasures, and afforded every facility for their study. In modern times, too, the Americans have taken great pains to investigate the early records of America, and have always been remarkably generous, in the use they have allowed to be made of the documents which they have rescued and brought together.*

There are few men to whom, up to the present time, the words which Shakespeare makes Mark Antony say of Cæsar, would more apply than to Las Casas:—

> " The evil that men do lives after them,
> The good is oft interred with their bones.'

At one inauspicious moment of his life he advised a course which has ever since been the one blot upon his well-earned fame, and too

---

* A short letter of Las Casas—of Las Casas who had very often not a maravedi in his pocket—has sometimes been bought by an enterprising American at a sum amounting to more than ten thousand maravedis, and the purchaser was but too glad if his purchase could be of any use to an historian.

often has this advice been the only thing which, when the name of Las Casas has been mentioned, has occurred to men's minds respecting him. He certainly did advise that negroes should be brought to the New World. I think, however, I have amply shown in the " Spanish Conquest" that he was not the first to give this advice, and that it had long before been largely acted upon. It is also to be remembered, that this advice, to introduce negroes, was but a very small part of his general scheme. Had that been carried into effect as a whole, it would have afforded the most efficient protection for negroes, Indians, and for all those who were to be subject to the Spanish Colonial Empire.

However, Las Casas makes no such defence for himself, but thus frankly owns his great error, saying, in his history, " This advice, that licence should be given to bring negro slaves to these lands, the Clerigo Casas first gave, not considering the injustice with which the Portuguese take them and make them slaves; which advice, after he had apprehended the nature of the thing, he would not have given for all he had in the world. For he always held that they had been made slaves unjustly, and tyrannically; for the same reason holds good of them as of the Indians."*

This one error must not be allowed to overshadow the long and noble career of one, who never, as far as I am aware, on any other occasion, yielded to worldly policy; who, for nearly sixty years, held fast to a grand cause, never growing weary of it; and who confronted great statesmen, potent churchmen, and mighty kings, with perfect fearlessness, in defence of an injured, a calumniated, and down-trodden race,—a race totally unable to protect themselves from the advance of a pseudo-civilization which destroyed as much as it civilized.

October, 1867.

---

* It is a curious fact in history, that this suggestion of Las Casas tended, as far as it was adopted, to check the importation of negroes into the New World. The licence to import was restricted, for a term of eight years, to the number of 4000, whereas the emperor had been requested to allow the importation of negroes without any restriction whatever.

The greater part of the subject-matter for this life is to be found in my " Spanish Conquest in America," but I am indebted to my son, Edmund Arthur Helps, for having utilized and added to it, with my assistance, in the preparation of the present biographical narrative.

CONTENTS.

Chapter I.
            Page

CHARACTER of Las Casas—His Parentage and Education—He joins with Narvaez in an Expedition to Cuba—He is summoned to Xagua 1

Chapter II.

The Conversion of Las Casas—His Voyage to Spain—He goes to Court—The Death of King Ferdinand   17

Chapter III.

Las Casas sees the Cardinal Ximenes—He is appointed to go out and inquire into the wrongs of the Indians, with the Jeronimite Fathers, and made " Protector of the Indians"—He returns to Spain   37

CHAPTER IV.

Page

Las Casas is introduced to the Grand Chancellor, and lays his Emigration Scheme before the King—His Plans are checked by the Death of the Chancellor—He holds a Controversy with the Bishop of Burgos . 55

CHAPTER V.

Las Casas brings forward his Plan for founding a Colony—After failing in gaining his point with the Council of the Indies, he goes to Court, and succeeds in obtaining full power to carry out his design . 92

CHAPTER VI.

Las Casas tries to detain Ocampo's Expedition—He complains to the Audiencia—He is put in command of an Expedition to the Terra-firma—His followers desert him on his arrival there 129

CHAPTER VII.

Las Casas alone in the land—He is received into the Franciscan Monastery—Fate of his Colony . . 144

CHAPTER VIII.

Las Casas becomes a Dominican Monk—He devotes himself to Literature 161

Chapter IX.

Las Casas in the Dominican Monastery—His Studies—He proposes to conquer the "Land of War" with the aid of his monks 178

Chapter X.

Las Casas succeeds in converting by peaceable means the "Land of War"—He is sent to Spain, and detained there by the Council of the Indies . . 199

Chapter XI.

Las Casas writes on Indian affairs—He is made Bishop of Chiapa—His troubles with his flock—He resigns the bishopric—His Controversy with Sepulveda . 232

Chapter XII.

Las Casas appeals to Philip II. through Carranza—He writes a Treatise on Peru—His Death—Review of his Life 277

THE LIFE OF LAS CASAS.

CHAPTER I.

Character of Las Casas—His Parentage and Education—He joins with Narvaez in an Expedition to Cuba—He is summoned to Xagua.

BARTHOLOMEW de Las Casas was the son of Antonio de Las Casas, one of Columbus's shipmates in his first voyage. Bartholomew was born at Seville in 1474. His father became rich, and sent him as a student to Salamanca, where he remained till he was eighteen, and took a licentiate's degree. We then hear nothing of importance concerning him till 1498, when he accompanied his father in an expedition under Columbus to the West Indies, returning to Cadiz with the expedition in 1500.

In 1502 he accompanied Nicholas de Ovando, a distinguished knight of Alacantara, who was going out to Hispaniola as governor of the Indies, was afterwards ordained priest,* and now, at the age of thirty-six, eight years after his arrival in the Indies, began to make his appearance on the stage of history. He was a very notable person, of that force of character and general ability, that he would have excelled in any career. Indeed, he did fulfil three or four vocations, being an eager man of business, a laborious and accurate historian, a great reformer, a great philanthropist, and a vigorous ecclesiastic. The utmost that friends or enemies, I imagine, could with the slightest truth allege against him, was an over-fervent temperament. If we had to arrange the faculties of great men, we should generally, according to our easy-working fancies, combine two characters to make our men of. And, in this case, we should not be sorry, if it might have been so, to have had a little of the wary nature of such a man as King Ferdinand the Second intermixed with the nobler elements of Las Casas. Considering, however, what great things Las Casas strove after, and how much he

---

* He sang the first "new mass" in the Indies, from which it appears that he was the first priest ordained there.

accomplished, it is ungracious to dwell more than is needful upon any defect or superfluity of his character. If it can be proved that he was on any occasion too impetuous in word or deed, it was in a cause that might have driven any man charged with it beyond all bounds of prudence in the expression of his indignation. His nature had the merit of being as constant as it was ardent. He was eloquent, acute, truthful, bold, self-sacrificing, pious. We need not do more in praise of such a character than show it in action.

In the whole course of West Indian colonization, a wise and humane forethought never could have been more wanted than at this period. Hispaniola was rapidly becoming depopulated of Indians, and on the mode of renewing the population, we may almost say, depended the future destinies of slavery. *A critical period in the West Indies.*

In the year 1511 the Admiral Don Diego Columbus, Ovando's successor as governor of Hispaniola, undertook the subjection of Cuba. He chose for his Captain, Diego Velazquez, one of the original conquerors, a man of wealth, whose possessions in Hispaniola were in that part of the island nearest to Cuba.

Las Casas joins Velazquez in an expedition to pacificate Cuba.

The earliest mention made of Las Casas in connection with West Indian history, is his being summoned by Diego Velazquez, to proceed to Cuba, where he arrived at the same time as Pamphilo de Narvaez, who had been selected by Velazquez as his lieutenant to join with Las Casas in the population and pacification— for such were the terms in vogue—of the island of Cuba.

One of the first expeditions of Narvaez was unsuccessful: it was in the province of Bayamo. He himself was nearly killed, and would never have escaped, but for the terror which his horse, an animal not hitherto seen by these Indians, inspired. These Indians, however, who had fled at the approach of the Spaniards, returned to beg pardon, and to be received into subjection. This appears astonishing, but may be easily explained. The territories into which they fled were occupied by other Indians, who had food enough for themselves only; and, therefore, after a brief sojourn, the unhappy fugitives, becoming most unwelcome guests, were tempted to return to their own country; for the Spaniards, though terrible visitors in other respects, did not at once create a famine in those parts which they occupied, by reason of the comparative smallness of their numbers.

By these means the province where the Spaniards first landed, called Maici, and the adjacent one of Bayamo, were brought into complete subjection; and the inhabitants were then divided into *repartimientos*,* and apportioned by Velazquez amongst his followers. After this Velazquez, who was about to be married, went to receive his bride, leaving his nephew, Juan de Grivalva, as his lieutenant (for Narvaez had not yet returned), and Las Casas as an adviser to the lieutenant. On the return of Narvaez, orders from Velazquez reached the place where Narvaez and Las Casas were stationed, directing them to make an expedition into the country of Camaguey, for the purpose of "assuring" it, to use their phrase. The

<small>Expedition of Las Casas and Narvaez, 1513 or 1514.</small>

---

* A *repartimiento* was a deed that ran thus:—"To you (such a one) is given an *encomienda* (or commandery) of so many Indians with such a Cacique, and you are to teach them the things of our Holy Catholic Faith." With respect to the implied condition of teaching the Indians the "Holy Catholic Faith," it was no more attended to from first to last than any formal clause in a deed which is supposed by the parties concerned to be a mere formality.

narrative of this expedition, which is given in full detail by Las Casas, an eye-witness and principal actor in the scene he describes, is very instructive.

And here I must say for Las Casas, that I have not the slightest doubt of the truth of any statement which he thus vouches for. He manifests throughout his writings, in various little things, his accuracy and truthfulness. For instance, he is careful to point out the exact pronunciation of the Indian names, and shows a fair appreciation of those persons he is most bitterly opposed to.

Nature of his testimony.

Before they reached the province of Camaguey they came to a place called Cueyba. This was the very spot where Ojeda—one of the explorers who followed Columbus—when shipwrecked, had left an image of the Virgin. Ojeda had been received with great kindness by the Indians in that vicinity, and the image which he left was now held in the highest reverence by the natives, who had built a church, adorning it inside with ornamental work made of cotton, and had set up an altar for the image. Moreover, they had composed couplets in honour of the Virgin, which they sang to sweet melodies, and accompanied with dancing. This image was also held in especial reverence by the Spaniards, and Las Casas being anxious on that account to obtain it in exchange for another image which he had brought with him, entered into treaty with the Cacique for that purpose. The Indian chief, however, was so alarmed at these overtures, that he fled by night, taking the beloved image with him. Las Casas, when he heard of this, was greatly disconcerted, fearing lest the neighbouring population should take up arms on behalf of their image. He managed, however, to quiet them, assuring them, that he would not only let them keep their own image, but that he would bestow upon them the one which he had brought with him.

Such gentle means as these were invariably pursued by Las Casas with the greatest effect; and it is evident from this story how very easy the conversion of the Indians would have been by mild means, instead of which it was made the pretext with some, and the real justification with others, for the greatest inhumanities.

The commands of Las Casas met with so much reverence from these simple people, that when he sent by a messenger any bit of paper inserted at

Las Casas reverenced by the natives of Cuba.

the end of a stick, and the messenger declared that the paper bore such and such orders, they were implicitly obeyed. The Indians had in general the greatest respect and wonder for the communication among the Spaniards by letter, for it appeared to them quite a miracle, how the information of what had been done in one place was made known in another by means of these mysterious pieces of paper.

One of the chief cares of the Clerigo (the title by which Las Casas describes himself) was, whenever they halted in any Indian town or village, to assign separate quarters to the Indians and the Spaniards. By this means he prevented many disorders and much cruelty. But his principal business was to assemble the children in order to baptize them; and, as he observes, there were many that God bestowed his sacred baptism upon in good time; for none, or scarcely any, of all those children remained alive a few months afterwards.

In the course of this journey of pacification, the Spaniards approached a large town of the Indians called Caonao, where an immense number of the natives had congregated together, chiefly to see the horses which the Spaniards brought with them. In the morning of the day on which the Spaniards under Narvaez and Las Casas, amounting to about a hundred men, arrived at Caonao, they stopped to breakfast in the dry bed of a stream where there were many stones suitable for grindstones; and they all took the opportunity of sharpening their swords. From thence a wide and arid plain led them to Caonao. They would have suffered terribly from thirst, but that some Indians kindly brought them water on the road. At last they reached Caonao at the time of vespers. Here they halted. The chief population of this Indian town and the vicinity was assembled together in one spot, sitting on the ground, and gazing, no doubt with wonder, at the horses of the Spaniards. Apart, in a large hut, were five hundred of the natives, who, being more timid than the others, were content to prepare victuals for their visitors, but declined any nearer approaches. The Spaniards had with them about a thousand of their own Indian attendants. The Clerigo was preparing for the division of the rations amongst the men, when suddenly a Spaniard, prompted, as was thought, by the Devil, drew his sword: the rest drew theirs; and immediately they all began to hack and hew the poor Indians, who were sitting quietly near them, and offering no more resistance than so many sheep. At the precise moment when the massacre began, the Clerigo was in the apartment where the Spaniards were to sleep for the night. He had five Spaniards with him: some Indians who had brought the baggage were lying on the ground, sunk in fatigue. The five Spaniards hearing the blows of the swords of their comrades without, immediately fell upon the Indians who had brought the baggage. Las Casas, however, was enabled to prevent that slaughter, and the five Spaniards rushed out to join their comrades. The Clerigo went also, and, to his grief and horror, saw heaps of dead bodies already strewed about, "like sheaves of corn," waiting to be gathered up. "What think you these Spaniards have been doing?" exclaimed Narvaez to Las Casas; and Las Casas replied, "I commend both you and them to the Devil."* The Clerigo did not stop, however, to

---

* "Que os ofresco á vos y á ellos el Diablo."—Las Casas, *Hist. de las Indias*, MS. lib iii. cap. 29.

bandy words with the Commander, but rushed hither and thither, endeavouring to prevent the indiscriminate slaughter which was going on, of men, women, and children. Then he entered the great hut, where he found that many Indians had already been slaughtered, but some had escaped by the pillars and the woodwork, and were up aloft. To them he exclaimed, "Fear not, there shall be no more slaughter — no more;" upon which, one of them, a young man of five-and-twenty, trusting to these words, came down. But, as Las Casas justly says, the Clerigo could not be in all places at once, and, as it happened, he left this hut directly, indeed, before the poor young man got down, upon which a Spaniard drew a short sword, and ran the Indian through the body. Las Casas was back in time to afford the last rites of the Church to the dying youth. To see the fearful wounds that were made, it seemed, the historian says, as if the Devil had guided the men that day to those stones in the dry bed of the river.

When inquiry was made as to who had been the author of this massacre, no one replied. This shows how causeless the massacre was, for if there

The massacre at Caonao causeless.

had been any good reason for it, the Spaniard who first drew his sword would have justified himself, and perhaps claimed merit for the action. It may have been panic in this one man; it may have been momentary madness, for such things are taken much less into account than is requisite; but, whatever the cause, the whole transaction shows the conduct of the Spaniards towards the Indians in a most unfavourable light.

<small>War, when most fatal in its consequences.</small>

The maxim, that the evil consequences of war depend, not so much upon the nature of the victory, or the rage of the combatants, or the cause of the quarrel, as upon the contempt, justifiable or not, which the victorious side has for the vanquished, seems to me applicable throughout history. The wars between nations that respect one another may have most sanguinary and cruel results, but not so injurious to humanity as when Spartan conquers Helot, Mahomedan conquers Christian, Spaniard conquers Moor or Indian; or as, in general, when one nation with much civilization, or much bigotry, conquers another nation of little civilization, or of another creed. The Romans may in some instances have offered a splendid exception to this rule; but in the general history of the world it holds good.

On the news of this massacre at Caonao,* all the inhabitants of the province deserted their towns, flying for refuge to the innumerable islets on that coast, called the " Garden of the Queen." The Spaniards, leaving the Indian town of Caonao, which they had desolated in the manner related above, formed a camp in the vicinity, or rather ordered the Indians to form it for them, for each Spaniard had at least eight or ten native attendants. Amongst those of Las Casas was an old Indian of much repute in the island, called Camacho, who had accompanied the Clerigo voluntarily, to be under his protection. One day, while the Spaniards were at this camp, a young Indian, sent as a spy from the former inhabitants of Caonao, came into tne camp, and making his way directly to the Clerigo's tent, addressed Camacho, begging to be taken into the Clerigo's service, and requesting that he might be allowed

{The Indians fly to the "Garden of the Queen."}

---

* " No quedó piante ni mamante."—Las Casas. A proverbial expression—" There remained neither the child that sucks nor the one that chirrups."

to bring his younger brother also. Camacho informed Las Casas of this, who was delighted with the news, as it gave an opportunity of communicating with those Indians who had fled. Accordingly he received the Indian very kindly, made him some trifling presents, and besought him to bring back his countrymen to their homes, and to assure them that they should not be further molested. The young man, to whom Camacho gave the name of Adrianico, took his leave, promising to bring his brother and the rest of the Indians. Some days passed away, and Las Casas began to think that Adrianico would not be able to perform his promise, when one evening he made his appearance with his brother and a hundred and eighty Indian men and women. Children are not mentioned, and I conjecture these Indians would not run the risk of bringing them within the power of the Spaniards.

It was a melancholy sight to see the little band of fugitives, with their small bundles of household things on their shoulders, and their strings of beads as presents for the Clerigo and the Spaniards, returning, perforce, for want of food— and perhaps too with some of that inextinguish-

People of Caonao return.

able fondness for home which endears so large a part of the world to its inhabitants—to the spot where they had but lately seen such cruelties perpetrated on their friends and relations. The Clerigo was delighted to see them, but very sad too, when he considered their gentleness, their humility, their poverty, and their sufferings. Pamphilo de Narvaez united with Las Casas in doing all he could to assure these poor people of their safety; and they were dismissed to their empty homes. This example of good treatment reassured the Indians of that vicinity, who in consequence returned to their houses.

The Spaniards pursued their purpose of pacificating Cuba, now taking to their vessels and coasting along the northern shore, and now traversing the interior of the country. When they came to the province of Havana, they found that the Indians, having heard of the massacre at Caonao and other such proceedings, had all fled; upon which Las Casas sent messengers to the different Caciques, the messengers bearing mysterious pieces of paper inserted at the end of sticks, which had before been found so efficacious, and assuring these Caciques of safety and protec-

Las Casas sends to the Caciques to assure them of safety.

tion. The result was, that eighteen or nineteen of these Caciques came and placed themselves in the power of the Spaniards; and it is an astonishing instance of the barbarity and folly of the Spanish captain Narvaez, that he put them in chains, and expressed an intention of burning them alive. Probably he thought that the province by this means, losing all its chiefs at one blow, would become hopeless and obedient. The Clerigo in the strongest manner protested against this monstrous treachery, to which he would have been so unwilling a party; and partly by entreaties, partly by threats, succeeded in procuring the release of all these Caciques except one, the most powerful, who was carried to Velazquez, but was afterwards set at liberty.

Las Casas joins Velazquez at Xagua.

This seems a strange method of assuring and pacificating the Indians; but their want of resources, and the absence of any experience of such war as they had now to encounter, if they made any resistance, caused them easily to succumb. The island of Cuba was now considered to be pacificated, and Pamphilo de Narvaez and Las Casas were ordered to join Velazquez at Xagua.

CHAPTER II.

The Conversion of Las Casas—His Voyage to Spain—He goes to Court—The Death of King Ferdinand.

LAS CASAS, as the reader will hereafter see, had many troubles and sorrows to bear; but at this particular period he was blessed with that which is always one of the greatest blessings, but which, like hospitality in a partially civilized country, seems to have flourished more, as being more needed, in rude, hard times. In a word, he had a real friend. This friend's name was Pedro de la Renteria. Their friendship was most intimate, and had subsisted for many years. De Renteria, as often happens in friendship, presented a curious contrast to Las Casas. He was a man who might well have been a monk—a devout, contemplative person, given much to solitude and

Las Casas had a friend.

C

prayer; and Las Casas mentions a trait in his character which exactly coincides with the rest of it, namely, that he was a most liberal man; but that his liberality seemed rather to flow from habit and a carelessness about worldly goods than from a deliberate judgment exercised in matters of benevolence. This good man's occupations, however, were entirely secular, and he was employed by Diego Velazquez as Alcalde.

<small>Partnership between Las Casas and Renteria.</small>

When the island was considered to be settled and the Governor began to give *repartimientos*, knowing the friendship that existed between Las Casas and Renteria, he gave them a large village in common, and Indians in *repartimiento*.* This land of theirs was about a league from Xagua, on the river Arimáo; and there they lived, the Clerigo

---

* "Dióle (á Pedro de Renteria) Indios de repartimiento juntamente con el Padre, dando á ambos un buen Pueblo y grande, con los cuales el Padre comenzó á entender en hacer grangerías y en echar parte de ellos en las minas, teniendo harto mas cuidado de ellas que de dar doctrina á los Indios, habiendo de sér como lo era principalmente aquel su oficio; pero en aquella materia tan ciego estaba por aquel tiempo el buen Padre como los Seglares todos que tenia por hijos."—LAS CASAS, *Hist. de las Indias*, MS., lib. iii. cap 32.

CONVERSION OF LAS CASAS. 19

having the greater part of the management of the joint affairs, as being much the more lively and the busier man. Indeed, he confesses that he was as much engaged as others in sending his Indians to the mines and making as large a profit of their labour as possible. At the same time, however, he was kind to them personally, and provided carefully for their sustenance; but, to use his own words, " he took no more heed than the other Spaniards to bethink himself that his Indians were unbelievers, and of the duty that there was on his part to give them instruction, and to bring them to the bosom of the Church of Christ."*

<small>Las Casas a busy, money-making man.</small>

As there was but one other clerigo in the whole island, and no friar, it was necessary for Las Casas occasionally to say mass and to preach. It happened that he had to do so on " the Feast of Pentecost," in the year 1514; and studying either the sermons that he preached himself, or that he heard the other clerigo preach at this time, he began to ponder over certain passages (" authorities" he calls them) of Scripture.

<small>Las Casas communes with himself.</small>

---

* LAS CASAS, *Hist. de las Indias*, MS., lib. iii. cap. 78

The 34th chapter of Ecclesiasticus, the 18th, 19th, 20th, 21st and 22nd verses, first arrested, and then enchained, his attention:—

"He that sacrificeth of a thing wrongfully gotten, his offering is ridiculous: and the gifts of unjust men are not accepted.

"The Most High is not pleased with the offerings of the wicked: neither is he pacified for sin by the multitude of sacrifices.

"Whoso bringeth an offering of the goods of the poor doeth as one that killeth the son before his father's eyes.

"The bread of the needy is their life; he that defraudeth him thereof is a man of blood.

"He that taketh away his neighbour's living slayeth him; and he that defraudeth the labourer of his hire is a bloodshedder."

I think that the Clerigo might have dwelt upon one of the remaining verses of the chapter with great profit:—

"When one prayeth, and another curseth, whose voice will the Lord hear?"

In recounting the steps which led to his conversion, Las Casas takes care to say, that what he had formerly heard the Dominicans preach in Hispaniola was, at this critical period of his life, of great service to him. Then he had only slighted their words; but he now particularly remembers a contest he had with a certain *Religioso*, who refused to give him absolution, because he possessed Indians. This is an instance of the great mistake it may be to hold your tongue about the truth, for fear it should provoke contest and harden an adversary in his opinion. The truths which he has heard sink into a man at some time or other: and, even when he retires from a contest, apparently fixed in his own conceits, it would often be found that if he had to renew the contest the next day, he would not take up quite the same position that he had maintained before. The good seed sown by the Dominicans had now, after having been buried for some years, found a most fruitful soil; and it shot up in the ardent soul of the Clerigo like grain in that warm land of the tropics upon which he stood. Las Casas studied the principles of the matter: from the principles he turned to considering the facts about him; and, with his candid mind thus fully aroused, he soon came to the conclusion that the system of *reparti-*

Good argument not lost upon men.

Las Casas convinced of the evil of *repartimientos*.

mientos was iniquitous,* and that he must preach against it.

What, then, must he do with his own Indians? Alas, it was necessary to give them up! Not that he grudged giving them up for any worldly motive, but he felt that no one in Cuba would be as considerate towards them as he, even in the days of his darkness, had been; and that they would be worked to death—as indeed they were. But still, the answer to all the sermons he might preach would be his own *repartimiento* of Indians. He resolved to give them up.

<small>Las Casas resolves to give up his own Indians.</small>

Now, as Las Casas was not only the friend, but the partner, of Pedro de Renteria, this determination on the part of the Clerigo was a matter which would affect the interests of his friend; and, unluckily, Renteria happened to be absent from home at this time, having gone to Jamaica

---

* " Pasados pues algunos dias en aquesta consideraçion, y cada dia mas y mas certificándola *por lo que leia cuánto al derecho, y via del hecho*, aplicándolo uno al otro, determinó en si mismo convencido de la misma verdad, ser injusto y tiránico todo cuanto cerca de los Indios en estas Indias se cometia."—LAS CASAS, *Hist. de las Indias*, MS., lib. iii. cap. 78.

upon their joint affairs. Las Casas, however, went to the Governor Velazquez, and laid open his mind to him upon the subject of the *repartimientos*, putting the matter boldly as it concerned his lordship's own salvation, as well as that of Las Casas and the rest of the Spaniards. The Clerigo added, that he must give up his own slaves, but wished that this determination might be kept secret till Pedro de Renteria should return. *[He informs the Governor.]*

The Governor was greatly astonished; for Las Casas, who, no doubt, took warmly in hand anything he did take up at all, passed for a man fond of gain, and very busy in the things of this world. Velazquez, in replying, besought the Clerigo to consider the matter well—to take fifteen days, indeed, to think of it—and to do nothing that he would repent of afterwards. Las Casas thanked his lordship for his kindness, but bade him count the fifteen days as already past; and added, that if he, Las Casas, were to repent, and were to ask for the Indians again, even with tears of blood, God would punish the Governor severely if he were to listen to such a request. Thus ended the interview; and it is to the Governor's credit that he ever afterwards held the Clerigo in greater esteem than before.

Las Casas, however, did not long confine his efforts at conversion to the Governor alone, nor did he conceal his intention until his partner had returned home; for, when preaching on the day of "The Assumption of Our Lady," he took occasion to mention publicly the conclusion he had come to as regards his own affairs, and also to urge upon his congregation in the strongest manner his conviction of the danger to their souls if they retained their *repartimientos* of Indians. All were amazed; some were struck with compunction; others were as much surprised to hear it called a sin to make use of the Indians as if they had been told it was sinful to make use of the beasts of the field.

Las Casas preaches against repartimientos.

After Las Casas had uttered many exhortations both in public and in private, and had found that they were of little avail, he meditated how to go to the fountain head of authority, the King of Spain. The Clerigo's resources were exhausted: he had not a *maravedi*,* or the means of getting one, ex-

---

* Equal to about two-thirds of a farthing.

CONVERSION OF LAS CASAS.

cept by selling a mare which was worth a hundred *pesos*.* Resolving, however, to go, he wrote to Renteria, telling him that business of importance was taking him to Castille, and that unless Renteria could return immediately, he, Las Casas, could not wait to see him—a thing, as he adds, not imaginable by the good Renteria, so firm was their friendship.

<small>Resolves to go to Spain.</small>

It was a singular coincidence that, not long before this time, the services of the Church had also brought into active existence very serious thoughts in the breast of Pedro de Renteria. There may be a community of thought not expressed in language; and, perhaps, these two good men, while apparently engaged in their ordinary secular business, had, unknown to themselves, been communicating to each other generous thoughts about their poor Indians, which had not hitherto been embodied in words. While Renteria was waiting in Jamaica for the despatch of his business, he went into a Franciscan monastery to spend his Lent in "retreat" (these pauses from the world are not to be despised!); and there thinking over the miseries

<small>A silent community of thought between the friends.</small>

---

* A *peso* was equivalent to four shillings and eight pence farthing.

of the Indians, the shape his thoughts had taken was, whether something for the children, at least, might not be done. Finally, he had come to the conclusion to ask the King's leave to found colleges where he might collect the young Indians, and have them instructed and brought up. For this purpose, Renteria resolved to go to Spain himself, in order to obtain the King's sanction; and, immediately after receiving the letter of the Clerigo, he hurried back to Cuba.

As the meeting of the friends took place in the presence of others, and as Renteria was welcomed back by the Governor in person, they had no opportunity for any explanation until they were alone together at night: then, in their dignified Spanish way, they agreed who should speak first, and after a friendly contention, the humble Renteria spoke first, which was the mark of the inferior. "I have thought sometimes," he said, "upon the miseries, sufferings, and evil life which these native people are leading; and how from day to day they are all being consumed, as the people were in Hispaniola. It has appeared to me that it would be an act of piety to go and inform the King of this—for he cannot

Conference between Las Casas and his friend Renteria.

know anything of it—and to ask him that at the least he should give us his royal licence to found some colleges, where the children might be brought up and taught, and where we may shelter them from such violent and vehement destruction."* Las Casas heard Renteria's words with astonishment and reverential joy, thinking it a sign of divine favour, that so good a man as Renteria should thus unexpectedly confirm his own resolve.

When it was the Clerigo's turn to speak, he thus began—"You must know, sir and brother" (for these people did not omit the courtesy which, however varied in its form, affection should not presume to dispense with), "that my purpose is no other than to go and seek a remedy for these unhappy men" (the Indians). The Clerigo then gave a full account of what he had already thought and done in this matter, during Renteria's absence. His friend replied in all humility, that it was not for him to go, but for Las Casas, who, as a lettered man (*letrado*), would know better how to establish what he should

They agree that Las Casas should go to Spain.

---

* LAS CASAS, *Hist. de las Indias*, MS., lib. iii. cap. 79.

urge. Renteria begged, therefore, that the stock and merchandize which he had just brought with him from Jamaica, and the farm, their joint property, might be turned into money to equip Las Casas for his journey and his stay at court; and he added, "May God our Lord be He who may ever keep you in the way and defend you."

The farm was sold, and in this manner Las Casas was provided for his journey. Bad as the world is said to be, there is always money forthcoming for any good purpose, when people really believe in the proposer.

At this time Pedro de Córdova, the prelate of the Dominicans in the New World, sent over four brethren of his order from Hispaniola to Cuba. They were very welcome to Las Casas, as he was to them. They listened with interest to his account of the state of the Indians in Cuba; and Brother Bernardo, the most eloquent and learned amongst them, preached to the same purpose and with fully as much animation, as the Clerigo himself had done. Their sermons terrified the hearers, but did not seem to change their way of proceeding. The Dominicans, ac-

First Dominicans in Cuba.

cordingly, resolved to send back one of their brotherhood, Gutierrez de Ampudia, to Pedro de Córdova, to inform him of the state of things at Cuba. It was arranged that Gutierrez should accompany Las Casas, who, by giving out that he was going to Paris, to study there and take a degree, contrived to leave Cuba without attracting the notice of the Governor, who might, perhaps, have detained him, had his true purpose and destination been known.

So Las Casas quitted the island of Cuba in company with Gutierrez de Ampudia and another Dominican, without being much observed by any one, or meeting with any hindrance.

Las Casas quits Cuba.

After their departure from the island, the cruelties of the Spaniards towards the Indians increased; and, as the Indians naturally enough sought for some refuge in flight, the Spaniards trained dogs to pursue them. The Indians then had recourse to suicide as a means of escape, for they believed in a future state of being, where ease and felicity, they thought, awaited them. Accordingly they put themselves to death, whole families doing so together, and villages inviting other villages to join them in their departure

Suicide of the Indians.

from a world that was no longer tolerable to them. Some hanged themselves; others drank the poisonous juice of the Yuca.

One pathetic and yet ludicrous occurrence is mentioned in connection with this practice of suicide amongst the Indians. A number of them belonging to one master had resolved to hang themselves, and so to escape from their labours and their sufferings. The master being made aware of their intention, came upon them just as they were about to carry it into effect. "Go seek me a rope, too," he exclaimed, "for I must hang myself with you." He then gave them to understand that he could not live without them, as they were so useful to him; and that he must go where they were going. They, believing that they would not get rid of him even in a future state of existence, agreed to remain where they were; and with sorrow laid aside their ropes to resume their labours.

Meanwhile, Las Casas and his companions were pursuing their journey, having arrived at the port of Hanaguana, in Hispaniola. Father Gutierrez, unhappily, fell ill of a fever and died on the road; but Las Casas reached St. Domingo in safety. On arriving there, he found that the Prelate of the Dominicans was absent, having just commenced a voyage for the purpose of founding monasteries in the Terra-firma, being accompanied not only by monks of his own order, but also by Franciscans, and by some monks from Picardy, who had lately come to the Indies. {Las Casas arrives at St. Domingo.}

It happened that a great storm compelled the Prelate and his company to return to port; and thus Las Casas was fortunate enough to obtain an interview with one of whom he ever speaks with great veneration, the Prelate of the Dominicans, Pedro de Córdova.

This excellent monk received Las Casas very kindly, and applauded his purpose greatly, but at the same time gave but little hope of its being brought to a successful termination in King Ferdinand's time, on account of the credit which, he said, the Bishop of Burgos and the Secretary, Lope Conchillos, had with the King, and their being entirely in favour of the system of *repartimientos*, and moreover possessing Indians themselves. {Interview between Las Casas and De Córdova.}

The Clerigo, grieved but not dismayed at

these words, declared his intention to persevere, to the delight of Pedro de Córdova, who, as the Dominican monastery was very poor, and only partly built, resolved to send Antonio Montesino, one of his monks, in company with Las Casas to the King, to solicit alms for completing the building. Moreover, if any opportunity should offer, he was to aid the Clerigo in his mission. And so, in September, 1515, Las Casas, Montesino, and another brother embarked at St. Domingo for Spain.

Las Casas embarks for Spain. Sept. 1515.

After their arrival at Seville, Montesino presented Las Casas to the Archbishop of Seville, Don Fray Diego de Deza, a prelate in great favour with King Ferdinand, who had been persuading the King to come to his diocese, as being an excellent climate for the aged. This advice Ferdinand had listened to, and was now making his way from Burgos to the South of Spain. The Archbishop received Las Casas graciously, and furnished him with letters to the King and to some of the courtiers. Armed with these letters, the Clerigo continued his journey, and found the King at Plasencia, arriving there a few days

Las Casas arrives at Seville.

before Christmas in the year 1515. Las Casas shunned the ministers Lope de Conchillos and the Bishop of Burgos, knowing how prejudiced they were likely to be; but he sought an interview with the King, and, obtaining it, spoke at large to the Monarch of the motives which had brought him to Spain. He had come, he said, to inform his Highness of the wrongs and sufferings of the Indians, and of how they died without a knowledge of the Faith and without the Sacraments, of the ruin of the country, of the diminution of the revenue; and he concluded by saying, that as these things concerned both the King's conscience and the welfare of his realm, and as to be understood they must be stated in detail, he begged for another and a long audience. Ferdinand, now an old and ailing man, whose death was near at hand, did not deny Las Casas the second audience he asked for, but said he would willingly hear him some day during the Christmas Festival. *Las Casas sees King Ferdinand. Dec. 1515.*

In the mean time, Las Casas poured his complaints against the King's ministers, and his narrative of the wrongs of the Indians, into the ears of the King's Confessor, Tomas de Matienzo, *Las Casas gains the King's Confessor.*

who, repeating them to the King, received orders to tell Las Casas to go to Seville and wait there for the King's coming (Ferdinand was about to set off immediately), when he would give him a long audience, and provide a remedy for the evils he complained of. The Confessor advised Las Casas to see the Bishop of Burgos,* who had the chief management of Indian affairs, and also Con-

---

* The Bishop of Burgos was one of those ready, bold, and dexterous men, with a great reputation for fidelity, who are such favourites with princes. He went through so many stages of preferment, that it is sometimes difficult to trace him; and the student of early American history will have a bad opinion of many Spanish bishops, if he does not discover that it is Bishop Fonseca who re-appears under various designations. He held successively the Archdiaconate of Seville, the Bishoprics of Badajoz, Córdova, Palencia, and Conde, the Archbishopric of Rosano (in Italy), with the Bishopric of Burgos, besides the office of Capellan mayor to Isabella, and afterwards to Ferdinand.

The Indies had a narrow escape of having him for their Patriarch. In the year 1513, Ferdinand instructed his ambassador at Rome to apply for the institution of a universal patriarchate of the Indies to be given to Archbishop Fonseca.

What answer the Pope gave to this application does not appear; but it is at any rate satisfactory to find that Bishop Fonseca was not appointed Patriarch of the Indies.

chillos, for, as he observed, the matter would ultimately have to come into their hands; and, perhaps, when they had heard all the miseries and evils which the Clerigo could tell them, they would soften. Las Casas, to show that he was not obstinate, sought out these ministers, and submitted his views and his information to them. Conchillos received the Clerigo with the utmost courtesy and kindness, and seems to have listened a little to what Las Casas had to tell him: the Bishop, on the contrary, was very rough. Las Casas finished his audience with the Bishop by informing him how seven thousand children had perished in three months;* and, as the Clerigo went on detailing the account of the death of these children, the ungodly Bishop broke in with these words, " Look you, what a droll fool; what is this to me, and what is it to the King?" To which Las Casas replied: "Is it nothing to your Lordship, or to the King, that all these souls should perish? Oh great and eternal God! And to whom then is it of any concern?" And, having said these words, he took his leave.

Interview between Las Casas and the Bishop of Burgos.

---

* I do not know to what transaction he alludes.

Considering the number of excellent churchmen whose conduct comes out nobly in the discovery and colonization of the Indies, it is not surprising that we should meet with one bad bishop; but it is almost heartbreaking to consider, that it is *the* one who could have done more than all the rest to redress the wrongs of the Indians, and to recover affairs in the New World. Let men in power see what one bad appointment may do!

Las Casas departs for Seville. Las Casas soon after left the court for Seville, where almost the first thing he heard of on his arrival, was the death of the King, which took place at Madrigalejos, a little village on the road to Seville, on the 23rd of January, 1516.

CHAPTER III.

Las Casas sees the Cardinal Ximenes—He is appointed to go out and inquire into the wrongs of the Indians, with the Jeronimite Fathers, and made "Protector of the Indians"— He returns to Spain.

AS soon as Las Casas heard of the King's death, he prepared to go to Flanders, to produce what impression he could upon the new King; but, previously to taking this step, he went to Madrid, to lay his statement of the wrongs of the Indians before the Cardinal-Governor Ximenes, and the Ambassador Adrian. They were governing conjointly, Ximenes having been appointed regent by Ferdinand during the minority of Charles the Fifth, and Adrian of Utrecht (who had been Charles's tutor) having been instructed by the young King to act in concert with the Cardinal.

Las Casas resolved to let them know of his intended journey, and to tell them that if they could remedy the evils he complained of he would stay with them; if not, he would go on to Flanders.

He drew up his statement in Latin, and began by laying it before Adrian. That good man was horrified at what he read; and without delay he went into the apartment of the Cardinal (for the two great men were lodged in the same building), to ask him if such things could be. The result of the conference was, that Las Casas was informed by Ximenes that he need not proceed to Flanders, but that a remedy for the evils he spoke of should be found there, at Madrid.

Las Casas sees Ximenes.

The associates whom the Cardinal took into council, to hear what Las Casas had to tell of Indian affairs, were the Ambassador Adrian, the Licentiate Zapata, Dr. Caravajal, Dr. Palacios Rubios, and the Bishop of Avila. These important personages summoned the Clerigo many times before them, and heard what he had to say. In the course of these hearings a curious circumstance took place, which is well worth recording. During one of these juntas* the cardinal ordered that the laws of Burgos (the last laws made touching the Indians) should be read. It is a slight circumstance, but serves to give some indication of the excellence of the Cardinal as a man of business and a member of a council, that he should wish to know exactly where the matter was, and what they were to start from. The Clerk of the Junta, an old retainer of Conchillos, when he came to the law about giving a pound of meat to the Indians on Sundays and feastdays, probably thinking that this in some way touched himself or his friends, read it wrongly. Las Casas, who knew the laws almost by heart, at once exclaimed, "The law does not say that." The Cardinal bade the clerk read it again. He gave the same reading. Las Casas said again, "That law says no such thing." The Cardinal, annoyed at these interruptions, exclaimed, "Be silent, or look to what you say." But Las Casas was not to be silenced by fear, when he knew himself to be in the right. "Your Lordship may order my head to be cut off," he exclaimed, "if

A junta to hear Las Casas.

---

* A junta was a council.

what the clerk reads is what the law says." Some members of the Council took the papers from the clerk's hands, and found that Las Casas was right. "You may imagine," he adds, "that that clerk (whose name, for his honour's sake, I will not mention) wished that he had not been born, so that he might not have met with the confusion of face he then met with." Las Casas concludes by remarking, "that the Clerigo lost nothing of the regard which the Cardinal had for him, and the credit which he gave to him."

Ximenes appoints Las Casas and Dr. Palacios to draw up a plan.

The result of these meetings was, that the Cardinal appointed Las Casas and Dr. Palacios Rubios, who had all along shown great interest in favour of the Indians, to draw up a plan for securing their liberty and arranging their government. At the request of Las Casas, Antonio Montesino was afterwards added to this committee. Their way of proceeding was as follows. Las Casas, as the more experienced in the matter, made the rough draft of any proposition, which he then showed to Antonio Montesino, who generally approved it, then to the doctor, who did the same, except that he perhaps added to it, and put it in official language. It was then taken to the

Cardinal and the Ambassador; and council held upon it.

The thing to be done and the mode of doing it were thus after much labour arrived at: the legislation was accordingly complete. And now the persons who were to have the great charge of administering the law had to be sought out. The Cardinal bade Las Casas find these persons; but the Clerigo, from his absence for so long a time from Castille, did not know fit persons, and begged to give the commission back into the Cardinal's hands, presenting at the same time a memorial in which he stated what in his opinion were the qualifications for the office in question. The Cardinal, smiling, observed to Las Casas, "Well, Father, we have some good persons."

The Cardinal resolved to look for his men amongst the Jeronimite monks, on account of their not being mixed up with the contention that had already taken place between the Franciscans and Dominicans touching the fitness of the Indians for freedom. Ximenes, accordingly, wrote to that effect to the General of the Order, who called a chapter, when twelve of the brethren were named, and a deputation of four priors was sent to the Cardinal to inform him of the nomination.

Jeronimites chosen to administer the law.

Las Casas, who was naturally anxious about the answer of the Jeronimites, went one Sunday morning to hear mass at their convent near to Madrid. There he found a venerable man praying in the cloister: upon asking him whether there was any reply to the Cardinal's missive, the old man told him, that he was one of the priors who had brought an answer, that they arrived last night, and that the Cardinal, having been made aware of their arrival, was to come to the convent that day.

Four of their priors come to Madrid.

Accordingly, in the course of the day, the Cardinal and Adrian came with a cavalcade of courtiers to the convent. The monks received the Junta in the sacristy, the main body of the courtiers remaining outside in the choir; amongst them, doubtless to his no small chagrin, the Bishop of Burgos, long accustomed to direct Indian affairs, but now of no authority in them.

Proceedings at the Jeronimite monastery.

The Cardinal, after thanking the Order for the tenor of their reply, and magnifying the work in hand, desired Las Casas to be called for, who, with great delight, walked through the assembled courtiers, much regarded by them, but most of all, as he conjectures, by the Bishop of Burgos.

Entering the sacristy, Las Casas knelt down before the Cardinal, who told him to thank God that the desires which God had given him were in the way of being accomplished. The Cardinal then informed him that the priors had brought twelve names of persons who might be chosen for the work, but that three would suffice. His Eminence added, that this night Las Casas should have letters of credit to the General of the Jeronimites and money for his journey, and that he was to go and confer with that Prelate about the choice of the three, informing the General of the requisite qualities for the office in question. Las Casas was then to bring to court the first Jeronimite of the chosen three whom he should find ready to accompany him. The despatches should thereupon be prepared, after which he might at once set off with them* for Seville.

Las Casas obtains letters of credit to the Jeronimite General.

We may observe throughout that nothing lingers in the Cardinal's hands. Commonplace statesmen live by delay, believe in it, hope in it,

---

* "Y habido el primero que de los tres mas presto hallaredes, venios con él á esta Corte, y hacerse han los Despachos, y de camino para Sevilla los podeis despues llevar."
—Las Casas, *Hist. de las Indias*, MS., lib. iii. cap. 85.

pray to it: but his Eminence worked as a man who knew that the night was coming, "in which no man can work."

Las Casas, almost in tears with joy, poured out his thanks and blessings on the Cardinal, and concluded by saying, that the money was not necessary, for that he had enough to sustain him in this business. The Cardinal smiled, and said, "Go to, Father, I am richer than you are." (*Andá, Padre, que yo soy mas rico que vos*). And then Las Casas went out, "the Cardinal saying many favourable things of some one who shall be nameless."[*]

The Clerigo received his letters, conferred with the General of the Order of St. Jerome, and three brethren were chosen. Their names were Luis de Figueroa, Prior of La Mejorada; Alonso de Santo Domingo, Prior of the Convent of Ortega; and Bernardino Manzanedo.

<small>The Jeronimites at Madrid.</small> Las Casas brought with him Bernardino Manzanedo to Madrid; the other two joined him there, and they all lived with him at his inn.

---

[*] "Diciendo multa favorabilia de Johanne." — L<small>AS</small> C<small>ASAS</small>, *Hist. de las Indias*, MS., lib. iii. cap. 85.

Afterwards, however, they went to a hospital of their own Order in that city. While staying there, they were waylaid, so to speak, by the agents for the Spanish colonists, who told them all manner of things against the Indians, and spoke ill of Las Casas; and, in the end, succeeded, as he thinks, in prejudicing the minds of the Fathers to that extent, that even before they set out, Las Casas and Dr. Palacios Rubios began to think that no good would come of this mission, which promised at the first so well.

The preparations, however, for their departure went on, and their orders and instructions were made ready. The first order was a *cedula*, to the effect that, on their arrival at St. Domingo, they should take away all the Indians belonging to members of the Council, or to any other absentees. The second was, that they should also deprive the judges and officers in the Indies of their Indians. The third was, that they should hold a court of impeachment upon all the judges and other officers in the colony, "who had lived, as the saying is, ' as Moors without a king.'"

Then came the main body of instructions, which I will not quote here, and concerning which it is sufficient to say that Las Casas was dissatisfied with many of them, and especially with regard to the compulsory* working at the mines, and the payment to be demanded from the Indians for whatever cattle and implements were to be furnished them. He was also averse to the provision for the capture of the Caribs, and declared that all these things were inserted contrary to his wishes. I hardly see how, without prophetic vision, any body of statesmen of that time, who had not themselves been in the Indies, could have been wise and foreseeing enough to leave the Indians alone in their settlements, not compelling them to go to the mines, but looking forward to the time when they would become civilized and taxable communities.

Las Casas' instructions and difficulties.

---

* The words of Las Casas on this subject, though somewhat unpractical, are very remarkable for the noble spirit they indicate:—"Y solo el pensamiento de que habian por fuerza de andar en las Minas la tercera parte bastaba para del todo acaballos. Manifiesto es que se les habia de dar las Haciendas y los Ganados y lo demas de valde para que comenzaran á respirar y saber que cosa era LIBERTAD (*sic* in MS.), ó á costa del Rey, ó de los Españoles que de ellos con tanto riesgo de sus vidas se habian aprovechado."— LAS CASAS, *Hist. de las Indias*, MS., lib. iii. cap. 88.

The despatches for the Jeronimite Fathers being now concluded, other matters connected with this great proposed reform were brought to a close. Las Casas was by a *cedula* formally appointed to advise and inform the Jeronimite Fathers, to be in correspondence with the government, and generally to take such steps in the matter as might be for the service of God and their Highnesses. All authorities were to abet him in the same. He was also named " Protector of the Indians," with a salary of a hundred *pesos* of gold, which he himself observes, " was then not little, as that hell of Peru " (*infierno del Peru*) " had not been discovered, which, with its multitude of *quintals* of gold, has impoverished and destroyed Spain." These are remarkable words for that time.

<small>Las Casas appointed Protector of the Indians.</small>

It now only remained that the legal part of the reform contemplated by Ximenes should be provided for. To ensure this, the Cardinal chose a lawyer of repute named Zuazo, giving him very large powers. He was to take a *residencia** of

---

* To take a *residencia* was equivalent to making an inquiry concerning, or calling to account, a public officer.

all the Judges in the Indies, and what was of more importance, his decisions were not to be appealed against. The Licentiate Zapata and Dr. Caravajal called these powers exorbitant, and refused to give their signature, which was necessary, to the instructions. This led to much delay. Zuazo threatened to return to Valladolid, saying, if he once returned to his college, no one should get him out of it again. Upon this Las Casas hurried off to the Cardinal, who supposed that Zuazo had already gone upon his mission, when the Clerigo informed his Eminence of the delay and the cause of it. The Cardinal, who, as Las Casas then observes, was not a man to be played with (*ninguno con él se burlaba*), sent for the Licentiate Zapata and Dr. Caravajal, and bade them in his presence sign all the provisions of the powers for Zuazo: which they did, putting, however, a certain private mark to their signatures, which was to denote what they intended afterwards to say, namely, that the Cardinal had forced them to sign.

Zuazo appointed.

At last, all was ready for these seeds of well-devised legislation to be taken out and sown in the Indies. Las Casas went to take leave of

Ximenes and to kiss hands. He could not on this occasion refrain from uttering his mind to the Cardinal, telling him that the Jeronimite Fathers would do no good thing, and informing him of their interviews with the agents from the colonies. It moves our pity to think that the sick old man, wearied enough with rapacious Flemish courtiers and untameable Spanish grandees, should now be told, after he had given so much time and attention to this business of the Indies, that the mission would do no good. Well may Las Casas add, that the Cardinal seemed struck with alarm; and that, after a short time, he said, " Whom then can we trust? You are going there: be watchful for all." Upon this, after receiving the Cardinal's benediction, Las Casas left for Seville.

Las Casas takes leave of the Cardinal.

The Jeronimite Fathers and the Clerigo then commenced their voyage,—in different vessels, however, for probably being somewhat tired of his discourses, and perhaps not wishing to alarm the colonists more than could be helped by being seen in such close contact with one so odious to them as Las Casas, the Fathers had contrived on some

E

pretext to prevent his going with them, though he much wished it; and when they arrived at St. Domingo, they seemed inclined there, too, to take a separate course from what he thought right. He speaks of them as gained over by the shrewd official men they fell amongst, such as the Treasurer Pasamonte. In discourse with Las Casas, the Fathers began, he says, to gild over and excuse the inhumanity of the colonists; and what was a shameful defect in their mode of proceeding according to his view of the case, they did not put in execution the charge they had received, to take away the Indians from the Spanish Judges and men in office, though they deprived the absentees of their Indians.

[margin: The Jeronimites arrive at St. Domingo. Dec. 1516.]

In three months' time Zuazo arrived. Las Casas now resolved on a bold, perhaps we may say, a violent step, though if we had been eye-witnesses of the cruelties that he had seen, our indignation, like his, might not always have been amenable to prudence. He resolved, himself, to impeach the Judges.* To use his own phrase, he brought against them a tremendous accusation

[margin: Las Casas impeaches the Judges.]

---

* The " Jueces de apelacion."

(*púsoles una terrible acusacion*), both in respect to their conduct in bringing Indians from the Lucayan islands, and also in reference to the infamous proceedings connected with an incident in Cumaná, where two poor Dominicans were left to be murdered by the natives. Certainly, if any charges were to be made against these Judges, it must be admitted that the subjects of accusation were well chosen.

The Jeronimite Fathers were much grieved at this bold step being taken by Las Casas. They evidently wished to manage things quietly; and were proceeding mainly with the second class of remedies for the Indians, giving them in *repartimiento* to such of the colonists as they thought well of, and publishing the orders for ameliorating the condition of the subject people. The Fathers seem on the whole to have made great efforts to do good, which must not pass without due recognition. I think with Las Casas, that if they had ventured to adopt the scheme, which he, Dr. Palacios Rubios, and Antonio Montesino, had planned (the main points of which were, the doing away with the system of *repartimientos* and compulsory working at the mines), it would have been better; and there is no doubt that, while Ximenes lived, they would have had a sufficiently powerful protector to enable them to carry out such a measure. But, though not determined enough to carry out such a bold undertaking, which few men, indeed, would have had courage for, and leaving many of the colonists in possession of their Indians, they still made great efforts to carry out the second class of measures for the relief of the Indians and the benefit of the colony.

Las Casas may complain of the Jeronimites, but I have no doubt they were more vigorous, and aimed at better purposes than almost any mere official persons would have done: and their conduct illustrates to my mind what I have long thought about government,—that there are occasions when those do best in it who are not strictly bred up for it, and who are not, therefore, likely to have the vigour and force of their natures encrusted with routine and deadened by a slavish belief in the incomplete traditions of the past.

The author hazards a remark about government.

Such measured proceedings as the Jeronimite Fathers at first adopted did not accord with the temperament of Las Casas; neither were they

Las Casas distrusts the Jeronimites.

such remedies as the fearful nature of the disease demanded. Moreover, in addition to his disapproval of their measures, he distrusted the men themselves. He states that they had relations whom they wished to benefit in the island of Hispaniola, but as they feared him too much to do so there, they recommended these relations to Diego Velazquez, the Governor of Cuba; and Las Casas observed, that in a letter which he happened to see when they were about to close it, they signed themselves, "Chaplains to Your Honour" (*Capellanes de Vuestra Merced*), a mode of describing themselves which seemed to him conclusive of the position the Fathers were going to take up with regard to this Governor. The Protector of the Indians, therefore, resolved to return to Castille and to appeal against the Fathers: and in this resolve he was strengthened by the opinion of Zuazo and of Pedro de Córdova, who still continued to be the head of the Dominican Order in those parts.

The Fathers were much disconcerted when they heard of the intention of Las Casas to return to court, saying that he was a torch that would set everything in a flame, and they had thoughts

ADMINISTRATION OF XIMENES.

of stopping him; but this was not within the scope of their powers. What they could do, and what they afterwards did, was to send one of their own body to court, to make representations on their behalf.

Las Casas returns to Spain, 1517.

Meanwhile the Clerigo left St. Domingo in May, 1517, and in July reached Aranda on the Douro, where he found Cardinal Ximenes at the point of death. Las Casas seems to have been fated to appear to great personages a few days before their death. This time, though, whatever complaints he might have been able to make of

Sees Ximenes.

the administration of Indian affairs, he had nothing to say which could wound the conscience of the dying statesman. The Clerigo's letters to Ximenes had, he says, been intercepted, and, in the little that passed between them then, the Protector of the Indians found the Cardinal ill-informed of what had occurred in Hispaniola.

CHAPTER IV.

Las Casas is introduced to the Grand Chancellor, and lays his Emigration Scheme before the King—His Plans are checked by the Death of the Chancellor—He holds a Controversy with the Bishop of Burgos.

THOSE who have never lived at courts have been very apt to magnify the vice and treachery of such places, just as those who dwell in the country are prone to believe in the singular wickedness of towns; but, after all, Virtue, like the rest of us, being sometimes very weary of dulness, quits groves and primeval settlements, to take up her abode with polished people. And, certainly, whenever the course of this narrative conducts us to the court of Spain, even the most cursory reader cannot fail to have the pleasure of observing that there was at least sympathy for the injured, and gene-

Always some redress at the court of Spain.

rally, in some quarter or other, an earnest endeavour to redress the wrong, which stand in striking and favourable contrast with the terrible oppressions and misdeeds that meet his eyes at every turn in the pages which record the proceedings of the Spanish colonists. It is like coming into daylight again after sudden darkness. I cannot illustrate this contrast better than by an incident which occurred in Trinidad about this time, and which will serve to show what enormities were occasionally perpetrated in the West Indies, even under the supervision of the Jeronimite Fathers. Such a narrative, moreover, will give us a deeper interest in the efforts of the Protector of the Indians, will explain his vehemence, and tend to justify his views.

Here, too, I must premise that Las Casas, according to my observation of his writings and character, may be thoroughly trusted whenever *Accuracy of Las Casas.* he is speaking of things of which he has competent knowledge. Seeing his vehemence, an ordinary observer might be apt to doubt his accuracy, though there has never been a greater mistake, or a much more common one, than to confound vehemence with inaccuracy. Far from being an inaccurate man, he was studiously accurate, which is to be seen throughout his history in all manner of little things. His countenance,* too, though benevolence may be its chief characteristic, gives strong indications of acuteness, firmness, and refinement, and is rather the face of a lawyer or a statesman than of an ecclesiastic. Indeed he was not especially fitted for an ecclesiastic,† excepting in so far as a man of the world, if essentially a good man, may make an excellent ecclesiastic, as often happens. He was, moreover, a gentleman, and in his history shows delicacy and kindness in suppressing names where there is no occasion to mention them, and where the bringing persons forward would give them or their descendants unnecessary pain.

<small>His portrait</small>

The following narrative of what occurred at

---

* The portrait of Las Casas is to be seen, if I recollect rightly, in a private collection at Seville.

† In a very naïve way he lets you see somehow or other in his history, that it was not so much care for the Faith, though he was a deeply religious man, as natural pity that led him to espouse the cause of the Indians, which, especially in those times, would have been thought so much the inferior motive.

Juan Bono's story.

Trinidad, to hear which we are going to quit the court of Spain for a time, is given on the authority of Las Casas.

There was a certain man named Juan Bono, and he was employed by the members of the *audiencia* of St. Domingo to go and obtain Indians. He and his men, to the number of fifty or sixty, landed on the island of Trinidad. Now the Indians of Trinidad were a mild, loving, credulous race, the enemies of the Caribs who ate human flesh. On Juan Bono's landing, the Indians, armed with bows and arrows, went to meet the Spaniards, and to ask them who they were, and what they wanted. Juan Bono replied, that his crew were good and peaceful people, who had come to live with the Indians; upon which, as the commencement of good fellowship, the natives offered to build houses for the Spaniards. The Spanish captain expressed a wish to have one large house built. The accommodating Indians set about building it. It was to be in the form of a bell, and to be large enough for a hundred persons to live in. On any great occasion it would hold many more. Every day, while this house was being built, the Spaniards were fed with fish, bread, and fruit by their good-natured hosts. Juan Bono was very anxious to see the roof on, and the Indians continued to work at the building with alacrity. At last it was completed, being two stories high, and so constructed that those within could not see those without. Upon a certain day Juan Bono collected the Indians together, men, women, and children, in the building, to see, as he told them, "what was to be done." Whether they thought they were coming to some festival, or that they were to do something more for the great house, does not appear. However, there they all were, four hundred of them, looking with much delight at their own handiwork. Meanwhile, Juan Bono brought his men round the building, with drawn swords in their hands: then, having thoroughly entrapped his Indian friends, he entered with a party of armed men, and bade the Indians keep still, or he would kill them. They did not listen to him, but rushed against the door. A horrible massacre ensued. Some of the Indians forced their way out, but many of them, stupified at what they saw, and losing heart, were captured and bound. A hundred, however, escaped, and,

Juan Bono's story.

snatching up their arms, assembled in one of their own houses, and prepared to defend themselves. Juan Bono summoned them to surrender: they would not hear of it; and then, as Las Casas says, "he resolved to pay them completely for the hospitality and kind treatment he had received," and so, setting fire to the house, the whole hundred men, together with some women and children, were burnt alive. The Spanish captain and his men retired to the ships with their captives: and his vessel happening to touch at Porto Rico when the Jeronimite Fathers were there, gave occasion to Las Casas to complain of this proceeding to the Fathers, who, however, did nothing in the way of remedy or punishment. The reader will be surprised to hear the Clerigo's authority for this deplorable narrative. It is Juan Bono himself. "From his own mouth I heard that which I write. Juan Bono acknowledged that never in his life had he met with the kindness of father and mother but in the island of Trinidad. 'Well, then, man of perdition, why did you reward them with such ungrateful wickedness and cruelty?' 'On my faith, Padre because they (he meant the auditors) gave me fo-

[marginalia: Juan Bono's story. His depth of ingratitude.]

destruction (he meant *instruction*) to take them in peace if I could not by war.'"

Such were the transactions which Las Casas must have had in his mind when he was pleading the cause of the Indians at the court of Spain; and that man would have been more than mortal, who, brooding over these things, and struggling to find a remedy for them, was always temperate in his language and courtly in his demeanour. I feel confident that St. Paul would not have been so.

Returning now to the court of Spain, I will recount what took place immediately after the death of the great Cardinal. On that event the administration of the affairs of Spain fell inevitably into much confusion. The King, as mentioned before, was only sixteen years old; and it could not be expected that he was yet to have much real weight in affairs. It has been a common saying, that he did not give promise, at this period of his life, of the sagacity which he afterwards manifested. This is a mistake. The truth is, that Charles was as a boy what he turned out to be as a man—grave, undemonstrative, cautious,

[margin: Spanish government on the death of Ximenes.]

[margin: Charles the Fifth as a boy.]

thoughtful, valiant. No doubt he was very observant; and I think it is manifest that the information he now obtained about Indian affairs, swayed him throughout his reign, and influenced him in the advice he gave in a great matter, connected with the government of the Spanish colonies, which occurred many years after, at a period when he had withdrawn for the most part from all human affairs. At this time of his life he trusted to his councillors, like a sensible boy, was very constant to them, and exceedingly liberal to all persons about him.

The two men who had now the supreme authority in Spain, were Chièvres,* the King's former Governor, and his present Lord Chamberlain—and the Grand Chancellor, Jean Salvage, called by the Spaniards Selvagius. The Chancellor settled all matters connected with justice; the other, those connected with patronage. Las Casas speaks well of the disposition of the Flemings, especially of their humanity; and he

Chièvres and Selvagius rule Spain.

---

* He is called familiarly Chièvres by writers of that period; but his name was William de Croy, Lord of Chièvres, in Hainault, afterwards Marquis or Duke of Aarschot.

seems to think that the Chancellor was an upright man.

These ministers were not without their especial perplexities. They did not know whom to trust, or what to do: and they were too cautious to act without sufficient knowledge. They did not even know the language of the country they governed. The King himself was busy learning it. In this state of things the public business languished.

<small>Perplexity of the Flemings.</small>

The affairs of the Indies, however, gained much more attention than might have been expected at this juncture. It happened thus: as Las Casas was at St. Domingo, on his way to appeal against the proceedings of the Jeronimite Fathers, he had seen those Franciscan monks from Picardy, who had now been some time in the island, and, as the reader may remember, had formed part of Pedro de Córdova's company, when he set out for the Terra-firma. These monks, with others, had signed letters of recommendation in favour of Las Casas, and by good fortune some of the foreign monks were known to the Grand Chancellor, and their signatures

<small>Las Casas made known to the Grand Chancellor.</small>

proved a favourable introduction for the Protector of the Indians. He soon enlarged the advantages arising from this introduction; and at last became on such terms with the Chancellor, that this great functionary used to give Las Casas all the letters and memorials from the colonists or their representatives, and the Clerigo then turned them into Latin, and made his remarks upon them, showing what was true and what was false, or wherein he approved, or dissented from, the views of the writer. Finally, the Grand Chancellor spoke of Las Casas to the King, and received his Highness's commands that they two should consult together, and provide a remedy for the bad government of the Indies.*

The Chancellor and Las Casas legislate for the Indies.

Again, therefore, great hopes might naturally be entertained that something effectual would now be done on behalf of the Indians. Las Casas prepared his memorials, taking for his basis the plan which the Jeronimites had carried out to Hispaniola, and which by this time they had partially acted upon. He added, however, some

---

* "Dominus noster jubet quod vos et ego apponamus remedia Indis—faciatis vestra memorialia."—LAS CASAS, *Hist. de las Indias*, MS., lib. iii. cap. 99.

other things; amongst them, that of securing to the Indians their entire liberty. And he provided a scheme for furnishing Hispaniola with labourers from the mother country.

The outline of this scheme was as follows:— The King was to give to every labourer willing to emigrate to Hispaniola his living during the journey from his place of abode to Seville, at the rate of half a *real* a day throughout the journey, for great and small, child and parent. At Seville the emigrants were to be lodged in the *Casa de la Contratacion* (the India House), and were to have from eleven to thirteen *maravedis* a day. From thence they were to have a free passage to Hispaniola, and to be provided with food for a year.* And if the climate " should try them so

<small>Proposed emigration from Spain.</small>

---

* "La órden de la poblacion della hizo de esta manera; que el Rey diese á cada labrador que quisiese venir á poblar en ella desde que partiese de su poblacion hasta Sevilla de comer, para lo qual se señaló á cada persona chico con grande medio real cada dia; y en Sevilla se les diese posada en la casa de la Contratacion, y once á trece maravedises para comer cada dia, de manera que tanto se dava al niño de teta, como á sus Padres.

"De allí pasage y matalotage hasta esta Isla, y en ella un año de comer hasta que ellos lo tuviesen de suyo. Y si la tierra los probase tanto que no estubiesen para trabajar

F

much," that at the expiration of this year they should not be able to work for themselves, the King was to continue to maintain them, but this extra maintenance was to be put down to the account of the emigrants, as a loan which they were to repay. The King was to give them lands (his own lands), furnish them with ploughshares and spades, and provide medicines for them. Lastly, whatever rights and profits accrued from their holdings were to become hereditary. This was certainly a most liberal plan of emigration. And, in addition, there were other privileges held out as inducements to these labourers.

<small>Licences to import negroes suggested by Las Casas.</small>

In connection with the above scheme, Las Casas, unfortunately for his reputation in after ages, added another provision, namely, that each Spanish resident in the island should have licence to import a dozen negro slaves.

The origin of this suggestion was, as he informs us, that the colonists had told him, that

---

mas tiempo de un año, que lo que demas de un año que el Rey les diese, fuese prestado para que se lo pagase quando pudiese."—LAS CASAS, *Hist. de las Indias*, MS., lib. iii. cap. 10.

if licence were given them to import a dozen negro slaves each, they, the colonists, would then set free the Indians. And so, recollecting that statement of the colonists, he added this provision. LAS CASAS, writing his history in his old age, thus frankly owns his error: " This advice, that licence should be given to bring negro slaves to these lands, the Clerigo Casas first gave, not considering the injustice with which the Portuguese take them, and make them slaves; which advice, after he had apprehended the nature of the thing, he would not have given for all he had in the world. For he always held that they had been made slaves unjustly and tyrannically; for the same reason holds good of them as of the Indians."* The above confession is delicately and truthfully worded—" not considering "—he does not say, not being aware of; but, though it

marginal note: He afterwards owns his error.

---

* " Este aviso de que se diese licencia para traer esclavos negros á estas tierras; dió primero el Clérigo Casas, no advirtiéndo la injusticia con que los Portugueses los toman y hacen esclavos; el qual despues de que cayó en ello no lo diera por quanto habia en el mundo. Porque siempre los tuvo por injusta y tiránicamente hechos esclavos : porque la misma razon es de ellos que de los Indios."—LAS CASAS, *Hist. de las Indias*, MS., lib. iii. cap. 101.

was a matter known to him, his moral sense was not watchful, as it were, about it. We must be careful not to press the admissions of a generous mind too far, or to exaggerate the importance of the suggestion of Las Casas.

It would be quite erroneous to look upon this suggestion as being the introduction of negro slavery. From the earliest times of the discovery of America, negroes had been sent there; and the young King Charles had, while in Flanders, granted licences to his courtiers for the importation of negroes into Hispaniola. But, what is of more significance, and what it is strange that Las Casas was not aware of, or did not mention, the Jeronimite Fathers had also come to the conclusion that negroes must be introduced into the West Indies. Writing in January, 1518, when the Fathers could not have known what was passing in Spain in relation to this subject, they recommended licences to be given to the inhabitants of Hispaniola, or to other persons, to bring negroes there. From the tenour of their letter it appears that they had before recommended the same thing. Zuazo, the judge of *residencia,* and the legal colleague of Las Casas, wrote to the same effect. He, however,

Negro slavery not introduced into the Indies by Las Casas.

The Jeronimites give the same advice as Las Casas.

suggested that the negroes should be placed in settlements, and married. Fray Bernandino de Manzanedo, the Jeronimite Father, who had been sent over to counteract Las Casas, gave the same advice as his brethren about the introduction of negroes. He added a proviso, which does not appear in their letter (perhaps it did exist in one of the earlier ones), that there should be as many women as men sent over, or more.

The suggestion of Las Casas was approved of by the Chancellor, and by Adrian, the colleague of the late Cardinal: and, indeed, it is probable there was hardly a man of that time who would have seen further than the excellent Clerigo did. Las Casas was asked, what number of negroes would suffice? He replied that he did not know; upon which a letter was sent to the officers of the India House at Seville, to ascertain the fit number in their opinion. They said that four thousand would at present suffice, being one thousand for each of the islands, Hispaniola, Porto Rico, Cuba, and Jamaica. Somebody now suggested to the Governor De Bresa, a Fleming of much influence and a member of the Council, that he should ask for this licence to be given to him. De Bresa

Selvagius and Adrian approve this advice.

Licence to De Bresa for 4000 negroes.

accordingly asked the King for it, who granted his request; and the Fleming sold this licence to certain Genoese merchants for twenty-five thousand ducats, having obtained from the King a pledge that for eight years he would give no other licence of this kind.

The consequence of this monopoly enjoyed by the Genoese merchants was, that negroes were sold at a great price, of which there are frequent complaints. Both Las Casas and Pasamonte (rarely found in accord) suggested to the King that it would be better to pay the twenty-five thousand ducats and resume the licence, or to abridge its term. Figueroa, writing to the Emperor from St. Domingo in July, 1520, says:— "Negroes are very much in request: none have come for about a year. It would have been better to have given De Bresa the customs' duties (*i. e.* the duties that had been usually paid on the importation of slaves) than to have placed a prohibition." I have scarcely a doubt that the immediate effect of the measure adopted in consequence of the Clerigo's suggestion was greatly to check that importation of negro slaves, which

Unexpected result of the monopoly.

otherwise, had the licence been general, would have been very abundant.

Before quitting this subject, something must be said for Las Casas which he does not allege for himself.* This suggestion of his about the negroes was not an isolated one. Had all his suggestions been carried out, and the Indians thereby been preserved, as I firmly believe they might have been, these negroes might have remained a very insignificant number in the general population. By the destruction of Indians a void in the laborious part of the community was being constantly created, which had to be filled up by the labour of negroes. The negroes could bear the labour in the mines much better than the Indians; and any man who perceived that a race, of whose Christian virtues and capabilities he thought highly, were fading away by reason of being subjected to labour which their natures were incompetent to endure, and

Excuses for Las Casas.

---

* Las Casas is much misrepresented by Herrera, who gives an account of the suggestion as if it were made, not in addition to, but in substitution for, other measures which they were most unjustly condemned to, might prefer the misery of the smaller number of another race treated with equal injustice, but more capable of enduring it. I do not say that Las Casas considered all these things; but, at any rate, in estimating his conduct, we must recollect, that we look at the matter centuries after it occurred, and see all the extent of the evil arising from circumstances which no man could then be expected to foresee, and which were inconsistent with the rest of the Clerigo's plans for the preservation of the Indians.

I suspect that the wisest amongst us would very likely have erred with him: and I am not sure that, taking all his plans together, and taking for granted, as he did then, that his influence at court was to last, his suggestion about the negroes was an impolitic one.

One more piece of advice Las Casas gave at this time, which, if it had been adopted, would have been most serviceable. He proposed that forts for mercantile purposes, containing about thirty persons, should be erected at intervals along the coast of the Terra-firma, to traffic with merchandize of Spain for gold, silver, and precious

Another suggestion made by Las Casas.

stones; and, in each of these forts, ecclesiastics were to be placed, to undertake the superintendence of spiritual matters. In this scheme may be seen an anticipation of our own plans for commercial intercourse with Africa. And, indeed, one is constantly reminded by the proceedings in those times of what has occurred much later and under the auspices of other nations.

Of all these suggestions, some of them certainly excellent, the only questionable one was at once adopted. Such is the irony of life. If we may imagine immortal beings beholding, with alternations of hope and fear, the great contests of the world, this fatal conclusion was a thing which all those who love mankind must have regarded with poignant sorrow and dismay.

Turning our thoughts from bad angels to bad men, it is vexatious to find the Bishop of Burgos creeping back to power just at this period. For a long time the Bishop had been quite in the background: and Conchillos, Ferdinand's minister, who also formerly had great weight in the government of the Indies, finding himself without any authority, had retired to his estate. But now, owing, it is said, to the effect of sixteen thousand ducats, or because the Bishop had been so long engaged in the Indian administration that his absence was felt (for Las Casas is by no means certain of the bribery), the Bishop was recalled to the Council; and he opposed, as quietly as he could, the excellent plans of Las Casas for colonization. The Bishop said, that for these twenty years he had been endeavouring to find labourers to go to the Indies, and that he had not yet found twenty men who would go. Las Casas engaged to find three thousand. The Clerigo, too, could give a reason why the Bishop had not succeeded in getting labourers, saying that it was because the Indies had been made a penal colony.

At the time of these altercations in the Council, the court had been moving from Valladolid, in order that the King might take formal possession of the throne of Aragon. In the course of the journey, at Aranda on the Douro, Las Casas fell ill, and was left behind, much regretted, as he tells us, even the boy King saying, " I wonder how Micer Bartholomew is" (*Oh qué tal estará Micer Bartolomé*). The King, young as he was,

was likely to approve of a sound-hearted man like Las Casas; and, though a person who has but one subject is apt to be rather troublesome, yet his devotedness elicits a certain interest for him. Moreover, anything that has life and earnestness in it is welcome to sombre people. I am particular in noticing this liking of the young King for Las Casas, as I cannot but attribute some of the King's future proceedings with regard to the Indians to the information he was silently acquiring from the Clerigo at this period. Thus it is that good seed is not lost, which should be a comfort to those who in their own time make great efforts, and seem to effect nothing. In a few days the Clerigo, whom the court left ill at Aranda, got better, and he overtook them before they reached Saragossa. The Grand Chancellor received him very kindly. The great business of the reformation of the Indian government, of which only the part that was no reformation at all had been accomplished, was now to be proceeded with. Again, however, it was delayed—this time by the illness of the Bishop of Burgos, who had now to be consulted; though, as Las Casas retained his full favour with the Chancellor, of

Las Casas recovers.

which there is good evidence, the Bishop was not able to thwart the views of the Clerigo. Las Casas received at this juncture the evidence of Father Roman concerning the horrible cruelties committed by one of the captains of Pedrarias, named Espinosa, which caused the destruction of 40,000 souls;* and Las Casas took care to bring this evidence before the Chancellor, who sent him with it to the Bishop.

At last, on the Bishop's recovery, the Junta for the business of the Indies was on the point of being called together—"to-morrow," it may be— (Las Casas is speaking of a certain Friday when he is to sup with the Chancellor), when, in the evening of that day, the Chancellor's servants tell him that a little page of his, a nephew, who was ill in the house, is dead, at which he appeared

<small>Father Roman's evidence.</small>

---

* "Entre tanto recibió una Carta el Clérigo de Sevilla del Padre Fray Reginaldo de quien arriba en el Capítulo noventa y ocho hizimos mencion, haciéndole saber, como habia llegado allí de la tierra firme un Religioso de San Francisco, llamado Fray Francisco de Sant Roman, que afirmaba por sus ojos, haver visto meter á espada, y echar á perros brabos sobre quarenta mill ánimas de Indios."—LAS CASAS. *Hist. de las Indias*, MS., lib. iii. cap. 102.

very sorrowful. "To-morrow" the Chancellor himself feels ill, and does not go to the palace. There are symptoms of fever. On Monday, however, he is well enough to go to the window of his room. We may imagine with what anxiety Las Casas heard of the illness: it may be that he was the very person who, ever on the watch, perceived the Chancellor at the window. But the fever was not to be baffled: they did not bleed the poor man in time, according to the theory of those days. He died, and on Wednesday he was not even on the face of the earth. "And the Grand Chancellor being dead, of a truth there died, for that time, all hope of a remedy for the Indians."

Illness and death of Selvagius.

This, as Las Casas remarks, was the second time* when the " salvation " of those nations (the

A second great reverse for the Indies.

---

* I suppose the first time was when, according to Las Casas, Ximenes took Indian affairs in hand; but I should name three occasions—1. The appointment of the Junta who made the laws of Burgos. 2. The appointment of Jeronimites. 3. The present one, viz. the appointment by the King of the Chancellor Selvagius and Las Casas to provide a remedy for the Indies.

Indians) seemed assured, and when a reverse occurred, and hope altogether vanished away. So fearfully valuable is the life of a great man in a despotic state: and it may console us, who live under representative governments, for a certain mediocrity and difficulty in the management of public affairs, that at least we are not subject to these dreadful reverses occasioned by the loss of one man. What is gained by us is mostly gained by the increase of insight in large bodies of men, and will live and augment itself with the advancement of the general thought of the nation.

<small>Bishop of Burgos in full power again.</small> Upon the Grand Chancellor's death, the Bishop of Burgos instantly regained all his old influence in the government of the Indies; and down went the Clerigo "into the abysses," as he expresses it. Nothing was to be done with the interim Chancellor, a very phlegmatic Dean,* who praised the Clerigo's unwearied efforts, but could not summon up energy enough to assist him: " and certainly," to use our historian's own words, " when a man of a choleric temperament, like the Clerigo, and

---

* The Dean of Besançon.

an excessively phlegmatic person, like the good
Dean, have to transact business together, it is no
slight torment to each of them. However," he
slyly adds, "it did not kill the Dean, such was
his phlegmatic patience."

At this time, on the Bishop of Burgos's sugges- *Council for the Indies. 1518.*
tion, an especial Council for Indian affairs was
formed. He was appointed president; Hernando
de Vega and Zapata, both of whom had connec-
tions in the colonies, and who had themselves
been deprived of Indians by the first law of
Ximenes, were of this Council; Peter Martyr,
the historian, was put upon it; also Don Garcia
de Padilla, the only person in the Council likely
to take up new views. The appointment of such
a council was very disheartening to Las Casas,
who, nevertheless, like a brave man as he was,
went about his work just as if all were smooth
before him and shining brightly upon him.

The first act of the Bishop was to recal the *Jeronimites recalled.*
Jeronimite Fathers. Though for some time be-
fore this they had possessed no real power (we
find that their letters to the authorities in Spain
were never answered), their presence and their
influence must still have been productive of

good, and must at least have been felt as a considerable restraint upon evil-doers. Those, therefore, who cared for the welfare of the Indies, must have been sorry to see the last vestige of the policy of the great Ximenes now altogether effaced from the Indian government.

<small>Effect of the small-pox in the Indies over-rated.</small>

It has been stated* that, on the Jeronimite Fathers placing the Indians in settlements, the small-pox came among them and carried off numbers. As I said before, I think this cause of the destruction of the Indians (a very convenient one for the conquerors to allege) has been exaggerated; and I am confirmed in this opinion by a letter written by Zuazo, which must have arrived at court about four or five months before this time, in which he says nothing of the small-pox, but assigns as one of the main causes of the decrease of the Indians the frequent change of government that there had been, which led to new *repartimientos,* and to changes of climate and water for the Indians, which were fatal to many of them;—" as in a number of small things, passed

---

* See Oviedo and Herrera.

rapidly from hand to hand, even with care, the number is soon diminished."

Just at this time, when the Bishop of Burgos was carrying it with a high hand in the Council of the Indies, a little gleam of good fortune broke most unexpectedly upon Las Casas and his cause. In all his affairs at court, he had principally been conversant with the late Chancellor; yet some knowledge of the business for which Las Casas worked at court with such indomitable perseverance was doubtless generally circulated amongst the courtiers. Amongst them there was a certain Monsieur de Bure (a young man, as I conjecture), who, it appears, had a desire to make himself acquainted with this business of the Indians. He caused his wish to be made known to the Clerigo: they had a meeting in the palace, and Las Casas acquainted him fully with the whole state of the case. Monsieur de Bure was much affected by the Clerigo's narration. De Bure was a powerful man, being the nephew of De Laxao,* who enjoyed great influence with the King, and who,

_{Flemish courtiers favour Las Casas.}

---

* Carl Puper, Lord of Laxao.

being the *sommelier du corps*,* slept in the King's room. De Laxao was a person celebrated for his wit, and probably on that account his society was exceedingly relished by the grave young King. Monsieur de Bure brought Las Casas to his uncle De Laxao, who also was much interested in the account which Las Casas gave of Indian affairs, and the result was, that he found protectors in these powerful men of the King's household and council.

Residencias taken of several authorities in the Indies.

At this time the Spanish court sent over Rodrigo de Figueroa to take a *residencia* of the auditors of St. Domingo, and of the judges appointed by the Admiral. A certain Doctor de la Gama was appointed to take a *residencia* of the Lieutenant-Governor of San Juan, and of Velaz-

---

* *Sommelier* was corrupted into *Sumiller* by the Spaniards. The following is the definition of the office:—" La persona muy distinguida en palacio, á cuyo cargo está la asistencia al rey en su retrete, para vestirle y desnudarle, y todo lo perteneciente á la cama real. *Summus præfectus cubiculi regis.*

" Es nombre introducido en Castilla con la casa de Borgoña."—*Diccionario de la Lengua Castellana por la Academia Española.*

quez in Cuba; and Lope de Sosa was sent to succeed Pedrarias as governor of the Terra-firma, and to take a *residencia* of the same Governor. Information having been given that the inhabitants of Trinidad were cannibals, the King's Council resolved to order war to be made upon them; but Las Casas prevailed upon the Council to insert in the instructions which Figueroa was to take with him, that, as the Clerigo Bartolomé de Las Casas asserted that the natives of Trinidad were not cannibals, Figueroa should, on arriving at St. Domingo, examine carefully into the truth of this statement. He did so, and found that these poor islanders were not cannibals, but very quiet people, as Figueroa himself afterwards bore testimony. *The natives of Trinidad not cannibals.*

At this period the Clerigo received a letter from Pedro de Córdova, in which, after telling of some horrible exploits of the Spaniards in the island of Trinidad, and expressing himself in a way that seems to show he was much dissatisfied with the proceedings of the Jeronimite Fathers, the good prelate of the Dominicans went on to say, that he wished the King would set apart one hundred leagues on the coast of the Terra-firma *Pedro de Córdova's letter.*

about Cumaná, to be entered solely by the Franciscan and Dominican monks, for the purpose of preaching the Gospel there. His desire was, that no layman might be permitted to enter, so that no hindrance might occur to the good work; and he suggested, that, if Las Casas could not obtain a hundred leagues, he should endeavour to obtain ten; and that, if he could not get such a tract of land on the Terra-firma set apart for this purpose, he should try and get some little islands, called the Islands of Alonso, about fifteen or twenty leagues from the coast. The object was,

Pedro de Córdova's plan.

that this land set apart might be a city of refuge for the poor Indians, and a place wherein to teach the Gospel to them. Pedro de Córdova added that, if none of these requests should be granted, he would recal the brethren of his Order from those parts, for it was of no use their preaching "when the Indians saw those who called themselves Christians acting in opposition to Christians."

The good Father imagined that Las Casas was very powerful at court, not knowing how things had been changed by the death of the Chancellor, and by the return of the Bishop of

Burgos to power. Las Casas, however, did what he could to further the request of Pedro de Córdova, but with no avail, the Bishop of Burgos saying, the King would be well advised indeed to grant a hundred leagues without any profit to himself. Such was the reply, as Las Casas notes, of one of the successors of the apostles, who laid down their lives for the sake of conversion. And, as for profit to the King, "no profit did he derive for forty years and more from those hundred leagues, or from eight thousand in addition, except to have them ravaged, desolated, and destroyed."*

As nothing could be done at present in the scheme suggested by Pedro de Córdova, Las Casas returned to the prosecution of his own plan, namely, the sending out of labourers to the West India islands. In this he was favoured by Cardinal Adrian and the other Flemings; and he succeeded in obtaining all the provisions and orders that he wanted for that purpose. Amongst others, he procured that a certain esquire called

margin: Emigration scheme of Las Casas.

---

* LAS CASAS, *Hist. de las Indias*, MS., lib. iii. cap. 104.

Berrio, an Italian, should be appointed by the King, and called the king's captain. He was to accompany Las Casas, to be under his orders, and to give notice by trumpet in the various towns of the purpose which Las Casas came to announce. This man, however, had no intention of really serving under the Clerigo, but he went to the Bishop of Burgos, and secretly got his orders altered from "Do what he shall desire you," to "Do what may seem good to you."*

<small>Las Casas pursues his emigration scheme.</small>

The Clerigo, with his squire and other attendants, set off on his expedition for procuring emigrant labourers. He directed his course from Saragossa towards Castille, assembling the people in the churches, and informing them of the benefits and privileges they would acquire by emigrating. Numbers consented to go, inscribing their names in a book. At Berlanga, out of a population of two hundred, more than seventy inscribed their names. It gives a curious insight into those times, to see that the inducement with these

---

* "Manda el Obispo luego que se raya la Cédula, y que donde decia hagais lo que él os dixere, hagais lo que os pareciere."—LAS CASAS, *Hist. de las Indias*, MS., lib. iii. cap. 104.

people to emigrate, was to get away from the seignorial rights over them. They came to Las Casas with the greatest secrecy; and he relates this speech made by four of them. "Señor, no one of us wishes to go to the Indies for want of means here, for each of us has a hundred thousand maravedis of *hacienda* and more, but we go to leave our children in a free land under royal jurisdiction."*

<small>A motive for emigration.</small>

As was to be expected, the lords of these places were very hostile to Las Casas; but their opposition was a trifling evil compared to the insubordination of Berrio. This man often requested leave to go to Andalucia, where his wife was. The Clerigo would not allow this; they would come, he said, to Andalucia in good time; they were upon duty now: but no remonstrances sufficed to retain Berrio, who came one day, booted and spurred, to the Clerigo, and asked if he had any orders for Andalucia. Las Casas then learnt for the first time that this Berrio was in fact no servant of his, but free to act for himself: and the man accordingly took his departure

---

* LAS CASAS, *Hist. de las Indias*, MS., lib. iii. cap. 104.

in this most wilful fashion. The mischief did not stop here. Berrio went to Andalucia, and, having collected about two hundred vagabonds, tapsters and roysterers and idle people, anything but labourers, went with them to the India House at Seville. The official persons there, having received no orders about them, were in complete perplexity what to do. They shipped them off, however, in two vessels which happened to be on the point of sailing at that time; and the unfortunate rabble of emigrants arrived in this way at St. Domingo. There again the official people had received no orders to provide anything for the emigrants, many of whom died; others crowded into the hospitals; others returned to their former mode of life; and others preyed upon the Indians. Thus ended this miserable expedition; and this ending may justly be attributed to the outrageous conduct of the Bishop of Burgos in altering a despatch, after it had been signed.

Failure of the emigration scheme.

Las Casas resolved to return to court. He was now fully assured of the facility of obtaining emigrants, but he did not wish to do any more at present than he had done in the matter, considering the probable opposition of the great lords and the defection of Berrio, and also taking into account the readiness of the common people to emigrate, which made it only a subject of more urgent concern to consider carefully what was to be done. When the Bishop of Burgos had heard the Clerigo's account of his expedition, in which he told his Lordship that he could answer for procuring not only three thousand but eight thousand labourers, the Bishop said it was "a great matter, a great matter indeed;" but, as usual, nothing came of this speech, only that by repeated and energetic remonstrances Las Casas prevailed upon the Council to send wine and provisions after the poor wretches who had already sailed. These supplies, however, came too late. And so ended this plan for the benefit of the Indies.

With all our aids and appliances of modern times, we, too, find emigration to be no light undertaking—one of the main difficulties being that the emigrants are generally of one class, so that the peculiarities of that one class are liable to be developed to the uttermost, and have to be provided for all at once.

A controversy that the Clerigo had at Barcelona with the Bishop of Burgos about the emigration scheme deserves to be mentioned. Las Casas would not in any way further the proposed emigration, without being assured of the emigrants receiving support for a year after their arrival. This was a fundamental part of his plan, and finding that it was not to be conceded, and that other persons were being sought for to take charge of the emigration, he wrote to the towns which he had previously visited, and warned the people against going. When Las Casas was arguing one day before the Council of the Indies for the allowance of a year's support to be made to the emigrants, the Bishop said that the King would spend more with those labourers, than with an armada of twenty thousand men (the Lord Bishop was much more versed in fitting out armadas than in saying masses), to which Las Casas replied: "It appears then to your Lordship, that after you have been the death of so many Indians, you wish to be the death of Christians also." "I do not know," he adds, "whether the Bishop, who was no fool, took it."

In fine, however, he could make nothing of this

obdurate Bishop, and, almost glad to be freed from the responsibility of the emigration scheme, he immediately turned his fertile mind to another plan, which he thought with worldly men might appear more feasible.

Las Casas abandons his emigration scheme.

CHAPTER V.

Las Casas brings forward his Plan for founding a Colony. After failing in gaining his point with the Council of the Indies, he goes to Court, and succeeds in obtaining full power to carry out his design.

LAS CASAS still pondered over the original plan of Pedro de Córdova, for enclosing, as it were, a hundred leagues along the coast of the Terra-firma, and forbidding the entrance of laymen into it. That scheme, however, was liable to the objection of the Bishop of Burgos, that it held out no solid pecuniary advantage to the crown. These two things, profit
Las Casas's new and notable plan. for the King and the preaching of the Gospel, must therefore be combined; and from this idea came the following ingenious proposition.

I may mention here, in the way of parenthesis, that a new Grand Chancellor, a learned and good man, according to our historian, had come from Flanders. This was Charles the Fifth's celebrated Chancellor, Arborio de Gattinara, a man whose name is found in connection with several of the greatest events of the age in which he lived. Just before his death, in 1529, he was made a cardinal.

The Chancellor Gattinara concerned in great affairs.

His moderation in reference to the Reformation is well known, and coincides with the high esteem which he had for Erasmus. I imagine him to have been one of the earliest of those professional statesmen, if the phrase may be used, who were afterwards so trustfully employed by Charles the Fifth, and in another generation by Elizabeth of England. Gattinara and Granvella correspond to Burleigh, the elder Bacon, and the other statesmen who stood round the throne of that Queen.

His moderation.

Gattinara favoured Las Casas almost as much as his predecessor in the chancellor's office, Selvagius, had done. The Clerigo says that the Chancellor loved him much; and as Las Casas was only a poor suitor, whose claims for attention were no other than the justness and the goodness of his cause, it is greatly to the credit of this Chancellor that he was always willing to give audience to Las Casas, and that he uniformly de-

He favours the Clerigo.

fended him. Whether, however, Gattinara had not quite as much influence as Selvagius (and it is certain he was not on such good terms with Chièvres), or whether he himself was won over to a certain extent by the Bishop of Burgos, it is clear that this mischievous prelate had more power now in Indian affairs than he had possessed under the former Chancellor.

Gattinara, though mixed up with so many great affairs in France, in Germany, in Italy, and in Spain, was never perhaps seen so closely, nor, I imagine, to such advantage, as he will be in the following pages.

The new proposition which Las Casas had to bring forward under this new dynasty (for the change of chancellors was almost a change of dynasty to him), is a very remarkable one. It formed the turning-point of the Clerigo's own life, and in its consequences had the widest influence upon the fortunes of the New World. The substance of it was as follows:—

Las Casas engaged to find fifty Spaniards, which he thought he could do amongst the colonists, moderate and reasonable men, who would undertake the good work he had in hand for them out of Christian motives, at the same time having a fair view to furthering their own interests by lawful means. He limited himself to fifty, because fifty would be more manageable than a greater number, and would be sufficient for peaceful converse with the Indians.

<small>The plan of Las Casas for colonizing the Terra-firma.</small>

These fifty were to subscribe two hundred ducats each, making ten thousand in the whole, which he thought would be enough to provide the requisite outfit and sustenance for a year, and presents for the Indians.

The fifty were to wear a peculiar dress, white cloth with red crosses, like that of the Knights of Calatrava, but having some additional ornament. Much ridicule was afterwards thrown on this part of the scheme; and the proposed knights obtained the name of *sanbenitos*,* in allusion to the dress of penitent convicts of the Inquisition. The object, however, of having a peculiar dress, was to distinguish this band from any Spaniards whom the Indians had seen before. They were also to bring a message to the Indians, of a new tenour, telling

<small>His knights.</small>

---

* The garment called a *sanbenito* had a large red and yellow cross before and behind.

them that they were sent to salute them from the King of Spain, who had heard of the evils and oppressions they (the Indians) had suffered, that they were to give them presents as a sign of amity, and to protect them from the other Spaniards who had done them injury.

Las Casas says that he had it in his mind, if God had prospered the work, to get the Pope and the King to allow this body to be formed into a religious fraternity.

Inducements to the King.

For the profit of the King, Las Casas held out the following inducements;—that he would pacify the country assigned to him, which he requested should begin a hundred leagues above Paria* and extend down the coast a thousand leagues;†

---

* That means a hundred leagues to the eastward of Paria, i. e., taking the river Dulce as the eastern limit. " Convienc á saber desde cien leguas arriba de Pária, del Rio que llamaban el rio dulce, que agora llamamos el Rio y la tierra de los Arvacas, la costa abajo hasta á donde las mill leguas llegasen."—LAS CASAS, *Hist. de las Indias*, MS., lib. iii. cap. 131.

† It was ultimately restricted to about two hundred and sixty leagues.

A letter has recently been brought to light, bearing the signature of Las Casas, but without date, which must, how-that after being settled there three years, he would contrive that the King should have fifteen thousand ducats of tribute from the Indians and the Spanish settlements, if there should be any; and that this tribute should increase gradually, until, at the tenth year, and thenceforward, it should amount to seventy thousand ducats.

---

ever, have been addressed by him to the Grand Chancellor in the course of these negociations.

It begins by stating that he does not wish to lose more time in a thing which is so manifestly good as this business, and so " practicable," unless, as he adds, the time which is lost here should prevent it (*sino que lo que aqui se pierde de tiempo pudiéndose escusar*).

He mentions that he first asked for a thousand leagues; that when the matter was referred to the Council of the Indies, they reduced it to six hundred, and in those six hundred there were only two provinces, namely Cenu and Santa Martha, which produced gold, and that these provinces were included in a hundred leagues. He also mentions that he had asked for the pearl fisheries, but that they had been " taken" from him. This, however, he had acceded to, on the condition that those Spaniards who had the permission to go to the pearl fisheries, should be prevented from injuring and scandalizing the Indians. He intimates, that now Cenu is about to be taken from him, and that, if so, it will greatly diminish the inducements which he can hold out to secular persons to join in his enterprize, and aid

H

Las Casas also offered to found three settlements in the course of five years, with a fortress in each of them. Moreover, he would obtain geographical knowledge about the country assigned to him, and give the King information on that head: and he would do what he could to convert the natives without its being any charge to the King.

---

him with their funds; "for," he adds, "as your Lordship may judge, we shall find few laymen who will be inclined to go and spend their estates, and to die and labour, solely to serve God, to convert souls, and to preach their faith to the infidels, (*porque, como v. s. puede juzgar, pocos seglares hallarémos que se quieran mover á yr á gastar sus haziendas y á morir y trabajar como dicho es solamente por servir á Dios y convertir animas y predicar su fee á los ynfieles*).

He puts it plainly to the Grand Chancellor, whether Lope de Sosa, who went out to supersede Pedrarias in the government of Darien, will not have enough to govern, and his people to destroy, without the province of Cenu. "Sin la provincia del Cenu queda á Lope de Sosa harta tierra y muy rica de oro desde el Darien versus occidentem para que él pueda governar y su gente destruyr."

After offering many good reasons to the Chancellor for the request being granted, he prays that, at least, the province of Cenu may be divided between himself and Lope de Sosa, or, if that be not possible, that the onerous conditions which he had undertaken for himself and his knights might be diminished accordingly.

The Clerigo on his part demanded, that the King should ask for a brief from the Pope, to allow the Clerigo to take with him twelve priests, Franciscans and Dominicans, who should come voluntarily: and that His Holiness should give a plenary indulgence to all those who should die on the voyage, or in the act of assisting in the said conversion. *(Demands of Las Casas.)*

He also demanded that he might take ten Indians from the islands, if they would come with him of their own accord.

He also made it a provision, that all the Indians who had been taken from that part of the Terra-firma which might be assigned to him, should be placed in his charge for the purpose of being restored to their own country.

We come now to the inducements for the fifty to combine in this enterprize. They were to have the twelfth part of the revenues accruing to the King, and to be enabled to leave this to their heirs for ever.*

---

* This was granted only for four descents.

Then they were to be made Knights of the Golden Spur, and to have a grant of arms. Such of them as the Clerigo should appoint were to have the government of the proposed fortresses and of the settlements. There were also many other provisions and exemptions made in their favour (such for instance as their salt being tax-free), which we need not recount.

Each of the fifty might import three negroes— half of the number men, half women,* and hereafter, if it should seem good to the Clerigo, they might have seven more negro slaves each. It is evident, therefore, that at this time Las Casas had not discovered his error with regard to the negroes.

No encomiendas to be in the settlement of Las Casas.

On behalf of the Indians, Las Casas demanded that the King should give assurance that, neither at this present nor at any future time, should the Indians within the limits agreed upon, being in due obedience and tributary, be given to the Spaniards in *repartimientos*, or in slavery of any kind.

---

* Rather a difficult matter; but I suppose it means that the total number brought over should consist of an equal number of males and females.

There was to be a treasurer, a contador, and a judge.

Also, as a false relation of what should take place in these territories might be carried to the King, the King was to promise, that on no account would he make any change in the order of things, as regarded this colony, without first hearing from the treasurer and the contador.

Several other matters of detail were provided for; but the above is an outline of the most important portions of this proposal made by Las Casas. Like any thing of long extent and large bearings, it presents certain points of attack; but, upon the whole, if sufficient power were given to the head of the colony, it was likely to work well. The plan may remind the reader of feudal times, and of an abbot with a large domain and a retinue of knights to do his bidding. Those abbacies, probably, did not work ill for the poor in their neighbourhood.

The great scheme being now ready, in which it may be observed that Las Casas asked nothing for himself, he explained it to the Grand Chancellor and the other Flemings, who received it

Las Casas lays his plan before the Council of the Indies.

favourably, and desired him to lay it before the Council of the Indies. There it was very ill received by the unflagging enemy of Las Casas, the Bishop of Burgos, and by the rest of the councillors. Still they did not utterly reject it, but sought by delay to put it aside. At this time the Grand Chancellor and Chièvres were obliged to go to the borders of France, to treat of peace with the French King. Las Casas urged the settlement of his business; and, on mentioning to the Flemings that he would have to leave the court on account of his poverty, a Monsieur de Bure and a relation of his advanced the Clerigo money, for fear he should have to leave while the Chancellor was absent. The favour of Las Casas with the Flemings on the King's arrival in Spain has been attributed to a wish to oppose the policy of Ximenes and the Spanish councillors. These gifts to Las Casas cannot be accounted for on this supposition. He says that these men had no interest to serve; and there is every reason to believe, that they acted from a regard for the man and a belief in the goodness of his cause. The Chancellor and Chièvres returned; but still Las Casas could

He receives gifts.

make no way in the Council of the Indies. Not daunted, however, his fertile genius and amazing vigour stirred up new means for furthering his cause, and there is thus brought before us one of the most interesting episodes in the whole of this narrative.

It has been a common practice at courts, to have certain set preachers. For the Spanish court at this time there were eight preachers to the King: and Las Casas bethought himself of laying his troubles and the wrongs of the Indians before these ecclesiastics, and beseeching their favour and assistance. I will here give their names, as I think we ought not to grudge naming men, who, though they come but once or twice before us, and speak but a few words in the great drama of history, do so in a way that ought to confer reputation upon them. First, then, there were the brothers Coronel, Maestro Luis and Maestro Antonio, both very learned men, doctors of the University of Paris; then there was Miguel de Salamanca, also a doctor of the same university, and a master in theology, afterwards Bishop of Cuba; then Doctor de la Fuente, a celebrated

The King's preachers.

man in the time of the late Cardinal Ximenes, of his University of Alcalá; then brother Alonso de Leon, of the Franciscan Order, very learned in theology; brother Dionysius, of the Order of St. Augustin, " a great preacher and very copious in eloquence:" the names of the other two Las Casas had forgotten.

<small>The preachers and Las Casas form a Junta.</small>

The King's preachers and Las Casas formed a Junta of their own. They admitted one or two other *religiosos* into it, a brother, as it was said, of the Queen of Scotland,* being one of them. This last mentioned noble monk was one of those who had come over from Picardy in the year 1516 or 1517; and who himself had gained experience of the proceedings of the Spaniards on the coast of Cumaná. The bold Scot wished to propose to the Junta a large question of the most searching

---

* " Por este tiempo (1516, or early in 1517,) vinieron quatorce religiosos de Sant Francisco, todos extrangeros de Picardia, personas muy religiosas, de muchas letras y muy principales, y de gran celo para emplearse en la conversion de estas gentes, y entre ellos vino un hermano de la Reyna de Escocia (segun se decia) varon de gran autoridad, viejo muy cano y todos ellos de edad madura, y que parecian como unos de los que imaginamos Senadores de Roma."— LAS CASAS, *Hist. de las Indias*, MS., lib. iii. cap. 94.

and fundamental nature, namely, "With what justice or right could an entrance be made into the Indies after the manner which the Spaniards adopted in entering those countries?"

Each day the Junta thus constituted met at the monastery of Santa Catalina, and formed, as the historian describes, a sort of antagonist Council to that held daily on Indian affairs under the auspices of the Bishop of Burgos. They met at the same hour as the Indian Council, perhaps the better to evade observation, for I imagine their proceedings were kept quite secret.

The court preachers employ themselves in Indian affairs.

The conclusion this Junta came to, was, that they were obliged by the Divine Law to undertake to procure a remedy for the evils of the Indies: and they bound themselves to each other by oath, that none of them were to be dismayed, or to desist from the undertaking until it should be accomplished.

They resolved to begin by "the evangelical form of fraternal correction." First, they would go and admonish the Council of the Indies; if this had no effect, they would then admonish the Chancellor; if he were obdurate they would admonish Monsieur Chièvres; and, if none of these admonitions addressed to the officers of the crown were of any avail, they would finally go to the King and admonish him.

If all these earthly powers turned a deaf ear to fraternal admonitions, they, the brethren, would then preach publicly against all of these great men, not omitting to give his due share of blame to the King himself.

This resolution, drawn up in writing, they subscribed to; and they swore upon the cross and the gospels to carry out their resolve.

On a certain day they entered the Council of the Indies, to the astonishment of the Bishop of Burgos, and the rest of the Council, and having requested leave to speak, laid before the Council their admonitions and suggestions, bringing their discourse to an end by urging upon their wisdom the careful consideration of the proposals they had advocated.

They admonish the Council of the Indies.

The Council received the paper with courtesy, and even with somewhat of approbation. To me it seems, as it did to Las Casas, that the scheme of the preachers for the regeneration of the Indies laboured under a great, if not a vital objection, in allowing too much work at the

The Council receive the preachers' suggestions.

mines. But, on the whole, it is a very remarkable state paper; sagacious, humane, and bold.

The Council of the Indies seems by quiet demeanour to have absorbed the opposition of the preachers; and these good men, thinking that they had produced the proper impression upon the minds of the statesmen, left the matter in their hands, considering themselves to have fulfilled their vow. As a body of men acting together, they are no more heard of in this history. Still we must not conclude that their labours and their boldness went for nothing. The river that carries civilization through a country, and creates a metropolis, is fed by many streams whose names and waters are lost in it; and in like manner, many are the unnoticed currents of thought and endeavour which go to form the main volume of wise legislation.

Legislation the work of many minds.

In the meanwhile the indefatigable Las Casas, having little hope of any good coming from the remonstrance of the preachers, pressed on with vigour his own scheme of colonization. The Bishop of Burgos and the Council of the Indies

Las Casas presses on his own scheme.

with equal vigour resisted it. The Clerigo, backed by many of the Flemings, and, as he intimates, having access to the young King and being favourably received by him, took up a position of attack in reference to the Council of the Indies, and inveighed against its proceedings with his usual boldness. The end of this contest was, that the King, with the advice of the Chancellor, appointed a special Council to judge between Las Casas and the Council of the Indies in the matter at issue between them, Las Casas being permitted to name some of the members of this judicial Council. The Bishop of Burgos, when summoned to attend this Council, evaded the summons, pleading indisposition : but, on another occasion, being summoned in general terms to a council, and supposing it to be a council of war or state, he came readily enough, and was dismayed to find that Indian affairs and the business of Las Casas were the questions to be discussed.

His success.   Being heard before this judicial Council, Las Casas eventually succeeded in obtaining a tract of land, extending from the province of Paria, to that of Santa Martha, about 260 leagues along the coast, and the proper official papers were put in course of preparation. The Clerigo thought now, that his business at court was really ended. But the Bishop had another arrow in his quiver. Oviedo, the historian, had just come over from the Indies; and he and two others offered to take the land that Las Casas asked for, agreeing to pay a much higher sum to the King. It is curious to look back and see these two men, who were to be the most celebrated historians of the Indies, bidding against each other for the land to found a colony there; but in those days men of letters were men of action, as perhaps they would be in any time, if they were not supposed to be unfitted for it. *New opposition.*

The Council, which I have described as the judicial Council, was summoned to hear this new proposition. Las Casas spoke out very boldly before it; and, in the course of the proceedings, Antonio de Fonseca, the brother of the Bishop of Burgos, a man of great authority, thus addressed Las Casas, interrupting him probably in the midst of some statement: " You cannot now say that the members of the Indian Council have been the death of the Indians, for you have taken all their Indians away." He alluded to the order issued by Ximenes, that the Indians should be taken *Las Casas heard before the Council.*

away from absentee proprietors, amongst whom were members of the Council. Las Casas replied, " My Lord, their Lordships have not been the death of all the Indians, but they have been the death of immense numbers where they possessed them: the principal destruction, however, of the Indians has been effected by private persons, which destruction their Lordships have abetted."

The Bishop in a furious manner then broke into the discussion with these words: " A fortunate man, indeed, is he who is of the Council of the King, if, being of the Council of the King, he is to put himself in contest with Casas." To this unmannerly speech the Clerigo replied with much readiness and dignity: " A more fortunate man is Casas, if, having come from the Indies two thousand leagues, encountering such risks and dangers, to advise the King and his Council, in order that they might not lose their souls (*que no se vayan a los Infiernos*) on account of the tyranny and destruction which is going on in the Indies, in place of being thanked and honoured for it, he should have to put himself in contest with the Council."

At the end of the proceedings the votes were taken, and were found to be in favour of Las

marginal note: Las Casas replies to the Bishop of Burgos in Council.

Casas. Still, the Council of the Indies, not likely to be much softened by the way in which he had spoken out before the great Council on this last occasion, continued to make resistance. Here we miss the late Cardinal, who would never have allowed for a day these mean endeavours to undermine a great undertaking. As a new device, the Council of the Indies drew up and presented to the Chancellor a memorial against the proposed grant being made to Las Casas, consisting of thirty articles, most of them of a very absurd character. Amongst them were such allegations as these:— that Las Casas, being a Clerigo, was not under the King's jurisdiction; and that he would league with the Genoese and Venetians, and make off to foreign countries with plunder. In their last article the Council alleged, that they had many other reasons which were secret, but which they would tell His Highness (for the memorial was addressed to the King), when he should be pleased to hear them.

Memorial against Las Casas.

The memorial was laid before the great Council; and the result was, that the Chancellor, upon coming out of it, said to Las Casas, that he must give an answer to this document. The difficulty then arose of getting the memorial, for the Council of the Indies made frivolous excuses for withholding it. Months were wasted about this trumpery affair, which may give us some notion of the perseverance and endurance of the Protector of the Indians. At last the Chancellor got the memorial into his hands. He then invited Las Casas to dinner, and afterwards, taking out of his escrutoire a large bundle of papers, he said to the Clerigo, " Answer now to these things they say against you." Las Casas replied, that the Council of the Indies had been months preparing this accusation, " and I have to answer them in a *credo*.* Give me the papers for as many hours as they had months, and your Lordship shall see that I will answer them." The Chancellor said, that he could not part with the papers, as he had promised he would not let them go out of his possession, but Las Casas might answer them there. So, of an evening, while the Chancellor was at his work, the Clerigo came, and sat in a corner of the room, and drew up his reply. Chancellors, even in those days, seem to have been greatly overworked; but, indeed, this

[Sidenote: The Chancellor obtains the memorial.]

---

* In the time he could recite his belief.

has always been the case, that the work of the world, of all kinds, gets into knots, as it were; and one man is often left to do the work of six men, who, with infinite dissatisfaction to themselves, are looking on and noting how ill the work is done. At eleven o'clock, a collation was always brought in; at twelve, the Clerigo took his leave, and went home to his *posada*, not without some fear of what might happen to him on the way from such powerful enemies as were ranged against him. In four evenings Las Casas had prepared his reply.

<small>Las Casas replies to the memorial.</small>

The Chancellor then summoned a council, and laid the reply before them. It seems to have been successful, for all the Bishop of Burgos could say against it was, "The preachers of the King have made these answers for him." This, of course, the Chancellor knew to be false. He reported to the King the whole course of the proceedings; and His Highness ordered that Micer Bartolomé should have the grant, and that no notice should be taken of the offers of those who wished to outbid him.

The reader will think that he has now accompanied the Clerigo to a triumphant conclusion of his present business at court; but, before he left, he was destined to have what he calls "a terrible combat;" and, as it will bring the young King into presence, upon whose disposition and knowledge of Indian affairs so much depended, it will be well to give an account of this combat.

Just at this time it happened that the Bishop of Darien came to court—upon what business will hereafter appear from a statement of his own. The court was still at Barcelona, but, on account of a pestilence that prevailed there, the King was lodged at a place called "Molins de Rey," three leagues from the town; and the great Lords occupied houses in the suburbs. Las Casas, seeing the Bishop of Darien for the first time, in the King's apartments, asked what prelate that was.

Altercation between the Bishop of Darien and Las Casas. They told him, "The Bishop of the Indies." Las Casas went up to him, and said, "My Lord, as I am concerned in the Indies, it is my duty to kiss the hands of your Lordship." The Bishop asked who it was that addressed him, and, being informed, rudely replied, "O, Señor Casas! and what sermon have you to preach to us?"

Las Casas, who was never daunted by bishop or councillor, answered at once, "There was a time, my Lord, when I desired to hear you preach" (the Bishop had been King's preacher in former days), " but I now declare to your Lordship, that I have two sermons ready for you, which, if you please to hear and well consider them, may be worth more than all the money that you bring from the Indies." " You have lost your senses; you have lost your senses," said the Bishop. An acquaintance of the Bishop said to his Lordship, " All these Lords approve of Señor Casas, and of his intentions." The Bishop replied, " With good intentions he may do a thing which shall be mortal sin." At this moment, when the Clerigo, once engaged in controversy, would doubtless have uttered some severe and angry speech, the doors of the council chamber, where the King was, opened, and the Bishop of Badajoz came out, for whom the other Bishop was waiting, as he was to dine with him.

Now the Bishop of Badajoz, who was in great credit with the King, had always favoured the Clerigo; and Las Casas, fearing that the Bishop of Darien might injure him with his brother Bishop, resolved to go to his house that day. He went there when the company had finished their dinner, and found the Bishop of Badajoz playing at backgammon (*a las tablas*) with the Admiral Don Diego Columbus, the Bishop recreating himself until it was the hour to return to the King's lodgings again. There was a knot of bystanders looking on at the game, and one of them happened to say to the Bishop of Darien, that wheat was grown in Hispaniola. The Bishop said that it was not possible. Now Las Casas happened to have in his purse some grains of wheat which had been grown under an orange tree in the garden of the Dominican Monastery of St. Domingo; and so, after controverting most respectfully the assertion of the Bishop, he produced the wheat. The Bishop replied with fierceness, and then launched into a general attack of the rudest kind upon Las Casas, declaring his unfitness for the business he had come to court upon. Great ecclesiastics have mostly been well-disposed and well-spoken men; but, when there has arisen an insolent one, his ill-breeding has always, I imagine, far outgone that of other men. The fervid Las Casas was not behindhand in the war of words, and told the Bishop that he drank the blood of his own flock, and that unless he

The Bishop in the wrong.

returned to the last farthing all the money he had brought over, he was no more likely to be saved than Judas Iscariot. The Bishop endeavoured to laugh down these violent sayings. The Clerigo told him he ought to weep rather than to laugh. At last the Bishop of Badajoz, using the authority of a host, interfered, saying, " No more, no more;" and after the Admiral and another great Lord had said some words in favour of Las Casas, the Clerigo retired.

The Bishop of Badajoz, when he saw the King in the afternoon, told him of what had taken place between the Bishop of Darien and the Clerigo, saying that His Highness would have been amused to hear what Micer Bartolomé said to the Bishop. I have but little doubt that there was supposed to be some truth in the hard sayings of the Clerigo. The King resolved to hear what they both had to say, and for that purpose fixed an hour of audience three days from that time. The Admiral of the Indies, as the matter concerned him, was requested to be present; and, as it happened that a Franciscan brother from Hispaniola had just arrived at court, he also was ordered by the King to attend this audience.

The King gives audience to persons concerned in the Indies.

The day came: the King took his seat on the throne, a few of his greatest councillors being ranged around him on benches below. The order of the proceedings was as follows. The Chancellor and the Lord of Croy ascended the *daïs* where the King was seated, and on their knees conferred with him and received his commands. Then, when they had returned to their places, the Chancellor gave utterance to these commands:—" Reverend Bishop, His Majesty" (Charles had just been elected Emperor, and was therefore styled Majesty) " commands you to speak, if you have anything to say touching the Indies."

Bishop of Darien's speech.

The Bishop of Darien then rose, and made, as Las Casas admits, an elegant exordium, saying how he had long desired to see that Royal Presence, and that now, God having complied with his desire, he knew that the face of Priam was worthy of his kingdom. Having finished this exordium, the Bishop went on to say, that he had come from the Indies, and had secret matters of much importance to communicate, which had better be told to His Majesty and the Council only, wherefore he begged that those who were not of the Council, might be ordered to depart. The King desired, through the Chancellor, that the Bishop should say there and then whatever he had to say. Part of the Bishop's speech is so remarkable, that it is better to give that in his own words.

"Very powerful Sir, the Catholic King your grandfather (may he be in glory!) determined to make an armada to go and people the Terrafirma of the Indies, and he begged our very holy Father to create me Bishop of that new settlement; and, not counting the time passed in going and returning, I have been five years there, and, as we were much people and took with us no more provisions than were necessary for the journey, the greatest part died of hunger, and we who remained, in order not to die as those did, have all this time done no other thing than rob and kill and eat. Seeing, then, that the land was going to destruction, and that the first Governor was bad, and the second much worse, and that Your Majesty had in a happy hour arrived in these kingdoms, I determined to come and give You intelligence of this, as to my Lord and King." Touching the Indians, the Bishop said,

His opinion of the governors of Darien.

that from what he had seen of them, both in his own diocese, and on his journey, his opinion was that they were by nature slaves.

Speech of Las Casas. Las Casas was now commanded to speak. It will be needless, however, to recount his speech, as his thoughts on these subjects, and the principal facts which he enumerated, have already been stated in various parts of this narrative. It appears that the Bishop of Darien, in the course of his argument, had quoted Plato, to which the Clerigo, I am sorry to say, made this reply: "Plato was a Gentile, and is now burning in Hell, and we are only to make use of his doctrine as far as it is consistent with our holy Faith and Christian customs."

Though the speech of the Clerigo need not be reported in full, one declaration that he made must not be omitted, in which he told the King, that he had not taken up his vocation to please him, but to please God, and in proof of this bold assertion, went on to say, "I renounce whatever temporal honour or reward Your Majesty may wish to confer upon me."*

---

* Indeed, he went so far as to say that, with all respect for so great a King, he would not go from where he stood

Las Casas having finished, the Franciscan Father was ordered to speak. "My Lord," he said, "I have been certain years in the island of Hispaniola, and I was commanded with others to go and visit and take the number of Indians in the island, and we found that they were so many thousand. Afterwards, at the end of two years, a similar charge was again given to me, and we found that there had perished so many thousand. And thus the infinity of people who were in that island has been destroyed. Now, if the blood of one person unjustly put to death was of such effect that it was not removed out of the sight of God until he had taken vengeance for it, and the blood of the others never ceases to exclaim ' *Vindica sanguinem nostrum, Deus noster*,' what will the blood do of such innumerable people as have

Speech of a Franciscan monk.

---

to the corner of the room, merely to serve His Majesty, unless it were to perform his duty as a subject, and unless he thought that it were consistent with the will of God to do so.—" Es cierto (hablando con todo acatamiento y reverencia que se deve á tan alto Rey é Señor) que de aquí á aquel rincon no me mudaré por servir á Vuestra Magestad, salva la fidelidad que como subdito devo, sino pensase y creyese hacer á Dios en ello gran sacrificio."—Las Casas, *Hist. de las Indias*, MS., lib. iii. cap. 148.

perished in those lands under such great tyranny and injustice? Then, by the blood of Jesus Christ and by the wounds* of St. Francis, I pray and entreat Your Majesty, that you would find a remedy for such wickedness and such destruction of people, as perish daily there, so that the divine justice may not pour out its severe indignation upon all of us."

It was a short speech, but uttered with such fervour, that it seemed to Las Casas as if all the persons there present were already listening to words pronounced in the Day of Judgment.

The Admiral was then requested to speak. He spoke prudently, acknowledging the evils, bearing witness as to what the *religiosos* had done in denouncing these evils, and praying also on his part for a remedy.

Upon the Admiral's ceasing to speak, the Bishop of Darien asked for leave to reply, but he was desired to deliver in writing what more he had to say. The King then rose, and retired into his room, and the audience was ended. It may be hoped that the young Emperor, who, we

Marginalia: Speech of the Admiral of the Indies. Audience ended.

---

* The *stigmata*.

are told, was unmoved by his new title,* but who had now begun to reign for himself,† found much to ponder over, from this his first audience in the affairs of the Indies.

It may be as well to mention here, that the Bishop of Darien did submit his information and his opinions about the Indies in writing, that his memorials were very much in accordance with the statements that Las Casas had already made, and that the Bishop, when asked his opinion respecting the Clerigo's plan, approved of it, to the great delight, as Las Casas tells us, of the Chancellor and Laxao, as men who loved to favour a good design, and had no mean ends of their own. It may be remarked that Peter Martyr, who is always sufficiently severe upon the Flemings, finds much to praise in this Chancellor.

Bishop of Darien gives his opinion in writing.

---

* "Rex, jam Cæsar, quicquid in humanis præstare fortuna potest visus est nihili facere. Tanta est ejus gravitas et animi magnitudo, ut habere sub pedibus universum præ se ferre videatur."—PETER MARTYR, *Epist.*, 648.

† "Porque, como el Rey comenzaba entonces á reinar, eran frecuentes los consejos."—LAS CASAS, *Hist. de las Indias*, MS., lib. iii. cap. 147.

Jeronimites.

At this time the Jeronimite Fathers came to court, on their return from Hispaniola; but, not being able to obtain an audience of the King, they retired to their monasteries, and, I believe, were no more heard of in the government of the Indies.

The King went to Coruña, in order to embark there, and to proceed to Germany for the purpose of being made Emperor with the due formalities, and the last seven days before his embarkation were given to the business of the Indies. In one of the Councils held on this occasion, the Cardinal Adrian (the former colleague of Ximenes) made a great speech in favour of the liberty of the Indians; and it was resolved that they ought to be free, and should be treated as free men. The

The grant to Las Casas.

grant to Las Casas was also concluded, and the King signed the necessary deed on the 19th of May, 1520. On the 20th he embarked for Flanders. It was during this voyage that he landed at Dover; and his object in making this visit was to prevent, if possible, the injury which he, or his councillors, foresaw might arise to his affairs from the meeting of the Kings of France and England at the proposed tourney, afterwards called the Field of the Cloth of Gold. Cardinal Adrian was nominated as Regent of Spain during the King's absence.

In the settlement of the details of the Clerigo's business, he was left to the mercy of the Bishop of Burgos, and a most formidable opposition might in consequence have been expected; but, strange to say, the Bishop facilitated the settlement of the affair, thus showing himself to have some nobleness of mind, for, the King and the Flemish ministers having departed, Las Casas was but a shadow of his former self. The Clerigo, too, meeting his old adversary's relentings with equal generosity, expresses a hope (though mingled with great fear about the result) that *all* the mischief the Bishop had been the cause of in the Indies might not come upon his soul; and Las Casas finds some excuse for the Bishop in his not having been a learned man, but having followed the ignorance of the learned. Each must have felt for the other as one of the chiefs in OSSIAN, who says, "I love a foe like Cathmor: his soul is great; his arm is strong; there is fame in his battles. But the little soul is like a vapour that hovers round a marshy lake. It never rises on the green hill, lest the winds meet it there."

<small>Bishop of Burgos favours the Clerigo.</small>

The Clerigo's purpose unchanged.

We must not suppose that, absorbed in all these secular negociations, the Clerigo had changed the main drift of his purpose. That was still spiritual, or, at the lowest, philanthropic, as we may gather from a remarkable answer which he made at an early stage of the proceedings to a certain licentiate, called Aguirre, a very good man, of great authority in those times, whom Queen Isabella had chosen for one of her executors. This man had always loved and favoured Las Casas, but when he found that the Clerigo was pursuing an enterprize in which Aguirre heard of rents being paid to the King, and of honours being sought for by Las Casas on behalf of his companions, the licentiate said "that such a manner of proceeding in preaching the gospel had scandalized him, for it evinced an aiming after temporal interests, which he had never hitherto suspected in the Clerigo."*

---

* " Dijo que le habia desedificado aquella manera de proceder en la predicacion Evangelica, porque mostraba pretender temporal interese, lo que nunca hasta entonces habia sospechado de él."—LAS CASAS, *Hist. de las Indias*, MS., lib. iii. cap. 137.

Las Casas, having heard what Aguirre had said, took occasion to speak to him one day in the following terms: "Señor, if you were to see our Lord Jesus Christ maltreated, vituperated, and afflicted, would you not implore with all your might that those who had him in their power would give him to you, that you might serve and worship him?" "Yes," said Aguirre. "Then," replied Las Casas, "if they would not give him to you, but would sell him, would you redeem him?" "Without a doubt." "Well, then, Señor," rejoined Las Casas, "that is what I have done, for I have left in the Indies Jesus Christ, our Lord, suffering stripes, and afflictions, and crucifixion, not once but thousands of times, at the hands of the Spaniards, who destroy and desolate those Indian nations, taking from them the opportunity of conversion and penitence, so that they die without faith and without sacraments."

His reply to the licentiate Aguirre.

Then Las Casas went on to explain how he had sought to remedy these things in the way that Aguirre would most have approved. To this the answer had been, that the King would have no rents, wherefore, when he, Las Casas, saw that his opponents would sell him the gospel, he had offered those temporal inducements which Aguirre had heard of and disapproved.

The licentiate considered this a sufficient answer, and so, I think, would any reasonable man.

CHAPTER VI.

Las Casas tries to detain Ocampo's Expedition—He complains to the Audiencia—He is put in command of an Expedition to the Terra-firma—His followers desert him on his arrival there.

BEFORE following Las Casas any farther, we must mention that in 1518 several monks, Franciscans, as well as Dominicans, founded two monasteries on the Pearl Coast, one called Santa Fé de Chiribichi and the other Cumaná. They were very successful in attracting to themselves the Indians, and lived a peaceful and unmolested life, till a Spaniard of the name of Ojeda, a pearl fisher, who dwelt in the neighbouring island of Cubagua, being in want of slaves, treacherously captured and carried off some of the Indians dwelling in their neighbourhood. Ojeda had previously visited the Dominicans, and it is supposed that the Indians

K

imagined the Dominicans (who, however, were perfectly innocent) to be connected in some way with this outrage, and resolved to revenge themselves. A few Sundays afterwards, as they were celebrating mass, the Indians rushed in, and murdered several of them. The Franciscans at Cumaná were also attacked, and the fury of the Indians, once excited, was such that they did not spare even the live creatures found in the monastery, down to the cats.

The Spaniards on the island of Cubagua, hearing that the infuriated Indians intended attacking them, were seized with a panic, and deserted the island, and when the Indians poured over it like a furious wave they found great stores of goods and merchandize which these wealthy pearl fishers had left behind them.

The authorities at St. Domingo send an expedition to Chiribichi.

When these events at Cubagua and on the Pearl Coast came to the knowledge of the *audiencia* at St. Domingo, they resolved to send an expedition to Chiribichi and its vicinity, to avenge the murder of the monks and the devastation of Cubagua,—and, as a matter of course, to enslave Indians. This expedition was now on its way, and was expected at Porto Rico, when Las Casas arrived there; and this is the news with which he was greeted. We may imagine the dismay that such tidings, appreciated by him in all their consequences, would cause in his mind. Fortunately for himself, he was one of those men who find some relief for their misfortunes in their indignation. Moreover, he probably entertained a hope that he would yet be able to prevent the mischief which he foresaw; and, accordingly, when the vessels arrived at Porto Rico, he showed his powers to Ocampo, whom the *audiencia* had entrusted with the command, and endeavoured to detain the expedition. But Ocampo, with all due expressions of civility to Las Casas, said, that he must execute his orders, and that the *audiencia* would bear him harmless. The expedition accordingly sailed on: and Las Casas, after distributing his labourers by threes and fours amongst the inhabitants of Porto Rico, hastened to St. Domingo.

His appearance there was very unwelcome. Indeed, from the exertions he had already made at the court of Spain and elsewhere in favour of the Indians, he was odious to all the Spanish

Las Casas seeks to detain Ocampo.

colonists.* He endeavoured to carry things with a high hand, but met with the usual hindrances and vexations that he had endured both at home and abroad from his countrymen in office. They did not dare, however, to oppose him openly, clothed as he was with the King's authority, and having the reputation of being in favour with the all-powerful Flemish ministers. He demanded that a proclamation should be made of the Royal Order of which he was the bearer: namely—that no one should dare to injure or affront any of the natives of those provinces which were within the limits granted to the Clerigo Las Casas. If they did do so, it would be at the peril of the confiscation of all their goods, and even of their lives. This was proclaimed in the usual manner, with sound of trumpet, in the principal streets, the Admiral and all the chief authorities being present.

He then demanded, that, with the least pos-

---

* " El que muchos no quisieron ver porque ya era por todas estas tierras odioso por saber que pretendia libertar los Indios y librallos de las manos de sus matadores."—LAS CASAS, *Hist. de las Indias*, MS., lib. iii. cap. 156.

sible delay, they should recal their fleet, discontinue the war, and cause their troops to quit the territory which had been given in charge to him. Again, they did not dare to refuse openly, but made answer that they were about to take the matter into consideration: and many days they spent in discourse about it without their coming to any conclusion.

Efforts of Las Casas to counteract Ocampo's expedition.

Meanwhile, a counter attack was very skilfully made by the Clerigo's enemies, which term probably included the whole population of the colony, with the exception of a few private friends, and of the Dominican monks, or any other persons in religious orders. There was a certain Biscayan shipwright who had two vessels of his own that were constantly engaged in the Cubaguan slave-trade, for so it may be called. This man no sooner saw Las Casas and knew the business upon which he had come, than, as the Clerigo expresses it, he would sooner have seen the Evil One. Scanning the ship of Las Casas with all the critical dislike of an enemy, the Biscayan pronounced that it was not sea-worthy, and that it could not be made sea-worthy. Here was a subject for enquiry which the authorities were willing should be investigated without delay. The King's subjects must not be permitted to go in vessels that were not sea-worthy. An examination was made, the hostile shipwright being, according to the Clerigo's recollection, one of the persons appointed to examine. The body thus constituted condemned the vessel, pronouncing it neither fit for navigation, nor capable of being made fit. "All this," as Las Casas declares, "was done to hinder the business of the Clerigo, as being odious to all; for all, both judges and official men, had a share in the business of man-stealing." By the condemnation of his vessel, Las Casas lost what was worth to him 500 pesos of gold, and, what were far more valuable at the present juncture,—time, reputation, and the means of transit.

Meanwhile, Ocampo had reached the port of Maracapána, in the territory of Gil Gonçalez, where the Spaniard took a very crafty method of securing the chief men of that district. On approaching the coast, Ocampo kept all his men but a few of the sailors, under hatches. The Indians, on hailing the vessels, enquired whence they came, to which the Spaniards answered

"Castilla." The Indians shouted out "Hayti, Hayti?" The Spaniards again replied "Castilla, Castilla," and made signs that they had wine and other things from Spain to barter. The Indians, thinking that they had to deal with Spaniards who did not know what had happened on that coast, no longer hesitated to enter the vessels and exchange goods. The Cacique himself, more wary than his followers, remained in a boat near to the vessel. But one of the sailors, who was an excellent swimmer, let himself down by a rope, sprung into the Cacique's canoe, plunged with him into the water, and, stabbing him in several places with a dagger, succeeded, with the help of some other sailors, in carrying him to the vessel. At the same time, a signal having been given on board, the concealed Spaniards rushed on deck, and the Indians in the vessel were captured. Gil Gonçalez and the principal chiefs were hung from the yard-arm as an example of terror to the Indians standing on the shore. Amongst these, it is said, was the Cacique of Cumaná. Now Ocampo had on board the wife, or one of the wives, of this Cacique, named Donna Maria, who had been carried by Flores from Cubagua to Hispaniola. The

Ocampo's success.

Spanish Commander gave her liberty and set her on shore, and through her means peace was ultimately restored between the Spaniards and the Indians of that coast, but not until Ocampo had thoroughly chastized the latter, and captured many slaves; carrying his incursions, I observe, into that mountainous country, the abode of the Tagares, where Ojeda had bought his maize and had committed the crime which caused the general rising of the inhabitants of the Pearl Coast.

Las Casas soon learnt by the surest means what was going on in his province of Cumaná, for, while he was endeavouring to adjust matters with the authorities of Hispaniola, Indian slaves were brought to St. Domingo, the first-fruits of Ocampo's campaigning. At this the Clerigo was excessively indignant:—to use his own expressive words — " he went raging, and with terrible sternness bore witness against this thing before the *audiencia*,"* pouring out all manner of threats against them. They thought it better to come

---

* "Viéndolos venir el Padre Clérigo, rabiaba, y con terrible rigor lo detestava delante el Audiencia."—LAS CASAS, *Hist. de las Indias*, MS., lib. iii. cap. 156

OCAMPO'S EXPEDITION.

to terms with him, and for this purpose they devised a plan which would not only remedy the past, but from which they might hope for some profit in the future. This was to offer to become partners with Las Casas in working out his grant from the King. They sent for him and made their proposition. He listened favourably to their terms; and it was finally agreed that Las Casas should go to the territories assigned to him; and that the expedition which had been sent out under Ocampo should now be placed under the Clerigo's command. Accordingly, two vessels were fitted out for him, and well provisioned. Ocampo's expedition consisted of three hundred men: out of them Las Casas was to choose a hundred and twenty, who were to be paid wages: the rest were to be sent back.

Scheme of the audiencia.

Adopted by Las Casas.

This agreement between the authorities of St. Domingo and Las Casas took the form of a commercial speculation. There was to be a company, and the venture was to be divided into twenty-four shares. The King was to have six shares in the concern, the Clerigo and his Knights six shares, the Admiral three shares, the Auditors, the Treasurer, the Contador and other official people, each a share. The means of profit were to be found in pearl-fishing, exchanging trifling commodities for gold, and making slaves, which last was a great object, for the following reason. Many of the principal persons in St. Domingo had bands of slaves employed under mayordomos in the pearl fishery at Cubagua; and human life was swiftly exhausted in procuring these diseased productions then so highly valued—the water mines, if we may so call them, being quite as injurious to the delicate Indian as those on land. A constant supply of slaves on the spot where their services were most valuable, was much to be desired.

This last mentioned means of profit was to be provided for in the following manner. Las Casas was to ascertain what Indians in those parts were cannibals, or would not be in amity and converse with the Spaniards, or would not receive the Faith and the preachers of it. Upon his pronouncing against the natives of any province upon either of the above points, these people were to be attacked by the hundred and twenty men under Ocampo, and were to be made slaves. Anybody who hoped that Las Casas would so pronounce must, as he intimates, have been somewhat mistaken in their man.*

The whole of this business must have been exceedingly distasteful to Las Casas; but he saw no other way of accomplishing any part of his object, and prudently availed himself of this.

Near at hand, there lay on his death-bed the man who, of all others, would have sympathized most with Las Casas in his efforts to civilize and convert the poor Indians of the Terra-firma. This was Pedro de Córdova, who, at the early age of thirty-eight, was now dying of consumption in the monastery of St. Domingo, worn out by the ascetic life he had led. We do not learn whether Las Casas was able to consult "that servant of God," as he always calls him, about

---

* " Y era tanta su ceguedad, que no advirtieron que habiendo andado cinco ó seis años el Clerigo (como todos sabian) trabajando y muriendo, yendo y viniendo á Castilla á Castilla, (sic in MS.) porque no hiciesen esclavos, y los que tenian hechos los libertasen, aunque fuesen de los Caribes ó que comian carne humana, oyéndole afirmar que hacellos aquellos esclavos era tiranía, que así engañasen á sí mismos, que pensasen que el Clérigo habia de ser causa de aquellas guerras."—LAS CASAS, *Hist. de las Indias*, MS., lib. iii. cap. 156.

the expedition; but, if he had done so, the dying Father could but have given one reply, as anything must have seemed advisable which promised to hinder the outrages which the men in Ocampo's expedition were inflicting upon the natives of the Terra-firma.

<small>Death of Pedro de Córdova.</small>

Pedro de Córdova departed this life in May, 1521. We know, however, that he left one worthy to succeed him in his office, for it is mentioned that Antonio Montesino, already well-known to the readers of this history, preached the funeral sermon on his late prelate, taking for the text, " Behold, how good and how pleasant it is for brethren to dwell together in unity." This resolute and noble monk, the especial friend of the Indians, no doubt felt as his late prelate would have done about the project of Las Casas. Another motive, too, which would have ensured the concurrence of Pedro de Córdova, Antonio Montesino, or any of the Dominican fraternity in Hispaniola, with the plans of Las Casas was, that in him they were certain of a protector to any monastery they might found again at Chiribichi, to replace the one which had been swept away in the late outbreak of the Indians.

Meanwhile the provisions were put on board the vessels intrusted to Las Casas by the *audiencia* of San Domingo. These provisions consisted of wine, oil, vinegar, and a great quantity of cheese from the Canary Islands. He had orders to go to the island of Mona, and take on board eleven hundred loaves of cassava bread from the King's stores in that island. He was also well provided with sea-stores of all kinds, and articles of merchandize; and, everything being now ready, in July of that year he set sail from San Domingo.

<small>Las Casas sets sail, July, 1521.</small>

Having received his cargo of bread at the island of Mona, he proceeded to Porto Rico for the labourers he had left there. But, as might have been expected, not a single man of them was to be found; and the Clerigo had not even the comfort of finding that his humble and simple followers had been employed in the cultivation of the earth, or in any good work, but he learnt that they had enlisted with certain freebooters, whose occupation it was to attack and pillage the Indians. It requires a large experience of mankind before we ascertain that gentle, simple, and ignorant people are not the best for keeping their promises. With some men it requires a certain training of the intel-

<small>What had become of his followers.</small>

lect, or an acquaintance with discipline, to make them faithful and true. Had Las Casas been enabled to bring out with him from Spain real knights, men worthy of wearing golden spurs, they might have been true to themselves and to him. Now he was left to prosecute his enterprize without any body of followers especially attached to him.

<small>Reaches the Terra-firma.</small>

Nothing was to be done, however, but to proceed in his voyage to the Terra-firma. When he arrived there, he found, as might have been foreseen, that Ocampo's men were pillaging and making slaves. They were in great want of provisions, as the Indians fled before them : and, without the assistance of the natives, the Spaniards were never able to purvey adequately for themselves. Ocampo

<small>Nueva Toledo founded.</small>

was busy founding a town about half a league above the river Cumaná, which he called Nueva Toledo; but even if it had been named New Seville, as Las Casas humorously remarks, the men would not have taken to it any the more. On the arrival of the Clerigo, they all resolved to avail themselves of the licence to return which had been granted beforehand for some of them, and to go home, having no fancy to continue with the Clerigo, being weary of the country, and looking upon him as a bad captain for marauding expeditions. So fearful were they of being detained, that they would never come on shore all at once, but took care to leave twenty men, whom they could depend upon, in the ships.

Ocampo's men will not stay with Las Casas.

Furnishing them with provisions for the voyage, Las Casas allowed them to go, but remained himself with a few servants and hired labourers. The polite and witty Ocampo, as might be expected from the feelings that one gentleman would have for another, showed regret at leaving the Clerigo in this deserted state; but was obliged, nevertheless, to take his departure. And now Las Casas, with his great projects, his immense territory, his scanty resources, was indeed alone. Never, perhaps, was there a position which the philanthropic part of mankind would have regarded with more profound concern and more solicitous apprehension.

CHAPTER VII.

Las Casas alone in the land—He is received into the Franciscan Monastery—Fate of his Colony.

THE Dominican community, to whom of course Las Casas would first have turned, had, as it appears, been entirely swept away. The Franciscans, however, had returned, and they were the sole nucleus of Christianity and of civilization in that immense expanse of country, a seventh part of the whole world. People are often seeking for romance in all kinds of fiction; but how really romantic such a situation as this was! The light from that monastery, the sound of its bell amidst the wilderness of idolatry, what signs of hope they were—which angels might have watched with unspeakable joy, and yet with apprehension.

It must have been no little comfort to Las

Casas, at this juncture, to find that the Franciscans had already repaired the ruin which had fallen upon them, together with the rest of the Spaniards in that part of the country. The monks must have re-established themselves under Ocampo's protection; and it does not seem as if their monastery could have suffered anything like the devastation which had come upon the unfortunate and equally innocent Dominicans.

When the Franciscans heard of the Clerigo's arrival, they came out to meet him with great joy, chanting a *Te Deum*. Their little monastery was on the river-side,* "a cross-bow-shot" from the sea-shore. It was constructed of wood and thatched with straw; and it had a pleasant garden with orange trees, vines, and melons in it. Las Casas built a large storehouse adjoining the monastery, and there he stowed away his goods. The first thing he did was to convey his message of peace to the Indians, which he accomplished by means of Donna Maria (before mentioned as the wife of the Cacique of Cumaná), who knew something of the Spanish language. Through

The Franciscans receive Las Casas.

---

* The river Cumaná, now called the Manzanares.

L

He sends a message of peace to the Indians.

this woman Las Casas informed the Indians that he had been sent by the new King of Spain, and that henceforth they were to experience nothing but kind treatment and good works from the Christians, as an earnest of which, he sent them some of the presents which he had brought from Castille, to gain their friendship.

The founding of a colony is always one of the most interesting things in the world; and it is surprizing that rich and powerful men in our own times do not more frequently give themselves to such splendid undertakings. But, in this particular case, the interest is doubled, from the feeling that the leader is no mere adventurer and has no private ambition, but is trying a great experiment for the good of the world. Moreover, one is always curious to see a man in a position which he has long sought for, where he has in some measure to fulfil the day-dreams of his life. The first proceedings of Las Casas seem to have been judicious; and, altogether, though this settlement at Cumaná was but a little one, a mere fragment of the great undertaking which Las Casas had originally designed, still much might have been hoped from it, if there had been no

Spaniards near to hinder the good work. Unfortunately, however, there was the island of Cubagua at a short distance from the coast, and, as there was no fresh water there, the Spaniards, engaged in pearl-fishing near that island, had a motive for coming frequently to the river Cumaná in the main land, which was but seven leagues off.

Spaniards at Cubagua a great detriment.

Las Casas, thinking to have some curb upon these Spaniards, engaged with a master mason at the rate of ten ducats a month, to build a fort at the mouth of the river; but the Spaniards of the island, the "apostles of Cubagua," as Las Casas sarcastically calls them, soon perceived the drift of the Clerigo's building, and the builder was bribed, or persuaded, by them, to desist from his work. The visits, therefore, of the Spaniards to the mainland were as uncontrolled as ever. The Indians had no love for these visitors, but then they brought wine with them, and this won over even those Indians who had most distaste to the Spaniards. And, just as a child cannot handle with any safety the arms of a grown-up man, so there is always danger for a people when, without fit preparation, it comes to use the products of an older state, whether it be strong wine, or a well-compacted political constitution. To obtain this all-seducing wine, which, or the like of which, has ever proved the subtlest and most destructive weapon against aborigines, clearing them off as fire consumes the dry herbage of the prairie, the Indians brought gold and slaves to the Spaniards, the slaves being youths and simple persons.

Of the light way in which such simple persons were made slaves among the Mexicans, and probably among these Indians too, we have a curious instance in the letter of Rodrigo de Albornoz to the Emperor in 1525.* He says, that "for very little things and almost in jest they became slaves to one another," and, as an instance, he mentions that when he was once officially examining some slaves, he asked one of them the origin of his

marginal note: Light way in which the Indians became slaves among their own people.

---

* " Dijo que no, sino que un dia que ellos estavan en sus areitos, que es su fiesta, tañia uno un ataval que ellos usan en sus fiestas, como los de España í que le tomó gana de tañer en él, í que el dueño no se lo quiso dexar tañer si no se lo pagaba, í como él no tenia que le dar, dixo seria su esclavo, í el otro le dejó tañer aquel dia, í de allí adelante quedó por su esclavo í despues le havia vendido tres ó quatro veces."—*Al* EMPERADOR CARLOS 5°. RODRIGO DE ALBORNOZ, *en Temistitan á 15 de diciembre, de 1525.— Coleccion de* MUÑOZ, MS., tom. 77.

slavery,—whether he was the son of slave parents, for instance; and the Indian replied, "No, but that one day when they were in the midst of their *areitos*, which is their festival, a man was beating an *ataval*, which they use in their feasts, like those of the Spaniards, and that he wished very much to play upon it, and that the owner would not let him without being paid for it; as he had nothing to give, he said that he would be his slave, and the other let him play the instrument for that one day, and thenceforward he was the other's slave." And Albornoz tells the Monarch, that the existence of such light modes of creating slavery is a thing to be considered " for the sake of Your Majesty's conscience as well as of Your Majesty's service."

But to return to the Cubaguans.—There is no doubt that their frequent communication with the Indians of Cumaná was likely to be fatal to the plans of the Clerigo: and so he felt it to be. Their conduct was a practical denial of his message from the King. He went to Cubagua and made most forcible appeals (*requerimientos terribles*) to the Alcalde there: but all to no effect. The chief monk of the Franciscans, Padre Joan de

Garceto, saw the matter in the same light as Las Casas, and urged him to go to St. Domingo and to appeal to the *audiencia,* in order to provide some remedy for the evils arising from the visits of the Cubaguans. Two vessels were lading with salt, and the Clerigo, he said, could go in one of them, which would be ready to sail in a month. Las Casas did not see the need for his going; but the Franciscan Father was very urgent about it. Every day they had mass and prayers for inspiration in this matter, and discoursed upon it after prayers. Father Garceto, with true Flemish perseverance, never swerved from his opinion, or from the same expression of it, winding up the discourse by saying, " It does not appear to me, Sir, but that you have to go and seek a remedy for these evils, in the cessation of which so much is at stake."*

But Las Casas was naturally very unwilling to leave his territory without the protection, slight as it might be, of his presence; and, besides,

Las Casas advised to go to St. Domingo.

---

* " No me parece, Señor, sino que vos habeis de ir á buscar el remedio de estos males en cuya cessacion tanto vá."—LAS CASAS, *Hist. de las Indias,* MS., lib. iii. cap. 157.

though this was a small matter, he had been entrusted with no small amount of merchandize. He accordingly prepared two sets of papers :—one being a memorandum naming Francisco de Soto captain in the Clerigo's absence, and giving him the necessary instructions; and the other being a despatch, in which an appeal was made to the *audiencia* of St. Domingo for protection from the visits of the Spaniards at Cubagua. This course left it open to Las Casas to change his mind at the final moment of the departure of the ships. At last the day came when it must be decided whether Las Casas was to go or not. Mass was said as usual, and the friends afterwards took counsel together as they were accustomed; when Father Garceto pronounced his unvarying opinion—" Sir, you have to go, and by no means to remain."

Father Garceto's pertinacity.

Overcome by this perseverance on the part of the Franciscan, which the Clerigo thought might be an expression of the will of God, he yielded, but still was not convinced. God knows," he exclaimed, " how much I do this against my judgment and also against my will, but I am willing to do it, since it seems good to your Reverence;

and if it be an error, I would rather err upon the opinion of another man, than succeed by taking my own. Wherefore I hope in God that, since I do not do this thing for any other intent than to perform my duty in that which I have undertaken for His service, He will convert even error into advantage." Hereupon we may remark, that a man seldom makes so signal a blunder as when he acts exceptionally, and contradicts the usual tenour of his life and character. Las Casas was not wont to defer much to other men's opinions, and why he should have given way to this good Franciscan, who knew much less of the world than the Clerigo did, is scarcely explicable, except upon the ground that the Franciscan's arguments were so weak, and his opinions so strong, as to give an appearance of mysterious significance to it, before which a pious man like Las Casas would be more likely to bow than to a well-connected train of reasoning. However, the decision was now arrived at, and he set sail in the salt-carrying vessel bound for St. Domingo, having parted from the Franciscan monks with great grief on their part, and he not being a man,

Las Casas quits his colony.

as he well says, alluding to his affectionate disposition, to feel less grief on his part.*

Las Casas was not fortunate, perhaps not wise, in his choice of agents. Francisco de Soto was a good and prudent man, but poor; and the Clerigo assigns to this poverty all the evils which De Soto was the cause of. The first thing after the departure of Las Casas that Francisco de Soto did, notwithstanding the express written orders (a copy of which orders De Soto had signed) of his master to the contrary, was to send away the only two boats the little colony had, to traffic for pearls, gold, and even for slaves, as some believe. Now the Clerigo, aware to some extent of the temper of the Indians, had given orders to De Soto, not on any account to send away these boats, so that if he should perceive symptoms of hostility in the Indians, he might be able to embark the men and goods in these boats, or the men at least, if there were not time to embark the goods, and thus to save the little colony. One

De Soto disobedient.

---

* "Así se partió con harto dolor de los Frailes, no siendo el qui él llevaba menos."—Las Casas, *Hist. de las Indias*, MS., lib. iii. cap. 157.

of these boats was fitted with sails; the other was a Moorish rowing-boat with many oars, which the Indians in their language called "the centipede," and of which they were much afraid.

The Indians had not had time to appreciate the motives or the purposes of Las Casas. Nothing but evil had hitherto come to them from converse with the Spaniards. The pearl-fishers of Cubagua had not ceased to molest the natives of Cumaná; and now, whether moved by former, yet recent, injuries, or by new insults received after the Clerigo's departure; or whether, as he also conjectures, they were by the decrees of Providence not destined to receive the blessings of the gospel, they resolved to make an onslaught upon the settlement. Twelve days had not elapsed since Las Casas had sailed, before the Franciscan brotherhood discerned the symptoms of coming danger; and they asked Donna Maria whether their suspicions were just or not, to which, as some of her countrymen were present, who might make out something of the conversation, she replied with her voice "No," but with her eyes she said "Yes."

At this point of time a Spanish vessel touched

Symptoms of danger from the natives.

at the coast, and the servants of the Clerigo begged to be taken on board; but, whether from fear or malice, the masters of the vessel would not listen to the request; and the little colony was left to its fate.

The poor Franciscan monks and the Clerigo's lieutenant roamed about now in all the agony of fear and indecision, endeavouring to find out, by going from one Indian hut to another, when the blow was to take place. On the fourteenth day after the departure of Las Casas, they discovered that the attack was to be made on the following morning; and then at last they resolved to fortify the monastery and the adjoining storehouse. With that purpose they placed round the building the twelve or fourteen guns which they possessed; but on examination they found at this critical juncture that their powder was damp. *The Spaniards take measures for defence.*

Early on the ensuing morning, (this was now the third day after warning had come to them from the eyes of the kind-hearted Indian woman), and while they were drying their powder in the sun, the Indians with a terrible war-whoop rushed down upon them. Two or three of the

Clerigo's servants were killed at the first onset: the rest, with the Franciscans, made good the entrance to the monastery. The Indians, however, succeeded in setting it on fire. But fortunately there was a postern door that led into the enclosed garden before mentioned, which was surrounded by a hedge of canes. Another door from the garden led out upon the bank of the river. At the moment of attack Francisco de Soto happened to be in the Indian *pueblo* of Cumanà, which was situated on the sea shore, a very short distance from the monastery. As soon as he perceived what was going on, he fled to the monastery, but in his flight was wounded by a poisoned arrow. He succeeded, however, in making his way into the garden with the other Spaniards. At the distance of a "stone's-throw" there was a little creek, where the monks had a canoe of their own which would hold fifty persons. They gained this canoe, and pushed off down the river, while the Indians thought they were being burnt in the monastery. The number of persons in the canoe was about fifteen, or twenty, including all of Las Casas's servants and all the Franciscan monks, with the exception of one lay-brother, who at the first war-whoop of the Indians had fled, and thrown himself into a bed of canes. He now made his appearance high up upon the bank: his friends in the boat did their utmost to get to the place where he was, but the stream was very strong against them. He, poor man, very nobly made signs to them, not to attempt to return; and they left him to his fate. All this must have taken some time, and the Indians now caught sight of the boat. Instantly they manned a light boat of their own, lighter than the canoe, called a *piragua*, set off in pursuit, and soon gained upon the Spaniards, whose object was to pull for the port of Araya, two leagues and a half across the gulf (of Cariaco). They pulled as men pulling for their lives, but the swift *piragua* still gained upon them; and they had not proceeded more than a league, when they saw that their only chance was to take to the shore again, and throw themselves into one of the dense beds of cactus with which that coast abounds. The *piragua* and the canoe landed not "a quoit's-throw" from each other. Happily there was time enough for the Spaniards to take refuge amongst the cactuses, pervious only to despair, Escape of the Spaniards.

but otherwise hardly to be penetrated by a fully-armed man. The Indians were naked, and though they made great efforts to get at the Spaniards in this "thorn fortress," they could not do so,* though they were at one time very near to them, so near that Father Joan Garceto lived to tell Las Casas,—how one Indian was close upon him, and lifted up his club (*macana*) to kill him, and the Father bent his knees, and shut his eyes, and raised his heart to God; but when he looked up, there was no one. Finally, in the course of the next day, they got to their countrymen's ships. De Soto died of the wounds which he had received, as the arrows were poisoned. The other servants of Las Casas, all but the two or three who perished at the first onset, together with the Franciscans, arrived in a short time at St. Domingo.

All this happened in little more than a fortnight after the Clerigo's departure. Meanwhile,

---

* " Y como los Indios eran, de los piés á las cabezas, desnudos, estubieron mucho tiempo en llegar aquella poca distancia en donde estaban los Seglares y Frailes. Y parece que habia tanta espesura que no pudieron menearse."— LAS CASAS, *Hist. de las Indias*, MS., lib. iii. cap. 158.

he himself had been carried by the ignorance of his mariners far beyond the port of St. Domingo: he had to waste two months in beating against contrary currents; and finally he landed on another part of the island of Hispaniola. As he was travelling thence to St. Domingo in company with other persons, and they were taking their *siesta* on the bank of a river, and he was asleep under a tree, a party from the city came up to them, and, being asked the news, said that the Indians of the Pearl Coast had killed the Clerigo Bartolomé de Las Casas and all his household. Those who journeyed with the Clerigo said, "We are witnesses that that is impossible." While they were disputing, Las Casas awoke to hear this news; and, versed in misfortune as he was, this must have been the most fatal intelligence he ever received, and the most difficult to bear, for, though he was sure enough that some of it was untrue, yet he could easily divine that some terrible disaster had happened to his little colony. Afterwards, he came to look upon the event as a judgment upon him for having acted in company with men whose only object had been self-enrichment, saying, "that though God uses

<small>Las Casas learns the fate of his colony.</small>

human means to bring about his ends, yet that such helps (*adminiculos*) are not needed for preaching the gospel." "Still," as he urges on the other side, " if he was in such haste to accept the offer of the *audiencia*, it was but to prevent the slaughter and destruction which Ocampo's expedition was occasioning."

Meanwhile, in great anxiety to hear the whole of the bad news, he approached the city of St. Domingo, and when near there, some "good Christians," friends of his, came out to meet and console him, offering him money, even as much as four or five thousand ducats, for a new attempt to colonize.

But none was to be made; and here, not without much regret at such a termination, we take leave of any further hopes from the Clerigo's noble attempt at colonization; and must content ourselves with being rejoiced that he returned in safety from the Indians of the Pearl Coast, who little knew the disservice they had been doing to their ill-fated race, in thrusting away from them its greatest benefactor.

CHAPTER VIII.

Las Casas becomes a Dominican Monk—He devotes himself to Literature.

THE transactions narrated in the preceding chapter did not pass without much comment, and, amongst other comment, that of contemporary historians, who have given a most unjust and inaccurate version of the whole affair. It affords them great amusement to talk of the "smock-frock soldiers" of the Clerigo, and of the labourers dressed like Knights of Calatrava; but, as we have seen from his own account, which he says is "the pure truth" (*la verdad pura*), none of these labourers went to Cumaná, and, if they had gone there, it was not from their body that the knights were to have been chosen. There were also other statements

Comments of contemporaries.

made by these historians equally false, which Las Casas takes the pains of refuting.

If the writer of this narrative may be permitted to fancy himself addressing Las Casas (and a fearful consideration it is, that biographers and the people they write about may some day be brought into each others' presence), he would say, "You need not have spent so many pages of your valuable history in confuting what has been written on the subject of your expedition, with manifest ill-nature, by Gomara, or, in the spirit of mere worldliness, by Oviedo. But I should like to suggest to you (having been made wise by the event), that, when you had once collected this body of labourers together, and had brought them to Porto Rico, you should not have let them disperse; but, instead of going to the *audiencia* at St. Domingo (never likely to be friendly to you), to prevent the ill effects of Ocampo's expedition, you should have accompanied him at once to Cumaná.

"It was certain that his expedition would render the Indians intolerant of your designs; and you could hardly hope to be in time to check his proceedings by orders from St. Domingo.

Address from the author to Las Casas; ex post eventu sapientia.

Besides, according to your own account, Ocampo was a witty, gracious, agreeable man, an old friend of yours; and had you accompanied him on the voyage, and told him the real feelings of powerful people at court, and then addressed such offers of personal advantage to himself, as I think you might have made, you would perhaps have gained him over. Then at the head of your two or three hundred colonists, and with your own vessels and outfit, you would have been more powerful than you ever were afterwards, though armed with letters from the *audiencia*. I speak, as I said before, with all the easy wisdom gained by knowing the event; and am aware of the foolishness of most criticism upon action. Moreover, I can thoroughly understand your aversion to bring your great scheme into any contact with what was avowedly an avenging, and was likely to be a marauding, expedition.

" I forbear to dwell much upon your rare and unfortunate modesty in yielding to the advice of Father Garceto, and forsaking your little colony, at a time when the presence of one earnest and vigorous man was worth a wilderness of orders from the *audiencia*, which, as you must have known, lost some of their force in every league that they were borne from the centre of authority, until at last in the *llanos,* or the forests, of the Terra-firma, these missives were little better than so much waste-paper."

<small>Las Casas informs the King of his misfortune.</small>

From the molestation of such remarks, in which, however, criticism is meant to be tempered by profound respect, Las Casas was, in all probability, quite free. He wrote to the King, to Cardinal Adrian (by this time advanced to the Papacy, though Las Casas did not know it), and to his other Flemish friends, to tell them what had happened; and then waited until their answers should arrive from Spain.

His thoughts at this period of his life must have been very bitter,—crowded with infinite regrets, and full of fearful anticipations. The prize that had been ever hovering before him was so great—the safety and pacification of vast territories and numerous populations:—the hinderances that had fatally thwarted him were so disproportionately, so malignantly small. The truth is, that for great enterprises, and even in the conduct of common life, it seems as if two souls were needed: the one to watch, while the other sleeps; one to do the worldly work, the other the spiritual; and each to cheer the other with a perfect sympathy. Had Las Casas met with but one man having a soul like his own, who would have been a real lieutenant to him, the obstacles in his way, fearful as they were, might have been doubled, and yet his end have been attained. But what could be hoped from men like Berrio or De Soto, who manifestly possessed none, or next to none, of the spirit and intelligence of their leader?

Harmonious conjoint action was then, as it is now, the greatest difficulty in the world.

Happily, there is an end to all things. Human endeavour ends in conquest, or in defeat, and, in case of either being carried to an extreme, is apt to sink into insensibility. There is the swooning limit to mental, as well as to bodily, endurance. It is most picturesque, and seems grandest, when this is the death-swoon; and when a man's good fortunes, his energies, and his life all unite in falling down together before some great calamity. And, if such had now been the case with the heroic Clerigo, it could have been no matter of surprise to any one who had traced his career up to this fatal period.

Of his power to endure and to persevere, the history of the Indies, if faithfully told, will convince every reader. Indeed, in this power lay the peculiarity of his character, and it was that which marked him out from other men of his time as much perhaps as his benevolence. This kind of perseverance is much more rare than people suppose, and is so hard to maintain, that we cannot but admire even bad men, who silently, resolutely, enduringly pursue some evil object of self-interest, or mere glory, through long and toilsome years. Rarer even than profound attention in the intellect is this kind of pertinacity in the moral powers. Each day brings its own interests with it, and makes its claims very loudly upon the men of that day. But a man with a great social purpose, like Las Casas, has to work on at something, which, for any given day, appears very irrelevant and makes him seem very obtrusive. This unwelcome part he must perform amidst the disgust and weariness of all other people,—through weeks, months, years perhaps, of the most dire discouragement,—when all the

The rarity of perseverance in a great cause.

while life seems too short for a great purpose, and when he feels the tide of events ebb by him, and nothing accomplished. The spectre of Death cowers in his pathway, and, whenever he has time to think away from his subject, occurs to threaten him. But all these vexations and hinderances are as nothing when compared with the weariness and want of elastic power which arise from that terrible familiarity with their subject, which, in the case of most persons, unless they have very deep and very imaginative souls, grows over and incrusts, like a fungus, the life of their original purposes. There are everywhere men of an immense capacity for labour, if their duties are such as come to them day by day to be done, and are connected with self-advancement or renown; but that man is somewhat of a prodigy who is found, in self-appointed labour, as earnest, as strenuous, and as fresh for his work, as those who receive impulses daily renewed which keep them up to their appointed tasks.

Such considerations demand our attention when contemplating the career of such a remarkable man as Las Casas. The age in which he lived was one of singular movement; and his was a

Much conversancy with a subject apt to destroy all care about it.

mind capable of great versatility, and inclined to take an interest in many things. Wars with France, conquests in Italy, contests with England, civil commotions about the liberties of the Spanish Parliaments, the suppression of heretics, dire strife throughout the Germanic Empire, and hard-contested battles with the Moors, were all of them subjects, that in their turn agitated Charles the Fifth and his ministers. Vast discoveries of unknown lands, unheard-of treasures in gold and precious stones, new animals, new men, new trees, the most wild and fanciful forms of life, extraordinary changes of fortune, and romantic adventures, were the daily topics in the Indies. This remarkable man, Las Casas, heard all these things, sympathized with all men's feelings about them; but hardly, I conceive, for any single day, omitted to do something in promoting the fixed purpose of his life. Walking about amongst his fellow men in that tremendous and saddening solitude in which a great idea enwraps a great man; feeling that all his efforts, even if successful, might be so too late; it is to be wondered that such a man retained his sanity, and that we are cognizant but of one long fit of dire despondency in a life of

Las Casas alone with his subject amidst the turmoil of the Empire.

such unwearied effort, such immense successes, and such overpowering disappointments.

The present was the lowest point of depression that the resolute mind of Las Casas ever sounded.

In recounting the latter part of his story as a colonist, a certain hopelessness creeps in upon his narrative. Perhaps the Indians are by the profound ways of Providence ordained to be destroyed, as many other nations have been; perhaps the Spaniards are not to be saved from the commission of great wickedness and from decay of their power; perhaps his own merits were not such as to warrant his being the man chosen to save the one nation, or to redeem the other.* Thus he argues. He intimates that he should have gone back to Spain to seek new

Despondency of Las Casas

---

* " Pero en la verdad no se lo puso Dios en el corazon que fuese, ó porque él no lo mereció, ó porque aquellas gentes segun los profundos juicios divinos se habian con otras muchas de perder, ó porque tambien los facinerosos pecados de nuestra Nacion que en aquellas gentes han cometido, no se habian tan presto de fenecer."—LAS CASAS, *Hist. de las Indias*, MS., lib. iii. cap. 159.

remedies, had he possessed the means; and that, if he had done so, the whole course of events in the Indies might have been greatly changed for the better. I think it is evident, however, that it was not strictly want of means (did not his friends come out to meet him, proffering money?), but that the hopeful spirit, which had been the mainstay of his life, was now deficient in him. Had he been a weak, a selfish, or not a religious man, he would have been absolutely broken-hearted. He was probably as utterly cast down as a good man can be: and I conjecture that he suffered under that abject, nervous depression which results from extreme distress of mind or prolonged overwork, and which none, but those who have suffered something like it, can imagine.

<small>Las Casas does not display his grief.</small>

There are but small indications of the mental sufferings which Las Casas went through at this period of his life. As a gentleman, a scholar, an ecclesiastic, above all, as a Castillian, Las Casas was not likely to spread out the sorrows of his soul on the pages of his history; but enough is there, even in the restrained tone of the narrative, to show how his ardent nature must for the moment have been crushed into torpor by misfortune.

The kind Dominicans, his old friends, received him into their monastery. There I fancy him sitting in some retired nook in their garden, thinking at times of the similar garden at Cumaná, or of the court at Barcelona, Valladolid, or Saragossa, and the great men he had seen and heard there;—then of his old enemy the Bishop of Burgos, whereupon the tears come into his eyes, for, in the bitterest encounters, there is a tenderness which is to come out hereafter. And, besides, he thinks the Bishop would not exult over him now, but would be rather sorry than otherwise. He has sat so long (the once restless man!) that the timid lizard has hurriedly rustled by him many times. And now, with measured step, comes one of his kind hosts, and seats himself on the bench beside him,—a certain Father Betanzos, whom the Clerigo had known for several years, a grey-haired young man, grey from his terrible penances in other lands, who was afterwards a most prominent figure in the history of the New World. And now the good monk, alluding perhaps to some speech which the Clerigo

His thoughts in the monastery.

Father Betanzos and Las Casas.

had uttered in the first bitterness of his disappointment, about retiring from the world, exalts the theme, impresses upon him the paramount necessity for a man to consider his own soul and what he can do to save that, tells him he has done enough for the Indians, and delicately hints that the Clerigo does not seem to be the chosen vessel for the conversion of these nations: to which, in his intense humiliation, Las Casas makes but a poor reply, and, indeed, thinks it must all be true. And then the severe young monk moves away, quite satisfied that he has done a very serviceable thing for the soul of his friend.

Whether the rest of the above picture is to the life, or not, at any rate we know that the brethren did solicit him to become one of themselves. He pleaded that he had written to the King, to Cardinal Adrian, and to others of his Flemish friends; and that he must await their answers. "What will it profit you, if you should die before their answers come?" replied Father Betanzos.* From this it appears as if Las Casas

---

* "Respondió el buen padre, si entre tanto vos os morís, quién rescivirá el mandato del Rey ó sus Cartas?"—Las Casas, *Hist. de las Indias*, MS., lib. iii. cap. 159.

had been ill, although he mentions no illness at this point of his narrative. I conjecture, therefore, that it was the temporary abeyance of the energy within him, which looked like the precursor of death. Hopeless for the moment of gaining his great object, sick of the world, and beginning to ponder more frequently on the state of his soul,* he yielded to the wishes of the friendly monks, and in 1522 received the tonsure from Father Betanzos, to the great joy of the brethren, and also of the inhabitants of St. Domingo, but for very different reasons, as he remarks—the former no doubt rejoicing to gain a distinguished and good man for their brotherhood, the latter delighting to see a man interred, as they thought, in a monastery, who had been in the habit of hindering them in all the robberies and wickedness which they had been wont to commit for their "iniquitous temporal interests." Las Casas takes the tonsure, 1522.

Afterwards letters for him did come from court, breathing kind encouragement and invitation from Not forgotten by his friends at court.

---

* "Estas palabras le atravesaron el alma al Clérigo Casas, y desde allí comenzó á pensar mas frequentemente de su estado."—LAS CASAS, *Hist. de las Indias*, MS., lib. iii. cap. 159.

his friends the Flemings; but his superiors did not show him these letters, for fear of disquieting his mind. Letters also came from Pope Adrian for the Clerigo, but it was when he could no longer dispose of himself.* If he had gone to Spain, it is probable, as he would have found King Charles there, that he might have succeeded in some new enterprise of colonization.† But this

---

* " Y el mismo Papa Adriano tambien le mandó escribir, sino que llegaron las Cartas cuando ya no podia determinar de sí."—Las Casas, *Hist. de las Indias*, MS., lib. iii. cap. 159.

† Las Casas would have been well able to prove that his failure had not arisen from any palpable fault of his. Although his own history has been the authority mainly referred to in the foregoing account of his attempt at colonization, it entirely coincides with what remains of the official narrative, sent in to the Emperor by his Majesty's contador, who accompanied Las Casas. This officer describes the opposition which Las Casas met with from the Governor of Cubagua, the desertion of Ocampo's armada, the ruin that on three occasions fell upon the monks, who, he says, have received glorious deaths (*han recibido muertes admirables;*) and he estimates the number of slaves at 600, who were made on that coast previously to Las Casas reaching it. " Ví en la Española que en obra de dos meses se trajeron mas de seiscientos esclavos de do habia de ir Casas y venderlos por los oficiales en Santo

was not to be; and he remained in the monastery of St. Domingo, moving in the narrow circle of his duties there, and, as we are told, writing his history* of the Indies.

Profiting so much as we do by this history,

Domingo." — *Representacion del Contador Real (Miguel Castellanos) que fué con Casas a Cumana.*—QUINTANA, *Apéndices á la Vida de Las Casas*, No. 9.

* It is generally said by Quintana, and other learned men, that Las Casas commenced his history at this period in the monastery of St. Domingo. Their assertion may be founded upon some fact which has escaped my observation. The only dates I can refer to, in reference to this point, where Las Casas speaks of the times of his writing, are as follows. In the Prologue there is a passage, quoted below, in which he speaks as if that were written in 1552. In lib. iii. cap. 155, he mentions the year 1560, as the time of his writing; and, in the last sentence but one of his history, he gives the date 1561, as the time at which he is then waiting. " No puede alguno rehusar con razon de conceder hacerse *hoy que es el año de* 1552 las mismas calamitosas obras que en los tiempos pasados se cometian." He may, however, at a very early period, have begun to collect and prepare his materials for writing, amongst which may be numbered some of the most valuable documents that ever existed as sources of early American history. The one which I should most like to have seen was *Tovilla's Historia Barbárica*, of which, I believe, there is now no trace.

still it must be regretted that Las Casas should have been thus occupied; and, however desirable it might be that he should regard his soul, I cannot but regret, in somewhat of a secular spirit, that he should have been taken away for the present from the civil administration of the Indies, which gained one more devout man, and lost that much rarer character, a profoundly and perseveringly philanthropic reformer, of which latter character the Indies had then far more need than all the rest of the world put together.

Studies of Las Casas in the monastery.

It is doubtful, moreover, whether his studies at the monastery did not do far more harm than good to his faculty for historical writing. It must, I conjecture, have been at this period, that he studied those works which enabled him to confuse his narrative with inappropriate learning. Before his becoming a monk, I imagine he knew little of what Pliny, Diodorus Siculus, Dionysius Halicarnassensis, Aristotle, the Master of the Sentences, or other learned writers, whose names infest his pages, had said upon any subject. It is not to be forgotten, however, that, while Las Casas dwelt in monastic retreat, he probably acquired that knowledge of the Fathers and the Schoolmen, which enabled him to battle so successfully before kings and princes with the most learned persons of his time, using the favourite scholastic weapons of that age.

CHAPTER IX.

Las Casas in the Dominican monastery—His studies—He goes to Mexico—Establishes himself in the monastery at Santiago de Guatemala—He proposes to conquer the "Land of War" with the aid of his monks.

Las Casas in the Dominican monastery.

LAS CASAS remained for eight years in the Dominican monastery of Hispaniola, during which time he led a life of extreme seclusion. In these eight years the bounds of the Indian Empire had been immensely enlarged.

What had happened in the Indies while Las Casas was in his monastery.

Cortes had completed his conquest of New Spain, Alvarado had conquered Guatemala, Pizarro had commenced the conquest of Peru, and the captains or the rivals of Pedrarias, exceeding all other Spaniards in cruelty, had devastated the fertile regions of Nicaragua.* Las Casas must have heard about all

---

* See LAS CASAS, *Brevíssima Relacion de la destruycion de las Indias,* "*De la Provincia de Nicaragua,*" p. 14.

these transactions, and we can well imagine what he must have thought of them. For five years of his life—namely, from 1522 to 1527, there is but one fact known about him; but that one is very significant. It is that he was not allowed to preach: probably, because the monastery wished to stand well with the town, and feared to allow Las Casas to enter the pulpit, knowing what terrible truths he would utter. We learn this fact in a very curious and authentic manner, from a witness in a legal process which, in after days, was instituted against Las Casas by the governor of Nicaragua. The witness says, that, having remained in San Domingo two years, he does not know that in the whole of that time brother Bartholomew preached; and the witness further deposes, that the Auditors of San Domingo had charged Las Casas not to preach. It may be doubted, however, whether any secular command would have been sufficient to restrain him.

In 1527, it is said, he commenced his history,*

---

* I am content to take the evidence of Remesal, referring as it does to Las Casas himself:—"Lo que no la (duda) tiene, porque el mismo lo afirma, es, que el año de 1527,

the most valuable groundwork for the history of America that exists.

The exact time and the particular cause of the re-entrance of Las Casas into the world are both very doubtful. A rebellion of the Indians in Hispaniola, under the cacique Enrique, is supposed to have engaged his attention; and it is stated by Oviedo that he was sent to negotiate with the revolted cacique. He is also said, upon some grounds, as it appears to me, to have gone to the Court of Spain in the year 1530. Moreover, it is alleged that, shortly before the second expedition of Pizarro to Peru, Las Casas, foreseeing the evils of that expedition, procured a royal decree, ordering that Pizarro and Almagro should abstain from making slaves of the Indians; and it is further stated that Las Casas himself travelled to Peru, and delivered this order into the hands of these captains.*

_{Occupations of Las Casas from 1529 to 1536.}

---

començó á escrivir la historia general de las Indias, coligida de los escritos mas ciertos y verdaderos de aquel tiempo, particularmente de los originales del Almirante don Christoval Colon."—REMESAL, *Hist. de Chiapa y Guatemala*, lib. iii. cap. 1.

* Quintana rejects all this part of the narrative, and, as Las Casas in his account of Peru never mentions himself as

There are few lives in which the main events, and the circumstances on which they depended, are clearer than in that of Las Casas. But, at this period of his life, from his entrance into the Dominican monastery in Hispaniola until his occupation of the Dominican monastery of Santiago in Guatemala, founded by Betanzos, there is great confusion and incertitude. If we abide by the account of Remesal, the writer from whom we learn most about Las Casas, the following is the order of events.

Las Casas having, by his presence at Court, obtained the decree in favour of the natives of Peru, returned to Hispaniola. Immediately after his return, a provincial Chapter of the Dominican Order was held in that island, and upon that occasion a prior was appointed for the Dominican

---

an eye-witness, I was at first inclined to reject it also. But, observing that, in his account of Nicaragua, where he certainly had been, and where the law-suit before alluded to was brought against him, he never makes the least allusion to himself, I am not inclined to pronounce hastily upon these statements, more especially as Remesal speaks of a letter written by the Bishop of Guatemala, which seems to allude to the circumstance of Las Casas passing through the town of Santiago on his way to Peru.

convent at Mexico,—the "Province," as it was called, of Mexico being dependent upon that of Hispaniola. That prior, Francisco de San Miguel, took Las Casas with him, intending to give him companions for passing on to Peru, not only to notify the royal decree, but to found convents in the newly-discovered country. Thus it was that Las Casas came to Mexico. The assumption of prelatical authority on the part of the convent at Hispaniola was the cause of great trouble to the Dominican brethren in New Spain. We have already seen how Domingo de Betanzos was suddenly summoned to attend a chapter, or meeting, of his Order in Mexico; and the cause of his being sent for was no other than the arrival, or the rumour of the arrival, of the new prior. Remesal states that Las Casas helped to allay the differences which arose on this occasion amongst the brethren; and then commenced his mission to Peru, accompanied by two Dominicans, who afterwards became celebrated men,—Bernardino de Minaya and Pedro de Angulo.

It was at the beginning of the year 1531 that Las Casas set out from Mexico with his companions, and traversing New Spain and Guatemala,

[margin: How Las Casas came to Mexico.]

[margin: Las Casas attends a Chapter in Mexico.]

[margin: Goes to Nicaragua, 1531.]

came to Nicaragua, in which province they took ship at the port of Realejo. There the good fathers were fortunate enough to find a vessel* which was going with men and provisions to Pizarro. They availed themselves of this means of transport, and notified the decree to the Spanish captains in Peru; but finding that the state of

---

* That Las Casas commenced a voyage to Peru is clear from the following passage in his *Historia Apologética*. He is speaking of tears being occasionally a mode of expressing joy.—" *Yo vide un plático soldado muy solemne taur y que segun presumimos iba con otros muchos á robar los Indios á los Reynos del Perú; handando que handabamos perdidos por la mar acordámos de hechar suertes sobre que camino tomariamos, ó' para ir al Perú, donde él y los demas iban, por que bullia el oro allí, enderezados, sino que nos era el tiempo contrario, ó' á la Provincia de Nicaragua, donde no habia oro, pero podiamos mas presto y matar la ambre allí á llegar: y por que salió la suerte que prosiguiesemos el camino del Perú, recibió tanta y tan veemente alegría que comenzo á llorar y derramar tantas lágrimas como una muy devota vieja ó veata, y dijo: por cierto no me parece sino que tengo tanto consuelo como si agora acabara de comulgar; y otra cosa no hacia en todo el dia sino jugar á los naipes y tan desenfrenadamente como los otros. Los que allí veniamos que deseabamos salir de allí donde quiera que la mar nos hechara, vista la causa de sus lágrimas reiamonos de su gran consuelo y devocion."—* LAS CASAS, *Historia Apologética*, MS., cap. 180.

the country did not then admit of the founding of monasteries, they returned to Panamá, and from thence went to Realejo, which port they reached in February or March of the year 1532.

Returns to Realejo, March, 1532.

A bishop, Diego Alvarez Osorio, had just been nominated by the Emperor for Nicaragua, who was also endowed with the office of Protector of the Indians. The bishop, naturally enough, saw in this advent of the good fathers from Peru an excellent opportunity for founding a Dominican convent in Leon, the chief Spanish town of Nicaragua, and he begged them to stay with him. They consented, and began to learn the language of the country, with the exception of Pedro de Angulo, who already knew Mexican well, and was therefore able at once to catechize the Indians, and to teach them the Christian Faith.*

---

* The foregoing details depend solely, or mainly, upon the authority of Remesal. They are liable to objections of considerable weight, which have, for the most part, been well stated by Quintana, the excellent modern biographer of Las Casas. On one point I am bound to confirm Quintana, namely, that in the account which Las Casas himself gives of the insurrection of Enrique (see chapters 124, 5, and 6, lib. iii. of his History), he does not assign to himself any such part as that given to him by Remesal.

IN NICARAGUA.

We are now, happily, on the firm ground of history, when we bring Las Casas into Nicaragua; though we must not suppose that he remained stationary there for any long period. In 1534, he undertook a second voyage to Peru, but was driven back by a storm, and did not renew the enterprise. Herrera makes him go to Spain, and though he gives a wrong date (1536) for this, yet the main statement may be true. Remesal makes Las Casas go in 1533 to the island of Hispaniola; and if this should be a true account (as it seems, from certain circumstances that are mentioned, a probable one),* it was then also that Las Casas may have interfered

He, however, promises to give further information in the next book, which he did not live to write. But still, what he has told us is by no means in accordance with Remesal.

With regard to the rest of the story, I do not feel at all disposed to throw over the authority of Remesal. He had access to the archives of Guatemala early in the seventeenth century, and he is one of those excellent writers, so dear to the students of history, who is not prone to declamation, or rhetoric, or picturesque writing, but indulges us largely by the introduction everywhere of most important historical documents, copied boldly into the text.

* See OVIEDO, "Hist Gen. y Nat. de Indias," lib. v cap. 2.

more potently in the affairs of the revolted cacique, Enrique, than is generally admitted by secular writers. There is no doubt, however, that, whilst at Nicaragua, Las Casas organized a formidable opposition to the governor, Rodrigo de Contreras, whom he prevented from undertaking one of those expeditions into the interior which were always most injurious to the native Indians.

Las Casas had great reason for opposing any such expedition in this country, as we learn from him that the most outrageous atrocities against the Indians had already taken place in this province. He mentions that it had been known to happen that, when a body of four thousand Indians accompanied an expedition to carry burdens, only six of them returned alive. He likewise describes how when an Indian was sick with weariness and hunger, and unable to proceed, as a quick way of getting the chain free from the Indian, his head was cut off, and so he was disengaged from the gang in which he travelled. "Imagine," he says, "what the others must have felt."*

<small>Atrocities in Nicaragua denounced by Las Casas.</small>

---

* " Y acaeció vez de muchas que esto hizo, que de

The Bishop of Nicaragua, who endeavoured to make peace between Las Casas and the governor, died; and their feud, consequently, raged more violently than before.

In passing through Guatemala on his way by land to Realejo, in his first attempt to reach Peru, Las Casas must have observed the deserted Dominican monastery in Guatemala; and, in all probability, he rested in one of its cells. He must also have made acquaintance with the curate of the town, Francisco de Marroquin. Marroquin had since become a bishop, and it seems certain that he now invited brother Bartholomew to come from Nicaragua to Guatemala. Las Casas probably finding that he could not resist the governor of Nicaragua, abandoned the convent there, and,

---

quatro mil Indios, no bolvieron seys vivos á sus casas, que todos los dexavan muertos por los caminos. E quando algunos cansavan, y se despeavan de las grandes cargas, y enfermavan de hambre, é trabajo, y flaqueza; por no desensartarlos de las cadenas les cortavan por la collera la cabeça, é caya la cabeça á un cabo, y el cuerpo á otro. Véase que sentirian los otros."—LAS CASAS, *Brevíssima Relacion de la Destruycion de las Indias*, p. 15. I do not know what governor or captain it was who authorized these cruelties. It was not Contreras, whose appointment was recent.

accompanied by his brethren, proceeded to Guatemala and took up his abode in the convent which Domingo de Betanzos had built, and which had remained vacant for six years.

It will be necessary now, to give a short review of the principal events which had occurred in Guatemala between the departure of Domingo de Betanzos and the arrival of Las Casas and his brethren to occupy the deserted monastery.

Alvarado, one of the most restless even of those restless men—the conquerors of the New World —had been devoting his energies to fitting out a fleet for the purpose of further discoveries. This fleet was built at a port called Iztapa, situated about seventeen leagues from the present city of Guatemala. When Alvarado was at the Court of Spain he had held out hopes of making further discoveries. But the great news of Pizarro's golden success reaching the greedy ears of the rapacious governor of Guatemala, he resolved to proceed southwards, and to join Pizarro in his enterprise. He was the more readily induced to do this, as he knew that Pizarro was but poorly equipped. It was in vain that the king's officers at Guatemala protested stoutly against Alvarado's expedition to Peru. They said that he would leave his own colony bare, and that it would, therefore, be in great peril, because a large part of it was in a state of war; and that even the subdued Indians, seeing themselves freed from the yoke of armed men, would rise in revolt. Moreover, they added, with a shrewd insight into the future, that the lieutenant-governor whom Alvarado was leaving would be continually obliged to be sending men and horses to assist his master; and, consequently, that the armed force of the country would, day by day, be growing weaker. To these sound arguments Alvarado replied that the government of Guatemala was a small matter for him, and that he wished to go and seek another greater one. With regard to the question of danger, he said that he intended to take with him the principal Indians, and so leave the province secure for the Spaniards.

The king's officers persevered in their remonstrances, and wrote both to the king, and to the *audiencia* of Mexico. The *audiencia* agreed with the king's officers of Guatemala, and wrote to Alvarado, forbidding the enterprise. He was not, however, to be daunted by their endeavours to restrain him, and he persevered in taking his departure for Peru.

The result of this expedition was disastrous, although Alvarado himself did not suffer much, as he received an ample sum for the forces which he made over to Pizarro. Alvarado returned to Guatemala at the end of the year 1535, not long before Las Casas with his Dominican monks established themselves in the monastery at Santiago de Guatemala.

Returns to Guatemala, 1535.

The Dominican brethren who accompanied Las Casas, and all of whom afterwards became celebrated men, were Luis Cancer, Pedro de Angulo, and Rodrigo de Ladrada. These grave and reverend monks might any time in the year 1537 have been found sitting in a little class round the Bishop of Guatemala, an elegant scholar, but whose scholarship was now solely employed to express Christian doctrines in the Utlatecan language, commonly called Quiché. As the chronicler says, " It was a delight to see the bishop, as a master of declensions and conjugations in the Indian tongue, teaching the good fathers of St. Dominic " This prelate afterwards published a

Las Casas and his brethren study the Quiché language.

work in Utlatecan, in the prologue of which he justly says, " It may, perchance, appear to some people a contemptible thing that prelates should be thus engaged in trifling things solely fitted for the teaching of children; but, if the matter be well looked into, it is a baser thing not to abase one's self to these apparent trifles, for such teaching is the 'marrow' of our Holy Faith." The bishop was quite right. It will soon be seen what an important end this study of the language led to; and, I doubt not—indeed, it might almost be proved—that there are territories, neighbouring to Guatemala, which would have been desert and barren as the sands of the sea but for the knowledge of the Utlatecan language acquired by these good fathers,—an acquisition, too, it must be recollected, not easy or welcome to men of their age and their habits.

It happened that a little before the year 1535, Las Casas had composed a treatise, which, though it was never printed, made a great noise at the time. It was entitled *De unico vocationis modo*. It was written in Latin, but was translated into Spanish, and so became current, not only amongst the monks and learned men, but also amongst the

<small>The treatise *De unico vocationis modo*.</small> common soldiers and colonists. It consisted of two propositions. The first was, that men were to be brought to Christianity by persuasion; and the second, which seems but a consequence of the first, that without special injury received on the part of the Christians, it was not lawful for them to carry on war against infidels, merely as infidels. The treatise, though requiring in parts to be passed quickly over, would, if we may judge by other works of the same author, be interesting even now, and having close reference to the daily affairs of life in the Indies, must at the time it was written have been read with eager and angry attention by the Spanish colonists possessing Indian slaves, whom they had won by their bows and their spears. To gain these slaves, they had toiled and bled. During long and harassing marches they had been alternately frozen, parched, and starved; sufferings only to be compensated for, and poorly compensated, by the large droves of captives which they had brought in triumph back with them. We may imagine the indignant manner in which these fierce veterans read what parts they could or would read of this wise and gentle treatise, *De unico vocationis modo*, written

by the great protector of the Indians, who had now indeed emerged to some purpose from his quiet cell in the Dominican monastery.

But the conquerors were not only indignant at the doctrines propounded in this treatise of Las Casas: they laughed at his theories—that mocking laugh of the so-called practical men,—a kind of laugh well known to all those who have attempted to do any new and good thing. "Try it," they said; "try with words only and sacred exhortations to bring the Indians to the true faith;" and Las Casas, who never said the thing he did not mean to abide by, took them at their word, and said he would try it.

The colonists of Guatemala deride Las Casas.

Now there was a neighbouring province called Tuzulutlan, which, amongst the Spanish inhabitants of Guatemala, had the ill name of the *Tierra de Guerra*, "The Land of War." This district was a terror to them; and the people in it were a "phantom of terror" to the Spaniards. Thrice they had attempted to penetrate this land; thrice they had returned defeated, with their hands up to their heads (*las manos en la cabeça*). Such is the statement of REMESAL. The land, therefore, was much more difficult to penetrate

The Tierra de Guerra.

O

than if no Spaniard had ever been there, being an irritated country, not merely an untried one. With all our knowledge hitherto acquired of Las Casas, we cannot but feel timid and apprehensive as to the result of this bold undertaking of his. We are not left in doubt as to the magnitude of the enterprise. The story is no monkish narrative to magnify the merits of the writer's Order. There was a formal compact entered into by the temporary governor of Guatemala with Las Casas, as vicar of the convent of San Domingo, in which it is admitted that the Indians in question were fierce men in revolt, whom no Spaniard dared to go near. Their country, too, was a most difficult one to conquer, where the ways were obstructed by mountains, intersected by rivers, and lost amidst dense forests.

The substance of the agreement is, that if Las Casas, or any of his monks, can bring these Indians into conditions of peace, so that they should recognize the Spanish monarch for their lord paramount, and pay him any moderate tribute, he, the governor, would place all those provinces under his majesty in chief (*en cabeça de su Magestad*), and would not give them to any private Spaniard

Tuzulutlan not an untried country.

Agreement between Las Casas and the governor, ad interim, of Guatemala. May, 1537.

in *encomienda*. Moreover, no Spaniard, under heavy penalties, except the governor himself in person, should be allowed for five years to enter into that territory. This agreement bears date the 2nd of May, 1537, and was signed by Alonzo Maldonado, the temporary governor of Guatemala.

Las Casas would hardly have been able to persuade the ruthless soldier, Pedro de Alvarado, to sign any such contract as the foregoing. It was, therefore, a singular felicity for the enterprise in hand, that Alvarado was at that time absent from the province, and powerless in it.

After the manner of pious men of those times, Las Casas and his monks did not fail to commence their undertaking by having recourse to the most fervent prayers, severe fasts, and other mortifications. These lasted several days. They then turned to the secular part of their enterprise, using all the skill that the most accomplished statesmen, or men of the world, could have brought to bear upon it. The first thing they did, was to translate into verse, in the Quiché language, the great doctrines of the Church. In these verses they described the creation of the world, the fall of man, his banishment from Paradise, and the

[margin: The Dominicans prepare for their enterprise in "the Land of War."]

[margin: Christian doctrines expressed in Quiché verse.]

mediation prepared for him; then the life of Christ, His passion, His death, His resurrection, His ascension; then His future return to judge all men, the punishment of the wicked and the reward of the good. They divided the work, which was very extensive, into *coplas*, after the Castillian fashion.* We might well wish, for many reasons, that this laudable work remained to us, but I am not aware of there being any traces of its existence.

The good fathers then began to study how they should introduce their poem to the notice of the Indians of Tuzulutlan; and, availing themselves of a happy thought for this purpose, they called to their aid four Indian merchants, who were in the habit of going with merchandise, several times a year, into this province called "the Land of War." The monks, with great care, taught these four men to repeat the couplets which they had composed. The pupils entered entirely into the views of their instructors. Indeed, they took such pains in learning their lessons,

marginalia: The Dominicans attach some Indian merchants,

marginalia: And teach them the Quiché verses.

---

* See BOUTERWEK's *History of Spanish Literature*, vol. i. p. 108; and TICKNOR, *History of Spanish Literature*, vol. i. pp. 371-2.

and (with the fine sense for musical intonation which the Indians generally possessed) repeated these verses so well, that there was nothing left to desire. The composition and the teaching occupied three months, and was not completed until the middle of August, 1537. Las Casas communicated his intended undertaking to Domingo de Betanzos, now the head of the Dominican Order in New Spain, who was delighted to give his sanction and his blessing to the good work. The monks and the merchants, however, were not satisfied until they had brought their labours to much greater perfection, until, indeed, they had set these verses to music, so that they might be accompanied by the Indian instruments; taking care, however, to give the voice parts a higher place in the scale than that of the deep-toned instruments of the natives.* No doubt,

<small>The poetry is set to music.</small>

---

* "Es de saber que no solo se contentaron con esto, sino que se las pusieron en tono y armonía música al son de los instrumentos que los Indios usan, accompañándolos con un tono vivo y atiplado para deleytar mas el oydo, por ser muy baxos y roncos los instrumentos músicos de que usan los Indios."—REMESAL, *Hist. de Chiapa y Guatemala*, lib. iii. cap. 15.

this music was a great improvement upon anything the Indians had ever heard in the way of sweet sounds.

The enterprise was now ready to be carried into action,—to be transplanted from the schools into the world. It was resolved that the merchants should commence their journey into " the Land of War," carrying with them not only their own merchandise, but being furnished by Las Casas with the usual small wares to please aborigines, such as scissors, knives, looking-glasses, and bells. The pupils and the teachers parted, the merchants making their accustomed journey into the territories of Quiché and Zacapula, their destination being a certain *pueblo* of a great cacique of those parts, a wise and warlike chief, who had many powerful alliances.*

---

* This must, I think, have been the Chief of Atitlan, for though, in Remesal's narrative he is never named directly, yet as he was baptized as Juan, and as the only cacique who is addressed as Don Juan, in a formal letter from the Emperor, thanking the caciques of those parts for the aid they had given to the Dominicans, is Don Juan de Atitlan, it is highly probable that Atitlan was the province visited by the merchants.

CHAPTER X.

Las Casas succeeds in converting by peaceable means " The Land of War"—He is sent to Spain, and detained there by the Council of the Indies.

BEHIND all ostensible efforts of much novelty and magnitude, what silent longings and unutterable expectations lie unnoticed or concealed! In the crowded theatre, or the cold, impatient senate, the voice that is raised for the first time—perhaps for ever afterwards to command an absolute attention—trembles with all the sensibility of genius, while great thoughts and vast aspirations, hurrying together in the agitated mind, obstruct and confuse the utterance. We pity, with an intense sympathy, the struggles of one who is about to be famous. Meanwhile, perhaps, in some dark corner or obscure passage, is the agonized and heart-sick mother, who can hardly think, or hope, or pray, convinced, as far as she is conscious of anything, that her child ought to succeed, and must succeed, but suffering all the timid anxiety that mature years will ever bring, and with the keenest appreciation of every difficulty and drawback that can prevent success.

It is a bold figure to illustrate the feelings of a monk by those of a mother; but it may be doubted whether many mothers have suffered a keener agony of apprehensive expectation than Las Casas and his brethren endured at this and other similar points of their career. They had the fullest faith in God and the utmost reliance upon Him; but they knew that He acts through secondary means, and how easily, they doubtless thought, might some failure in their own preparation — some unworthiness in themselves — some unfortunate conjunction of political affairs in the Indies — some dreadful wile of the Evil One — frustrate all their long enduring hopes. In an age when private and individual success is made too much of, and success for others too little, it may be difficult for many persons to imagine the intense interest with which these

The anxieties of Las Casas and his brethren.

childless men looked forward to the realization of their great religious enterprise—the bringing of the Indians by peaceful means into the fold of Christ.

The merchants were received, as was the custom in a country without inns, into the palace of the cacique, where they met with a better reception than usual, being enabled to make him presents of these new things from Castille. They then set up their tent, and began to sell their goods as they were wont to do, their customers thronging about them to see the Spanish novelties. When the sale was over for that day, the chief men amongst the Indians remained with the cacique, to do him honour. In the evening, the merchants asked for a "*teplanastle*," an instrument of music which we may suppose to have been the same as the Mexican *teponaztli*,* or

Reception of the merchants in Tuzulutlan.

---

* "The *teponaztli*, which is used to this day among the Indians, is cylindrical and hollow, but all of wood, having no skin about it, nor any opening but two slits lengthways in the middle, parallel to, and at a little distance from each other. It is sounded by beating the space between those two slits with two little sticks, similar to those which are drum. They then produced some timbrels and bells, which they had brought with them, and began to sing the verses which they had learned by heart, accompanying themselves on the musical instruments. The effect produced was very great. The sudden change of character, not often made, from a merchant to a priest, at once arrested the attention of the assemblage. Then, if the music was beyond anything that these Indians had heard, the words were still more extraordinary; for the good fathers had not hesitated to put into their verses the question-

<small>The merchants commence their chant.</small>

---

made use of for modern drums, only that their points are covered with *ule* or elastic gum, to soften the sound. The size of this instrument is various: some are so small as to be hung about the neck; some of a middling size; and others so large as to be upwards of five feet long. The sound which they yield is melancholy, and that of the largest so loud, that it may be heard at the distance of two or three miles. To the accompaniment of these instruments . . . . the Mexicans sung their hymns and sacred music. Their singing was harsh and offensive to European ears; but they took so much pleasure in it themselves, that on festivals they continued singing the whole day. This was unquestionably the art in which the Mexicans were least successful."—CLAVIGERO, *Hist. of Mexico*, vol. i. pp. 398-9. English translation.

able assertion that idols were demons, and the certain fact that human sacrifices were abominable. The main body of the audience was delighted, and pronounced these merchants to be ambassadors from new gods.

The cacique, with the caution of a man in authority, suspended his judgment until he had heard more of the matter. The next day, and for seven succeeding days, this sermon in song was repeated. In public and in private, the person who insisted most on this repetition was the cacique; and he expressed a wish to fathom the matter, and to know the origin and meaning of these things. The prudent merchants replied, that they only sang what they had heard; that it was not their business to explain these verses, for that office belonged to certain *padres*, who instructed the people. "And who are *padres?*" asked the chief. In answer to this question, the merchants painted pictures of the Dominican monks, in their robes of black and white, and with their tonsured heads. The merchants then described the lives of these *padres:* how they did not eat meat, and how they did not desire gold, or feathers, or cocoa; that they were not married,

Curiosity of the cacique.

Explanation given by the merchants.

and had no communication with women; that night and day they sang the praises of God; and that they knelt before very beautiful images. Such were the persons, the merchants said, who could and would explain these couplets: they were such good people, and so ready to teach, that if the cacique were to send for them, they would most willingly come.

The Indian chief resolved to see and hear these marvellous men in black and white, with their hair in the form of a garland, who were so different from other men; and for this purpose, when the merchants returned, he sent in company with them a brother of his, a young man twenty-two years of age, who was to invite the Dominicans to visit his brother's country, and to carry them presents. The cautious cacique

The cacique sends his brother back with the merchants. instructed his brother to look well to the ways of these *padres*, to observe whether they had gold and silver like the other Christians, and whether there were women in their houses. These instructions having been given, and his brother having taken his departure, the cacique made large offerings of incense and great sacrifices to his idols for the success of the embassage.

On the arrival of this company at Santiago, Las Casas and the Dominican monks received the young Indian chief with every demonstration of welcome: and it need hardly be said with what joy they heard from the merchants who accompanied him of the success of their mission.

While the Indian prince was occupied in visiting the town of Santiago, the monks debated amongst themselves what course they should pursue in reference to the invitation which they had received from the cacique. Guided throughout by great prudence, they resolved not to risk the safety of the whole of their body, but to send only one monk at first as an ambassador and explorer. Their choice fell upon Father Luis Cancér, who probably was the most skilled of all the four in the language that was likely to be best understood in Tuzulutlan. Meanwhile the cacique's brother and his attendants made their observations on the mode of life of the monks, who gratified him and them by little presents. It was time now to return; and the whole party, consisting of Luis Cancér, the cacique's brother, his Indians, and the four merchants of Guatemala, set off from Santiago on their way to the cacique's country.

Father LuisCancér chosen for the mission to Tuzulutlan.

Luis Cancér carried with him a present for the cacique in fabrics of Castille, and also some crosses and images. The reason given for carrying these latter is, " That the cacique might read in them that which he might forget in the sermons that would be preached to him."*

<small>Father Luis well received.</small>

The journey of Father Luis was a continued triumph. Everywhere the difference was noticed between his dress, customs, and manners, and those of the Spaniards who had already been seen in Tuzulutlan. When he came into the cacique's territory he was received under triumphal arches, and the ways were made clean before him as if he had been a monarch, traversing his kingdom. At the entrance of the cacique's own town, the chief himself came out to meet Father Luis, and bending before him, cast down his eyes, showing him the same mark of reverence that he would have shown to the priests of that country. More substantial and abiding honours soon followed. At the cacique's orders a church was

---

* " Para que leyesse en ellas lo que de los sermones que le avia de hazer se le olvidasse."—REMESAL, *Hist. de Chiapa y Guatemala*, lib. iii. cap. 15.

built, and in it the father said mass in the presence of the chief, who was especially delighted with the cleanliness of the sacerdotal garments, for the priests of his own country, like those of Mexico, affected filth and darkness, the fitting accompaniments for a religion of terror.

A church built in Tuzulutlan.

Meanwhile, Father Luis continued to explain the Christian creed, having always a most attentive and favourable hearer in the cacique. The good monk had taken the precaution to bring with him the written agreement signed by the governor, and he explained to the chief the favourable conditions that it contained for the welfare of the Indians. The merchants were witnesses who might be appealed to for the meaning of this document; and that they were faithful to the monks—indeed, a sort of lay-brotherhood—may be inferred from the fact of their continuing to chaunt every evening the verses which had won for them at first the title of ambassadors from new gods. The cacique's brother gave a favourable report of what he had seen at Santiago, and the result of all these influences on the mind of the Indian chieftain was such, that he determined to embrace the Christian faith. No sooner had he

The cacique becomes a proselyte.

become a proselyte, than, with all the zeal and energy belonging to that character, he began to preach the new doctrine to his own vassals. He was the first to pull down and to burn his idols; and many of his chiefs, in imitation of their master, likewise became iconoclasts.

In a word, the mission of Father Luis was supremely successful, and after he had visited other parts of the country subject to the converted cacique, he returned, according to the plan that had been determined upon by the brethren, to the town of Santiago, where Las Casas and the other monks received with ineffable delight the good tidings which their brother had to communicate to them. Even if the result of this mission be looked at as a mere matter of worldly success, all persons of any power of sympathy will be glad to find that some enterprise projected by Las Casas met with its due reward, and such a reward, indeed, as might well serve to efface the remembrance of the terrible disaster at Cumaná, which had driven him from secular into monastic life. How often, perhaps, in the solitude of his cell at St. Domingo, had he regretted taking that irremediable step, especially when he found from

Father Luis returns to Santiago, Oct., 1537.

letters, that his friends at Court had not forgotten him; and how often had he painted to himself, according to the fancies we all indulge in, the good that he might have done had he taken " the other course."

It was at the end of October, 1537, at the close of the rainy season, when those provinces could best be traversed, that father Luis returned to Santiago. Las Casas himself now resolved to go into " the Land of War," taking as a companion father Pedro de Angulo, who also was well acquainted with the language of that district. As might be expected, the cacique (whom we shall hereafter call by his baptismal name, Don Juan) received Las Casas with all due honours. In the interval of time that had elapsed between the departure of father Luis and the arrival of father Bartholomew, the new convert's sincerity and energy had been sorely tried. Indeed, it was hardly to be expected that this sudden conversion could go on with all the success that had attended it in the beginning. The first great difficulty that he encountered arose from the following circumstances.

Las Casas takes his place, Dec., 1537.

There happened to be a treaty of marriage for a daughter of the cacique of Coban with the brother of the converted cacique—that same brother who had visited the Dominicans at Santiago. It was a custom on such occasions for those who had charge of the bride to sacrifice certain birds and animals, on arriving at the confines of the bridegroom's territory. Don Juan's conscience would not allow even these innocent sacrifices to be made. The ambassadors from Coban were in the highest degree vexed and affronted; but at last, after much consideration, they resolved not to break off an alliance with so powerful a prince upon a mere matter of form, and the princess of Coban was conducted into the bridegroom's country.

<small>The cacique finds it difficult to convert his people.</small>

This difficulty, therefore, was for the present surmounted; but his own people now gave Don Juan far more trouble than the ambassadors from Coban. An ignorant mob is sometimes very conservative. Pagans, as the scholar knows from the derivation of the name, were but the inhabitants of country villages, whose ignorance and unimpressibility kept off the influence of any new doctrine, however good. In Don Juan's territories similar causes would produce similar effects.

and there would be a body of dull and fierce fanatics who would pride themselves on being the last to quit the old heathen ways, and the slowest to appreciate the merits of Christianity. Moreover, we cannot doubt that in this case the unclean priests, seeing their vocation falling from them, stirred up the common people, who, thus acted upon, contrived furtively to burn the church. This was not done without suspicion of the ambassadors from Coban being concerned in the matter. The cacique, however, undaunted by all this opposition, rebuilt the church. Las Casas and his brother monk, Pedro de Angulo, said mass in it, and preached in the open plain to the people, who came in great numbers, some from curiosity and from favour to the new religion, and others with a gluttonous longing to devour the monks, who, they thought, would taste well if flavoured with sauce of Chili.* Las Casas and his companion, anxious to extend their knowledge of these regions, traversed, with a guard of sixty

marginal note: Resistance to the new doctrines.

---

* "Otros con golosina de comérselos, pareciéndoles que tendrian buen gusto con salsa de Chile."—REMESAL, lib. iii. cap. 16.

of his new friends the neighbouring territories, but yielded to the wishes of Don Juan in not going as far as Coban. The fathers were well received on their journey, and they returned to the *pueblo* of Don Juan at the beginning of the year 1538.

1538.

At this juncture Las Casas and all lovers of the Indians received a very seasonable aid from the Court of Rome. That accomplished and refined pope, Paul the Third (Alexander Farnese), was moved to a consideration of Indian affairs by a letter, which the learned bishop of Tlascala had addressed to him, and also by a mission sent at the instance of Betanzos and the chief Dominicans in New Spain. This mission was conducted by father Bernardino de Minaya, who in former days had travelled with Las Casas through Guatemala and Nicaragua. The pope answered the requisitions of the bishop and the monks in the most favourable and forcible manner; and must have shown a rapidity in giving this answer which his Holiness—who was celebrated for delay in business, usually waiting for some happy conjuncture of affairs,—was seldom known to manifest. He issued a brief, founded on the great text *Euntes docete omnes gentes*, in which he declared in the

The Dominicans in New Spain send to Paul III.

Brief of Pope Paul III. in

most absolute manner the fitness of the Indians for receiving Christianity, considering them, to use the words of the brief, "as veritable men, not only capable of receiving the Christian faith, but as we have learnt, most ready to embrace that faith." He also pronounced in very strong language against their being reduced into slavery.

favour of the Indians. June, 1537.

Nor was Paul the Third content with issuing this brief, but he addressed a letter to the Archbishop of Toledo, the primate of Spain, in which his holiness said, "It has come to our knowledge that our dearest son in Christ, Charles, the ever august emperor of the Romans, king of Castille and Leon, in order to repress those who, boiling over with cupidity, bear an inhuman mind against the human race, has by public edict forbidden all his subjects from making slaves of the Western and Southern Indians, or depriving them of their goods."*

His letter to the Primate of Spain. June, 1537.

---

* "Ad nostrum siquidem pervenit auditum, quòd charissimus in Christo filius noster Carolus Romanorum Imperator semper Augustus, qui etiam Castellæ et Legionis Rex existit, ad reprimendos eos, qui cupiditate æstuantes contra humanum genus inhumanum gerunt animum, publico edicto omnibus sibi subditis prohibuit, ne quisquam Occidentales

The pope then pronounced a sentence of excommunication of the most absolute kind* against all those who should reduce the Indians to slavery, or deprive them of their goods.

<small>Las Casas translates the pope's brief.</small>

The men who throw themselves most earnestly into public affairs, if they meet with terrible rebuffs, have, on the other hand, at rare intervals, signal joys and triumphs—triumphs unknown to those who commit their hopes to private ventures only. Thus it fared with Las Casas on the present occasion. His delight on the arrival in the Indies of these missives from the pope was very keen; and he soon found a practical way of expressing it, by translating the brief into Spanish, and sending it to many parts of the Indies, in order that the monks might notify its contents to the lay colonists.

In his own particular mission, however, Las

---

aut Meridionales Indos in servitutem redigere, aut bonis suis privare præsumant."—REMESAL, *Hist. de Chiapa y Guatemala*, lib. iii. cap. 17.

* " Sub excommunicationis latæ sententiæ pœnâ, si secùs fecerint, eo ipso incurrendâ."—REMESAL, lib. iii. cap. 17.

Casas found something else, beyond the papal declaration of freedom, that was wanting, and without which the welfare of the Indians of Tuzulutlan could not, in his opinion, be secured. According to a proposition which he maintained most stoutly, it appeared to him, that for any nation to receive a law, two conditions were necessary: first, that there should be a *pueblo*, by which he means a collection of families; and secondly, that the nation should have perfect liberty; for, not being free, he says, they cannot form part of a community. This last is a great doctrine. The arguments of Las Casas were founded upon biblical history—as, for instance, that God gave no law in the time of Abraham, because there was no community, but a single household only. On the other hand, when the Israelites were in Egypt, although they formed a great community, they received no law, because they were captives. God gave the law only when the two conditions were combined—namely, the existence of a community, and freedom for the people who dwelt in it. Now, looking around him in Tuzulutlan, Las Casas found the element of liberty sufficiently developed, but that of the

Conditions requisite for political life.

existence of communities lamentably deficient. The Indians, under the government of his friend, the cacique Don Juan, were scattered over the country in very small villages, seldom consisting of so many as six houses, and these villages were generally more than "a musket-shot" apart. This state of things seemed to him intolerable, and certainly, with a view to instruction, it was so. But instruction and preservation are different things; and it was afterwards found that collecting the Indians together in settlements did not always favour their preservation.

<small>Danger of bringing the Indians together in settlements.</small>

One evil effect of these settlements was, that it exposed the Indians to the attack of contagious diseases, like the small-pox, which, being caught from a strong people, the Spaniards, was a strong disease, and carried off the infirmly-constituted Indians by thousands. In reference to this subject, a Mexican ecclesiastic, writing a century afterwards, quotes with great significance, a common Spanish proverb, "If the stone strikes against the earthen jar, woe to the jar: and if the jar strikes against the stone, woe not the less to the jar."* We cannot wonder, however, that Las

---

* "Que si la piedra da en el cántaro, mal para el cán-

Casas, whose first aim at this period was conversion, should have insisted so much upon collecting the people into *pueblos*, as it enabled them to hear mass and to receive the sacraments. But the Tuzulutlans were not at all of his mind. They could not bear the idea of quitting the spots where they had been born—their forests, their mountains, and their clefts,—for the purpose of forming a *pueblo*, which could not unite in itself the peculiarities of each man's birth-place, and would be likely to be chosen with a view to dull convenience mainly. This measure, therefore, second only in difficulty to that of winning a people from a nomadic state to one of settled habitation, was hard to effect in Tuzulutlan. Though Las Casas was seconded in all his efforts by the cacique, the people were almost inclined to take up arms. At last, after great labours and sufferings, Las Casas and Pedro de Angulo contrived to make a beginning of a settlement, at a place called Rabinal, having wisely chosen a spot which some few Indians, at least, were attached to, as Rabinal had been inhabited before. There

Las Casas desires to found pueblos in the converted country.

Founding of the town of Rabinal. 1538

---

taro: y si el cántaro da en la piedra, mal tambien para el cántaro."—DAVILA PADILLA, lib. i. cap. 33, p. 103.

they built a church, and there they preached and taught the people, teaching not only spiritual things, but manual arts, and having to instruct their flock in the elementary processes of washing and dressing. These good fathers were not of that school which holds that this life, God's gift, is to be left uncomely because the next is to be sublime.

<small>What the mass at first appeared to the Indians.</small>
It is admitted that the Indians, at first, regarded the mass rather as a religious ceremony which was new to them than for what, as Remesal says, " that most divine Sacrifice in itself is." But it must have had its attractions; and the active, kindly teaching of brother Bartholomew and brother Pedro about things the Indians could understand must have given weight and influence to their words in all matters. The town began to grow, one Indian family attracting another, until, at last, a hundred families were collected together.

<small>Indians of Coban come to see the new town.</small>
This strange experiment of forming a *pueblo* was not likely to go unnoticed long, and accordingly the inhabitants of Rabinal found their neighbours of Coban stealing in to see this new mode of life. It seems that their impressions of

it were favourable, for Luis Cancér, who had been sent for by Las Casas to aid in founding the town, took occasion now to penetrate as far as Coban, and, finding himself well received, and that the Indians there listened with pleasure to what he told them of the Christian faith, returned to Rabinal more contented, it is said, than if he had discovered very rich mines of silver and of gold. His joy was shared by Las Casas and Pedro de Angulo, and they all commenced with great vigour studying the language of Coban. Each success was with these brave monks a step gained for continued exertion. *Father Luis penetrates to Coban.*

The little town of Rabinal, which consisted of five hundred inhabitants, having now been put into some kind of order, Las Casas and Pedro de Angulo resolved to return to Guatemala, for the purpose of concerting measures with the bishop for the further spread of the faith in those parts. Las Casas bethought him of taking back with them their principal convert, the cacique Don Juan. It was not found difficult to induce the cacique to accompany the fathers, but they were obliged to persuade him to reduce his retinue, which he would have made very large, as they *Las Casas induces the cacique to accompany him.*

feared that any injury or affront which any Indian in the chief's train might meet with, would bring down a torrent of trouble and reproaches upon themselves, and they thought that, the smaller the number of Indians, the less chance there would be of anything untoward happening between them and the Spaniards of Santiago. Finally, the fathers and the cacique Don Juan, with a moderate number of attendants, set off on their journey, leaving Luis Cancer in charge of the Christianized town of Rabinal.

Persuades the cacique to reduce his retinue.

Las Casas had given due notice to his friends at Santiago of his intended return, and also of what notable company was coming with him. Rodrigo de Ladrada, the only monk left in the convent of the Dominicans at Santiago, did the best he could to prepare their poor house for the reception of the chief and his retinue, by adding huts to it, and collecting maize.

Return of Las Casas, with his convert, to Guatemala, 1538.

It was with more delight, and certainly with more reason for being delighted, than many a Roman conqueror has had on the day of his ascent to the capitol, that Las Casas and his brother monk brought the cacique Don Juan in triumph to their humble monastery. The moment they had arrived, the Bishop of Guatemala hurried forth to welcome the good fathers, and also to salute the Indian chief. As the bishop knew the language very well, he was able to conduct the reception with all fitting courtesy, and also to discourse with the new convert about religious matters, upon which the bishop found him well informed.

The bishop, being much pleased at this interview, felt sure the governor would be no less so; and he sent a message, begging his lordship (Alvarado had returned from Spain) to come and join them. The governor came forthwith. Now, Alvarado, though a fierce and cruel personage, was not without that power of rapid appreciation which belongs to great commanders, and knew well when he saw a noble and true man before him.

When, therefore, the bold Adelantado met the cacique, the Indian chieftain's air and manner, his repose, the gravity and modesty of his countenance, his severe look and weighty speech, won so instantaneously upon the Spaniard, that, having nothing else at hand, he took off his own plumed

The bishop and the governor do honour to the cacique.

hat, and put it on the head of the cacique. The soldiers who stood around wondered and murmured at the strange fact, that a lieutenant-governor of the emperor should take his own hat off, and put it, as they said, on a dog of an Indian. But Alvarado was not a man to care for their murmurs, and so, on some ensuing day, far from showing less favour to the grave cacique, he placed the Indian between himself and the bishop, and they traversed the town together, the governor having previously ordered the merchants to display their goods to the greatest advantage, and the bishop having told them that, if the cacique should seem to take a fancy to anything, they should offer it to him, and he, the bishop, would be answerable for the payment. But those whom we call savages, and people of the highest breeding in civilized life, alike pride themselves upon the coolness and composure with which they regard any new thing that may be offered for their wonder or their admiration. The cacique walked through the tents of the Guatemalan merchants with such gravity and apparent indifference that it seemed as if the goods he saw were no novelty to him—" as if, indeed, he had

The cacique's gravity of demeanour.

been born in Milan." Finding that he did not seem to admire anything particularly, the governor and the bishop changed their tactics, and began to press articles of value upon him; but he would not receive any of them. At last he fixed his eyes upon an image of "Our Lady," and condescended to ask what that was. The bishop informed him; when the Indian remarked that the bishop's words agreed with what the *padres* had told him. The bishop then ordered the image to be taken down, and begged the cacique to accept it. The cacique seemed pleased with this, and received the image on his knees. He then delivered it to one of his principal attendants, ordering him to carry it with much veneration. The chieftain's suite, not so dignified and self-restrained as their master, were pleased at receiving little presents; and, after a short stay at Santiago, they all returned into their own country, accompanied by Las Casas and Ladrada, who were anxious to continue the good work they had begun, and, if possible, to go together into the territory of Coban. This they succeeded in doing, and they found the people of that country very ready to receive them. They found, also, that it was well governed, and that the

Las Casas returns to Rabinal.

sacrifices there were less offensive than in any other part of the Indies.

Las Casas penetrates into Coban.

Las Casas and his companions were not left long to investigate this part of the country, as they were recalled by their brethren at Santiago, who told them "that certain good thoughts had occurred to the Bishop of Guatemala, who wished to communicate them to Brother Bartholomew and his companions." They accordingly returned to Santiago in the beginning of May, 1539.

Returns to Guatemala, May, 1539.

When they were all met together in junta, they found that the business upon which the bishop wished to confer with them was the paucity of ecclesiastics in that diocese; to remedy which defect he stated his intention of sending to Spain. He mentioned also that for this purpose he had collected some money, and was ready to apply some more which he had in the hands of an agent at Seville. His present difficulty was in the selection of a person to whom he might intrust this business, and he begged the assembled churchmen to help him to decide that point. There was also a chapter of their order about to be held at Mexico, and the clergy of Guatemala must be represented there. It was soon agreed that Las

Casas and Ladrada should go to Spain, and that Luis Cancér and Pedro de Angulo should attend the chapter at Mexico. They lost no time in setting out upon their journey. The two monks, who were to attend the chapter, took the road by the sea-shore, which passed through Soconusco. Las Casas and Ladrada went by Rabinal and Coban, an arduous undertaking, but one which they thought necessary in order to re-assure their friendly Indians, who would otherwise be dismayed by their absence. And, in truth, the cacique, Don Juan, was greatly disheartened when Las Casas and Ladrada came into his country, and told him that they were going to Spain. He feared that the surrounding tribes, many of whom were displeased with him for becoming a convert to Christianity, would now, in the absence of his protectors, the monks, no longer hesitate to make war upon him. They consoled him with the promise of a quick return, and he accompanied them to the bounds of his own country, furnishing them with an escort who were to see them safe as far as Chiapa.*

Las Casas sent to Spain.

---

* That the cacique was most zealous in the cause of the

Thus the Dominican monastery at Guatemala was again left desolate. Certainly this monkish fraternity was no pedantic institution, which could not conform itself to the wants and the necessities of the people amongst whom its lot was cast. A faithful layman took charge of the convent, probably with such orders as had been given many years ago, on a similar occasion, by Betanzos,—

---

monks, may be gathered from the following account of a transaction which took place in the year 1555, and which we conclude, by the date, relates to the cacique Don Juan, mentioned in the text.

"Sabida, pues, la cruel barbaridad de los Idolatras en toda aquella Tierra, el Indio Don Juan Cazique, Governador de la Vera-Paz, tomó tan por su quenta la vengança de la Muerte de los Religiosos, que con las compañías de sus Indios, acaudillándolos él en Persona, empezó à guerrear crudamente . . . .

" . . . . Y dezia públicamente á todos, y en especial á los Padres del Convento de Santo Domingo de Coban : Que no descansaria su Coraçon, ni tendria sossiego alguna, hasta que acabasse de raiz con todos los Acalanes, y Lacandones, en satisfacion, y vengança de la Muerte, que avian dado al Padre Prior Fray Domingo de Vico, y al Padre Fray Andrés Lopez, su Compañero: Tan excessivo era el amor, que al Padre Prior tenia; y tal el dolor, que labró en su sentimiento la alevosa Muerte que á los dos dieron aquellos Barbaros!"
—JUAN DE VILLAGUTIERRE SOTO-MAYOR, *Historia de la Conquista de la Provincia de el Itza*, lib. i. cap. 10.

to open the convent church to any one who wished to pray there; and this lay friend of the monastery employed his leisure, somewhat as the other laymen had done, in preparing unburnt bricks for the future building materials of the monastery.

The four monks reached Mexico safely, and were very kindly received by Domingo de Betanzos. A chapter of the Dominicans was held on the 24th day of August, 1539; and, though the demand for Christian instruction was very urgent in Mexico, the chapter, having been informed of the proceedings in Guatemala and "the Land of War," determined that four monks and two novices should be appointed to go to Guatemala; that Pedro de Angulo should be named as Vicar of the Dominican convent at Guatemala, and that Las Casas, with Ladrada and Luis Cancér, should be allowed to go to Spain. Las Casas and his companions accordingly pursued their way to the mother country.

We are left in no doubt of the activity of Brother Bartholomew after he had arrived at the Spanish Court; for there are a number of royal orders and letters, about this period, all bearing upon

Royal orders and letters fathe conversion of the inhabitants of Tuzulutlan. There is an order sanctioning the promise which had been made on the Emperor's part, that no lay Spaniard should enter that province within five years, unless with the permission of the Dominican monks. There are letters, addressed, by command of the emperor, to each of the principal caciques of "the Land of War" who had favoured the Dominicans, in which letters Charles thanks them for what they had done, and charges them to continue in the same course.* There are orders to the Governor of Guatemala to favour these caciques in their endeavours to help the Dominican monks, and instructions to the Governor of Mexico to allow Indians to be taken from that

---

* The letter of the Emperor to one of the caciques commences thus:—" EL REY. Don Jorge, Principal del pueblo de Tegpanatitan, que es en la Provincia de Guatemala. Por relacion de fray Bartolomé de las Casas e sido informado, que aveys travajado en pacificar, y traer de paz, los naturales de las Provincias de Taçulutlan, que estavan de guerra, y el favor y ayuda que para ello aveys dado al dicho fray Bartolomé de las Casas, y fray Pedro de Angulo, y á los otros Religiosos que en ello han entendido. . . . . Oct. 17, 1540."—REMESAL, *Hist. de Chiapa y Guatemala,* lib. iii. cap. 21.

province by the Dominican monks, if they should find such Indians useful in their entry into Tuzulutlan. Music, the means by which Las Casas and his friends had accomplished so much good, was not forgotten; and the emperor commands the head of the Franciscans in New Spain to allow some of the Indians who could play and sing church music in the monasteries of that order, to be taken by Las Casas into the province of Tuzulutlan. And, finally, there is a general order to the authorities in America to punish those who should transgress the provisions which had been made in favour of Las Casas and his Dominicans.

We learn from one of these letters who were the chiefs that favoured the introduction of Christianity, and the names of their provinces, which is a valuable contribution to the history, and perhaps to the ethnology, of Central America. They were Don Juan, Governor (so he is called) of the town of Atitlan, Don Jorge, Principal of the town of Tecpanatitan, Don Miguel, Principal of the town of Zizicaztenango, and Don Gaspar, Principal of the town of Tequizistlan.

The business of Las Casas at court was finished, and the monks, for whose sustenance the good

Bishop of Guatemala had provided, were ready to leave Spain, when the President of the Council of the Indies detained Las Casas, in order that he might assist at certain councils which were about to be held, concerning the Government of the Indies. This is the second time within a short period, that we have seen the authorities in Spain anxious to avail themselves of the local knowledge and experience of eminent persons who had lived in the Indies.

The monks chosen to aid in the conversion of Guatemala consisted of Franciscans and Dominicans. The Dominicans were detained in Spain, as Las Casas was their vicar-general. But the Franciscans were sent on, and with them went Luis Cancér, carrying all the letters and royal orders relating to the province of Tuzulutlan, still called "the Land of War," but which now deserved that name less than any part of the Indies. Before sailing, a very solemn proclamation was made on the steps of the Cathedral at Seville of that royal order which sternly forbad the entrance for the present of any lay Spaniards into the favoured province of Tuzulutlan. This was a precaution adopted by Las Casas, who well knew that the provincial governors, though they kissed the royal orders very dutifully, and were wont to put them, after the eastern fashion, upon their heads, with every demonstration of respect, were extremely dexterous in disobeying them, on the pretext that His Majesty had been misinformed, or had been informed in a left-hand manner (*siniestramente*). Las Casas, therefore, was anxious to give all possible publicity to this royal order in Spain, where its validity could not be denied.

CHAPTER XI.

Las Casas writes on Indian affairs—He is made Bishop of Chiapa—His troubles with his flock—He resigns the bishopric—His controversy with Sepulveda.

WE left Las Casas detained at the court of Spain by the Council of the Indies, who wished to profit by his knowledge of Indian affairs. It is easy to imagine with what force he could then speak in favour of his Indians, having, for once, a great practical success to appeal to in the conquest of Tuzulutlan: he who had never been even daunted when the course of affairs had apparently been most decisive against him.

The Emperor Charles the Fifth was absent in Germany, contending against Luther and the German princes who favoured the great reformer, and Las Casas employed his time in writing the work, which of all his works has become most celebrated, namely, *The Destruction of the Indies*. This was afterwards translated into several languages, and has been read throughout Europe. It gives a short account of what had taken place in each colony, and is one of the boldest works that ever issued from the press. At that time it was not published, but submitted to the Emperor and his ministers. It is possible that in this its first form it was a still more daring production than it appears to be now; for in the printed copies there is not a single name given of the persons inculpated. These are generally spoken of as this or that "tyrant." The work was not published in its present form until twelve years afterwards, when it was addressed with a dedication to Philip, the heir to the throne.

He writes the Destruction of the Indies.

The above, however, was not the only, or, perhaps, the most important, work Las Casas wrote about this time. He also drew up a memorial, which is in itself an elaborate work, consisting of twenty reasons to prove that the Indians ought not to be given to the Spaniards either in encomienda, in fee, in vassalage, or in any other

He writes a memorial called Veynte Razones.

manner. It appears from the title (*Veynte Razones*), that it was written at the Emperor's command for the information of a certain great junta which was to be held at Valladolid, in the year 1542. There is one very striking passage in the Memorial, in which Las Casas states that the Indians were subjected to four masters, namely, first, His majesty the Emperor; secondly, their own caciques; thirdly, their Encomendero; and fourthly, his manager, who, as Las Casas said, " weighed more upon them than an hundred towers."

Among the achievements of the statesmen, churchmen, and lawyers, who distinguished themselves as Protectors of the Indians during the first half of the sixteenth century, those of Las Casas are incomparably the most prominent. It cannot even be said of any other protector, as was said of the second competitor in the race in Virgil's *Æneid*, that he was next to the foremost man, " though next after a long interval;"* for Las

---

* " Primus abit, longeque ante omnia corpora Nisus
   Emicat, et ventis et fulminis ocior alis.
Proximus huic, longo sed proximus intervallo,
Insequitur Salius."—*Æneid*, lib. v. 318.

Casas was entirely alone in his pre-eminence, and was the prime mover on almost all the great occasions when the welfare of the Indians occupied the attention of the court of Spain.

Gonzalo Pizarro's rebellion in Peru, which the remarkable sagacity of the licentiate Pedro de la Gasca only just sufficed to quell, was directly traceable to the disinclination to adopt the New Laws; and two minor rebellions which followed were also caused by these same ordinances. The New Laws had been a signal triumph for Las Casas. Without him, without his untiring energy and singular influence over those whom he came near, these laws would not have been enacted. The mere bodily fatigue which he endured was such as hardly any man of his time, not a conqueror, had encountered. He had crossed the ocean twelve times. Four times he had made his way into Germany, to see the Emperor. Had a record been kept of his wanderings, such as that which exists of the journeys of Charles the Fifth, it would have shown that Las Casas had led a much more active life than even that energetic monarch. Moreover, the journeyings of Las Casas were often made with all the inconvenience of

New Laws due to the energy of Las Casas.

The labours of Las Casas.

poverty, and were not in any respect like a royal progress.

Narrative of his life resumed at the year 1543.

It was in 1543 that Las Casas, being at Barcelona, whither he had gone to thank the Emperor for the promulgation of the New Laws, was surprised by an offer which would have delighted most other men, but which to him was singularly unwelcome. One Sunday evening he was honoured by receiving a visit from the Emperor's secretary, Francisco de los Cobos, who came to press upon his acceptance the bishopric of Cusco (a town in the province of New Toledo), vacant by the death of Bishop Valverde. Now, there were weighty reasons why this offer of a bishopric should be unwelcome to Las Casas. To prove that he was moved by no private interest in his advocacy of the cause of the Indians, he had publicly and solemnly renounced all personal favour or gratification that Charles the Fifth could bestow upon him. Moreover, his flock was already larger than that in any bishopric; and to become a bishop was, for Las Casas, a limitation of the sphere of his philanthropic endeavours.

Las Casas is offered the bishopric of Cusco.

Las Casas refuses the bishopric of Cusco.

Accordingly he refused the bishopric of Cusco, and quitted Barcelona.

He was not, however, to escape being raised to the episcopal dignity. The province of Chiapa had recently been constituted into a diocese; and the first bishop who had been appointed had died on his way to the seat of his bishopric. The Council of the Indies felt that it would be desirable to have a bishop in that diocese who would look to the execution of the New Laws. The province of Chiapa was at a great distance from Mexico, where there was an *audiencia,* and also from Honduras, where a new one was about to be constituted, to be called the *Audiencia* of the Confines. Chiapa, therefore, might be much misgoverned, unless it had a vigorous bishop. The Council resolved that Las Casas should have this bishopric pressed upon him. The heads of the Dominican order were of opinion that Las Casas ought not to refuse this offer; and, after being exposed to entreaty of all kinds, it being pressed upon him as a matter of conscience that he should accept the bishopric, he at last conquered his repugnance, and submitted himself to the will of his superiors.

Chiapa made a diocese.

Las Casas accepts the bishopric of Chiapa.

Having accepted the bishopric, Las Casas instantly set off for Toledo, where a chapter of his order was about to be held, and where he resolved to ask permission to carry out with him a number of Dominican monks, who might assist him in christianising his diocèse. The permission was granted. Several monks were chosen, who with Las Casas prepared themselves for their journey and voyage to the New World. Las Casas was consecrated at Seville; and on a Wednesday, the 4th of July, 1544, the new bishop, with his friend Rodrigo de Ladrada, and some clerigos, took his departure from Spain. The monks who accompanied him were forty-four in number, and were under the orders of their vicar, Thomas Casillas. They all set sail from San Lucar; and, after touching at the Canary Islands, arrived at the island of Hispaniola. The bishop was exceedingly ill received there. Indeed, he was the most unpopular man in the New World, as being the one who had done most to restrain the cruelty and curb the power of the Spanish conquerors. We cannot pursue the voyages and the journeyings of the bishop and the monks until they reached the province of Chiapa, and were installed in the town of Ciudad Real, the capital of that province. There exists, however, a minute account of all their proceedings, which is most interesting, and serves to show the hardships which such men underwent at that period before they could establish themselves in the Indies.

The episcopal dignity made no change in the ways or manners of Las Casas. His dress was that of a simple monk, often torn and patched. He ate no meat himself, though it was provided for the clergy who sat at table with him. There was no plate to be seen in his house, nothing but earthenware; and in all respects his household was maintained in the simplest manner.* He had lost all his books, which had been on board a vessel that had sunk in Campeachy Bay. This was a great grief to the good bishop, who, amidst all his other labours, was a diligent student giving especial attention to the voluminous works of

margin: The habits of Las Casas as a bishop.

margin: The bishop a student.

---

* " En su persona se trató siempre como frayle, un habito humilde, y algunas vezes roto y remendado. Jamas se puso tunica de lienço, ni durmió sino en sabanas de estameña, y una fraçada por colcha rica. No comia carne, aunque para los clérigos que assistian á su mesa se servia con mucha moderacion, coma se ha dicho. Comia en platos de varro, y las alhajas de su casa eran muy pocas."—REMESAL, *Hist. de Chiapa y Guatemala*, lib. vi. cap. 2.

Thomas Aquinas, which were a needful armoury to all those who had any controversy to maintain in that age.

It was only at rare intervals that Las Casas achieved success, or knew happiness; and the sufferings of the Indians oppressed his soul here, in Chiapa, as they had done in other parts of the New World. The members of his household could often hear him sighing and groaning in his own room at night. His grief used to reach its height when some poor Indian woman would come to him, and, throwing herself at his feet, exclaim with tears, "My father, great lord, I am free. Look at me; I have no mark of the brand on my face; and yet I have been sold for a slave. Defend me, you, who are our father." And Las Casas resolved to defend these poor people. His way of doing so was by forbidding absolution to be given to those Spaniards who held slaves, contrary to the provisions contained in the New Laws. This bold measure raised a perfect storm in his diocese. Some of the colonists and conquerors put the question as a point of honour. "If we dismiss these Indians," they said, "and cease to buy and sell them as we have hitherto done, they will say that we have been tyrants from the beginning, and that we cannot do with them what we have done, since a simple monk like this restores them to their liberty. They will laugh at us, mock at us, and cry after us in the streets; and there will not be an Indian who will do what a Spaniard may command him."

There was nothing that the Spaniards in Ciudad Real did not say and do to molest the bishop. They called him a "Bachelor by the Tiles;" a phrase of that time, signifying one who had not been a regular student of theology, who had entered by the roof, and not by the door. They made verses upon him, of an opprobrious kind, which the children sang in the streets. An arquebuse, without ball, was discharged at his window, to alarm him. His dean would not obey him, and gave absolution to some persons who notoriously had Indians for slaves. The Dominican monks partook of the unpopularity of the bishop. Finally, Las Casas resolved to seek redress, not for his own wrongs, but for those of his Indian flock, from the Royal *Audiencia* of the Confines; and he made a journey to Honduras for that purpose. There is a letter of his, dated

Hostility to the bishop in his diocese.

He appeals to the nearest audiencia.

the 22nd of October, 1545, addressed to that *audiencia*, in which he threatened the Auditors with excommunication unless they should provide a remedy for the evils which existed in his diocese. When he appeared before them, the president, far from listening favourably to the protestations of Las Casas, poured forth a torrent of abuse upon him: "You are a scoundrel, a bad man, a bad monk, a bad bishop, a shameless fellow; and you deserve to be chastised." "I do deserve all that your lordship says," Las Casas replied. The bishop said this ironically, recollecting how much he had laboured to obtain for this judge his place.

<small>Reply of the president to Las Casas.</small>

Notwithstanding his bad reception in the first instance from the Auditors of the Confines, the bishop at last succeeded in persuading them to agree to send an Auditor to Ciudad Real, who should see to the execution of the new laws. The inhabitants of Ciudad Real were informed by letter of this fact; and they determined to make the most strenuous resistance to the return of their bishop into the city. They prepared a protest, in which they said that he had never shown any bull from the pope, or mandate from the em-

<small>His flock determine to resist Las Casas.</small>

peror, authorizing him to exercise the rights of a bishop. They insisted upon his proceeding like the other bishops of New Spain, and not introducing innovations. If he did not assent to this, they would deprive him of his temporalities, and refuse to admit him as their bishop. They placed a body of Indians on the road that he would have to traverse in returning to their city, having determined that they would not let him enter, unless, as they said, he would treat them as Christians, allowing them absolution, and not endeavour to take away their slaves, nor to fix the tribute of their *encomiendas*. Against the bishop, who would come " unguarded and on foot, with only a stick in his hand, and a breviary in his girdle," they prepared coats of mail and corslets, arquebuses, lances, and swords. The Indians were posted some way out of the city, as sentinels, to give notice of his approach. Meanwhile Las Casas had arrived at Copanabastla, where there was a Dominican monastery, and where he learnt what reception was awaiting him in his diocese. The Dominicans counselled him not to proceed; but the bishop's opinion was that he should fearlessly prosecute his journey. "For," he said, " if

<small>Their preparations for resistance.</small>

<small>The bishop resolves to enter his diocese.</small>

I do not go to Ciudad Real, I banish myself from my church; and it will be said of me, with much reason, 'The wicked fleeth; and no man pursueth.'" He did not deny that the intelligence was true, and that his flock were prepared to kill him. "But," he said, "the minds of men change from hour to hour, from minute to minute, from moment to moment. Is it possible that God has been so chary with the men of Ciudad Real as to deny His holy assistance in causing them to abstain from so great a crime as putting me to death? If I do not endeavour to enter my church, of whom shall I have to complain to the king, or to the pope, as having thrust me out of it? Are my adversaries so bitter against me that the first word will be a deadly thrust through my heart, without giving me the chance of soothing them? In conclusion, reverend fathers, I am resolved, trusting in the mercy of God and in your holy prayers, to set out for my diocese. To tarry here, or to go elsewhere, has all the inconveniences which have just been stated." So saying, he rose from his seat; and, gathering up the folds of his scapulary, he commenced his journey.

Now the Indian sentinels had heard that the

bishop's baggage, which had preceded him, had been taken back, and they were consequently quite at their ease. The inhabitants of Ciudad Real had also heard of this, and there was great joy in the city; as they thought that their preparations had daunted the bishop.

Suddenly the bishop in his journey came upon these Indian sentinels. They fell at his feet, and with tears besought his pardon. "It was beautiful to hear the harangue which each of them made, clinging to the feet of the bishop, and speaking in the Mexican language, which is very expressive of the affections."* The kind bishop was not angry with the Indians, and his only fear was lest they should be scourged or put to death for not having given notice of his approach. He, therefore, with his own hands, assisted by a certain Father Vicente who was with him, tied these Indians to one another, and made them follow behind him, as if they were his prisoners. He did this partly with his own hands, in order

The Indian sentinels fall at the bishop's feet.

---

* "Y era donoso el modo de la arenga que cada uno abraçado con los pies del Obispo dezia en lengua Mexicana, que es muy significativa de afectos."—REMESAL, *Hist. de Chiapa y Guatemala*, lib. vii. cap. 8.

that two or three Spaniards who were with him, and a negro, who always accompanied him because he was very tall and could carry the bishop across the rivers, might not be subject to the charge of having bound the Indians. That same night, as the bishop journeyed, there was an earthquake at Ciudad Real; and the citizens said, " The bishop must be coming, and those dogs of Indians have not told us of it:—this earthquake is a sign of the destruction that is to come upon the city when he arrives in it."

The bishop enters Ciudad Real.

The bishop travelled all night, and reached Ciudad Real at day-break. He went straight to the church; and thither he summoned the alcaldes and regidors to meet him. They came, followed by all the inhabitants of the city, and seated themselves, as if to hear a sermon. When the bishop advanced from the sacristy, no man asked his benediction, or spoke a word to him, or made any sign of courtesy. Then the notary to the Town Council rose, and read a paper containing the requisitions which had been agreed upon. To this the bishop replied in a speech of much gentleness and modesty; and his words were producing a considerable effect on his hearers, when one of

Proceedings in the cathedral.

the regidors, without rising, or taking off his cap, commenced a speech, blaming the bishop, whom he described as a private individual, for presuming to summon them there instead of coming to the Town Council.

"Look you, sir," the bishop replied, "when I have to ask you anything from your estates, I will go to your houses to speak to you; but, when the things which I have to speak about relate to the service of God and the good of your souls, I have to send and summon you, and to command that you should come wherever I may be; and if you are Christians, you have to come trooping there in haste, lest evil fall upon you." These words, spoken with great animation, had the effect of dismaying and silencing the bishop's opponents.

He rose and prepared to go into the sacristy, when the secretary of the Town Council went up to him, and presented a petition that he would name confessors. "I shall willingly do so," said the bishop; and with a loud voice he named two confessors. They were, however, well known to be of his own way of thinking. The people, therefore, were not satisfied. The bishop then named two others, of whose good disposition he was well aware, but who were not so well known as his partizans. The monk who had accompanied him on his journey, Fray Vicente de Ferrer, laid hold of the bishop's vestments, and exclaimed, "Let your lordship die rather than do this," for he was not aware of the character of these men whom the bishop had named, and thought he was giving way to clamour. Immediately a great tumult arose in the church; and, at that juncture, two monks of the Order of Mercy entered it, who persuaded the bishop and his companion to withdraw from the crowd, and to accompany them to their convent.

Las Casas, having journeyed on foot all night, was exceedingly exhausted; and the monks were giving him some bread, when they heard a great noise, and found that an armed populace had surrounded the convent. Some of the armed men forced their way even to the cell where the bishop was. A new grievance, which had infuriated them, was that their Indian sentinels had been bound and treated as prisoners. The bishop said that he alone was to blame in the matter, that he had come upon these Indians suddenly,

<small>The convent beset by armed men.</small>

and had bound them with his own hands, lest they should be suspected of having voluntarily favoured him, and be accordingly maltreated. One of the rioters, a certain Pedro de Pando, said, " You see here the way of the world. He is the saviour of the Indians, and look, he it is who binds them. Yet this same man will send memorials against us to Spain, declaring that we maltreat them." After this, another of the inhabitants of Ciudad Real poured out most foul language against the bishop. Las Casas only said, "I do not choose, sir, to answer you, in order not to take out of God's hands your chastisement; for these insults are not addressed to me, but to Him."

While this was going on in the cell of the bishop, one of the mob in the courtyard had been quarrelling with Juanillo, the bishop's negro, saying that it was he who had tied the Indians, and he gave the negro a thrust with a pike which stretched him on the ground. The monks rushed forward to assist the negro; and two of them, who were youths, showed such courage that the Fathers of Mercy succeeded in clearing, by main force, their convent from its invaders. It was now nine o'clock in the morning. But by mid-

<small>The convent is cleared of its invaders</small>

Change of mood in the rioters of Ciudad Real.

day so great a change had been wrought in the minds of the inhabitants of Ciudad Real, so completely had they come to a sense of the turbulence and shamefulness of their conduct, that nearly all of them proceeded to the convent, and, on their knees, besought the bishop's pardon, kissed his hands, and said that they were his children. The alcaldes, as a sign of submission, would not carry their wands of office in his presence; others took off their swords; and, in festal procession, they brought the bishop out of the convent, carried him to the house of one of the principal inhabitants, and sent him various costly presents. Nay more, they resolved to hold a tournament in honour of their bishop, a mark of their favour and esteem he could, perhaps, have dispensed with. Certainly few men have ever experienced stranger turns of fortune than Las Casas did in the course of this memorable day of his return to his diocese. The very suddenness of the change of feeling in his flock was a circumstance that might well have engendered in his mind misgivings as to the future, and have disgusted him with the office of ruling as bishop over the turbulent and versatile citizens of Ciudad Real, the chief city of Chiapa.

But, indeed, in no part of the New World would Las Casas have had an easy life. It was at this time that Gonzalo Pizarro's rebellion in Peru was at its height, and that the resistance to the New Laws was so great that Charles the Fifth was obliged to revoke them. What anguish must have been caused to Las Casas by the revocation of these laws is known to no man. Notwithstanding the disasters he experienced, which would have crushed the spirit of almost any other person, his zeal never slackened, and his practical sagacity taught him not to reproach Charles the Fifth or his ministers for a backward course of legislation, which he knew had been forced upon them by calamity. For himself, he maintained his ground that the granting of *encomiendas* to private persons was a great injustice to the native Indians; but he seems to have accepted the new position of affairs, and to have bent his efforts to improving that system which he must have felt could not now be destroyed by a mere mandate from the court of Spain. At any rate, he did not protest against the revocation of the new laws as an act of folly or weakness on the part of the Spanish authorities at home. This revocation, could not have been known at this

Revocation of the New Laws.

How Las Casas bore the revocation of the New Laws.

time to the *audiencia* of the confines, for they fulfilled their promise of sending one of their body to Chiapa.

The Auditor's address to the bishop.

This Auditor heard, with attention and respect, the representations that Las Casas made to him on behalf of the Indians. But one day he thus replied:—" Your lordship well knows that although these new laws were framed at Valladolid, with the accordances of sundry grave personages (as your lordship and I saw), one of the reasons that has made these laws hateful in the Indies has been the fact of your having had a hand in them. The conquerors consider your lordship as so prejudiced against them, that they believe that what you do in favour of the natives is not so much from love of the Indians as from hatred of the Spaniards. As they entertain this opinion, if I have to deprive any of them of their slaves or estates, they will feel more its being done in your presence than they will the loss itself. Don Tello de Sandoval (the president of the *Audiencia* at Mexico) has summoned your lordship for a synod of prelates; and I shall be glad, if you will hasten your departure, for, until you have gone, I can do nothing."

The bishop had been preparing to attend this synod, and he now took his departure. He never beheld his diocese again.

The bishop goes to a Synod at Mexico.

When he approached the city of Mexico there was a tumult as if a hostile army were about to occupy the city. The authorities were obliged to write to him, begging him to defer his entry until the minds of men should be somewhat quieted.* He afterwards entered in the daytime, without receiving any insult. He took up his abode in the Dominican monastery; and on the first day of his arrival, the viceroy and the Auditors sent word that they were ready to receive a visit from him. His reply evinced his habitual boldness, but, at the same time, betrayed the want of worldly wisdom that was occasionally manifest

His reception in that city.

---

* The hatred to Las Casas throughout the New World amounted to a passion. Letters were written to the residents in Chiapa, expressing pity for them as having met the greatest misfortune that could occur to them, in being placed under such a bishop. They did not name him, but spoke of him as " That Devil who has come to you for a bishop." The following is an extract from one of these letters. " We say here, that very great must be the sins of your country, when God chastises it with such a scourge as sending that Antichrist for a bishop."

in him. There was quite enough difficulty in the affairs which he had to manage, on his own account; but he felt it his duty to inform the king's officers that they must excuse his visiting them, as they were excommunicated, since they had given orders for cutting off the head of a priest at Anteguera. This answer was soon made known throughout the city of Mexico, and increased the odium under which Las Casas laboured.

He refuses to visit the king's Officers in Mexico.

The synod of prelates and other learned men commenced its proceedings, and laid down as a basis five principal points. 1st, That all unbelievers, of whatever sect or religion they might be, and whatever sins they might have committed against natural, national, or divine law, have nevertheless a just lordship over their own possessions. 2nd, That there are four different kinds of unbelievers. The object of laying down this maxim is not obvious at first, and requires a knowledge of the controversies of that age. The object was to place the Indians in the second class of unbelievers; and more than once, on great occasions, Las Casas placed them in the same

Proceedings of the Synod at Mexico.

The principles laid down by the Synod.

division as the ancient British, thus dividing them from those barbarians who had no arts or polity whatever. 3rd, That the final and only reason why the Apostolic See had given supreme jurisdiction in the Indies to the Kings of Castile and Leon was, that the gospel might be preached, and the Indians be converted It was not to make those kings greater lords and richer princes than they were. 4th, That the Apostolic See, in granting this supremacy to the Kings of Castile and Leon, did not mean thereby to deprive the lords of the Indians of their estates, lordships, jurisdictions, or dignities. 5th, That the Kings of Castile and Leon were bound to provide the requisite expenses for the conversion of the Indians to the true faith.

Taking the foregoing as their main principles, the synod made many deductions very unfavourable to the claims of the conquerors; and especially they pronounced what were the conditions upon which absolution should be granted by confessors to the Spanish colonists, into which conditions restitution entered.

The proceedings of this synod were very bold, but Las Casas was not satisfied with them, because the particular point of slavery, though much discussed, was not resolved upon. He therefore summoned a junta, which was attended by all the learned men except the bishops; and this junta pronounced that the Spaniards who had made slaves were "tyrants;" that the slaves were to be considered as illegally made; and that all those who possessed them were bound to liberate them. They also pronounced against the personal service of the Indians.

<small>Las Casas summons another junta.</small>

It must not be supposed that the members of this junta imagined that their decisions would immediately insure the liberation of the Indians. These learned men contented themselves with declaring to their countrymen what they held to be the truth, and informing them of what was necessary for the salvation of their souls. They were not bound to do anything more.

Las Casas did not return from Mexico to his bishopric. Ever since his interview with the Auditors of the Confines he had resolved to go back to Spain; and the reason which he gave to one of his reverend brethren was, that when at court, and near the king and his council, he would be able to do more good service, both to

<small>Las Casas resolves to go to Spain.</small>

great authority of the middle ages, Thomas Aquinas. He appeals to history, citing the law of capital punishment enacted by "that most pious emperor," Constantine, against those pagans who should persevere in their rites and sacrifices. He maintains that men who are in a grievous state of error are to be recalled to the truth, whether they like it or not. He urges that more can be effected in a month by conquest than in a hundred years by mere preaching. Miracles are not to be asked for, when human means, having the sanction of divine authority, can attain the same end. "The preachers of our time," he says, "without miracles, cannot effect more than the apostles did, blessed with the co-operation of the Lord, and their words being confirmed by miracles." War, therefore, was a necessity. If the natives were taught without being terrified, being obdurate in their old ways, they would be much more slowly moved to adopt the true faith.

If Las Casas had been ardent in his opposition to Sepulveda's doctrines, when they were not printed, and while they could be read by those only who understood Latin, his ardour was redoubled when they were translated into Spanish, and could be joyfully perused by the conquerors in the Indies and their adherents at court, who would pronounce them to be most comfortable doctrines, and readily assign the palm of knowledge and of wisdom to this learned doctor, who justified the ways of his countrymen to themselves.

<small>The government prohibit the publication of the *Apology*.</small>

It is true that the government were not remiss. They seized upon whatever copies of Sepulveda's *Apology* they could lay hold of, and strictly forbade its circulation.* But prohibited works are often not the less read on account of the prohibition. It is not likely that any of the numerous band of agents and proctors who thronged the court of Spain, and besieged it with applications on behalf of the conquerors and colonists of the New World, were ignorant of the arguments which Sepulveda had urged, and which might

---

* It is worthy of notice that there could have been no personal hostility to Sepulveda on the part of the government. He was not punished for the publication of the *Apology*. Charles the Fifth's friendship was not withdrawn from him; and he was one of the few persons who afterwards visited that monarch in his retreat at Yuste, where he was kindly welcomed by Charles. See the graphic account of *The Cloister Life of Charles the Fifth*, written by Mr. STIRLING, p. 124.

salve the troubled consciences, if troubled they were, of these conquerors and colonists. Las Casas set himself more seriously to work than ever to refute doctrines so fatal to his cause, and which had thus obtained extended publication and currency.

A great ferment arose about the controversy. In times like our own, when there is so much that is exciting and amusing in literature, it is difficult to imagine the interest that was felt in learned controversy in those ages, when controversy was the chief excitement and amusement of learned men. In this case, moreover, there were many and great interests concerned.

Las Casas was not the only person who had been shocked by the doctrines or the expressions in Sepulveda's work, and who had sought to controvert them. Melchior Cano, a Dominican, renowned in those times for learning, had found passages in the *Democrates Secundus* " which were offensive to pious ears." The Bishop of Segovia had also been an ardent opponent to Sepulveda; and it was to him that the *Apology* for the work was addressed. Cano's objection to the book seems mainly to have turned upon an expression

Melchior Cano and the Bishop of Segovia oppose Sepulveda.

which had been used by the author in reference to St. Paul, Sepulveda having said that St. Paul had borne contumely with impatience, or words to that effect. A long correspondence ensued between the friends, for Cano was a friend of Sepulveda; but the real gist of the question is not touched upon in this correspondence. Las Casas was the opponent whom Sepulveda had most to fear; and he seems to have had somewhat of the same feeling towards him that his friend Erasmus must have had for the impetuous Luther. The refined scholar Sepulveda, "the Livy of Spain," as he has been called, looked upon the earnest Las Casas as a furious and dangerous person, " of better intentions than judgment;" yet (for he seems to have been an amiable man) declared that he bore no enmity to the bishop, and only prayed " that God would grant him a calmer mind, that he might learn sometimes to prefer quiet cogitations to turbulent designs."

Sepulveda might feel disgust at the uncontrolled temper of his opponent, and might despise his lesser acquisitions of learning, and his comparatively rude Latinity. But he was soon to learn what strength there was in an adversary whose practical knowledge of the subject in dispute was greater than that of any living man; whose eloquence was equal to his vehemence, and not hindered by it; and who brought a fervour to the cause which exceeded even that of an author publicly defending his own work, and one who must have thought himself most ungratefully used by the court and the universities in Spain.

Charles the Fifth convoked at Valladolid, in 1550, a junta of theologians and other learned men to hear this great cause argued, " Whether war of the kind that is called a war of conquest could be lawfully undertaken against the nations of the New World, if they had not committed any new faults other than those they had committed in the times of their infidelity." The Council of the Indies was associated with this junta; and altogether it consisted of fourteen persons. This practice of summoning persons of special knowledge to assist the authorities in the determination of difficult questions, was one of the greatest advantages which the government of Spain possessed at that period.

Junta at Valladolid to hear the dispute between Sepulveda and Las Casas.

Las Casas and Sepulveda appear before the junta.

Doctor Sepulveda appeared before the junta, and delivered a statement of the arguments on his side. The bishop was then summoned for a hearing; and, in five consecutive days, he read that laborious work of his, which is called the *Historia Apologética*. It is rich in facts and arguments of every description, and he had been many years preparing it.

The junta had deputed Domingo de Soto,* Charles's Confessor, to give a summary of the arguments on both sides. This he did in a very masterly manner. The summary was then submitted to Doctor Sepulveda, who made a reply before the junta, containing twelve objections to the arguments of the bishop. The bishop then gave twelve answers to these objections, and the proceedings terminated. They were afterwards published as a work entitled " A Dispute or Con-

---

* Mr. HALLAM, speaking of the *Relectiones Theologicæ* of Francis á Victoria, says, " The whole relection, as well as that on the Indians, displays an intrepid spirit of justice and humanity, which seems to have been rather a general characteristic of the Spanish theologians. Domingo Soto, always inflexibly on the side of right, had already sustained by his authority the noble enthusiasm of Las Casas."— *Literature of Europe*, part ii. chap. iv. sect. 3.

troversy between the Bishop Don Fray Bartolomé de las Casas, lately Bishop of Ciudad Real in Chiapa, and Doctor Ginés Sepulveda, Historiographer to our Lord the Emperor."

It would be impossible, and perhaps tedious to our readers, to attempt a full account of this important controversy within the limits which this biography must occupy. The work which Las Casas read in five days embodies much of the knowledge and experience which he had been acquiring for fifty years. We can hardly doubt, moreover, that both the controversialists were aided by other learned men, for an astonishing weight of learning is brought to bear upon the disputed points. The skill with which it is summed up by Charles's Confessor is marvellous, considering the immense mass of material with which he had to deal, and that Las Casas was a man who sought to exhaust his subject by an appeal to facts and arguments drawn from every conceivable source. *Nature of the controversy between Sepulveda and Las Casas.*

Doctor Sepulveda divided his statement of the case into four heads. It was lawful, he said, to commence war upon the natives in the New World for the four following reasons:— *Sepulveda's statement of the case.*

1st. For the gravity of the sins which the Indians had committed, especially their idolatries and their sins against nature.

Sins of the Indians.

2nd. On account of the rudeness of their natures, which brought upon them the necessity of serving persons of a more refined nature, such as that which the Spaniards possessed.

Rudeness of their nature.

3rd. In order to spread the faith, which would be more readily accomplished by the prior subjugation of the natives.

Must be conquered before they are converted.

4th. To protect the weak amongst the natives themselves, duly considering the cruelties which the Indians exercised upon one another, slaying numbers in sacrifices to false gods, and practising cannibalism.

Cruelties to one another.

It would have been difficult to make a better division of the subject than that adopted by Sepulveda. His fourth reason was well thought of, and put with much skill. He adduced in evidence the immense loss of life which had taken place in the sacrifices to idols amongst the Mexicans, and was enabled to argue that it exceeded the loss of life in war. This was not so; but still the argument was a very plausible one.

The dealings of the Israelites with the neighbouring idolaters formed the basis of the controversy upon the first reason, and gave room for elaborate argument. The doctor relied upon the command given to the Israelites, in the 20th chapter of *Deuteronomy*, to destroy the male inhabitants of those cities which should not be delivered up to them upon their demanding a surrender of the cities.* He dwelt especially on the 15th verse of that chapter, which says, " Thus shalt thou do unto all the cities which are

---

* " When thou comest nigh unto a city to fight against it, then proclaim peace unto it.

"And it shall be, if it make thee answer of peace, and open unto thee, then it shall be, that all the people that is found therein shall be tributaries unto thee, and they shall serve thee.

" And if it will make no peace with thee, but will make war against thee, then thou shalt besiege it :

"And when the Lord thy God hath delivered it into thine hands, thou shalt smite every male thereof with the edge of the sword.

" But the women, and the little ones, and the cattle, and all that is in the city, even all the spoil thereof, shalt thou take unto thyself; and thou shalt eat the spoil of thine enemies, which the Lord thy God hath given thee."—*Deut.* chap. xx. ver. 10-14.

very far off from thee, which are not of the cities of these nations." Upon this verse there is a gloss which declares that the words "far off" mean "of a different religion." Sepulveda consequently inferred that the Spaniards might make war upon any nation of a different religion from their own; and he supported this view by other passages quoted from *Deuteronomy.*

Sepulveda's arguments from Deuteronomy.

The bishop replied that the wars commanded by God against certain nations were not commanded in respect of their idolatry, as in that case the whole world, except Judæa, would have had to be conquered and chastised; but it was only against the Canaanites, the Jebusites, and other tribes who possessed the Land of Promise that the Israelites were commanded to make war. The bishop relied upon the 7th verse of the 23rd chapter, which says, "Thou shalt not abhor an Edomite; for he is thy brother: thou shalt not abhor an Egyptian, because thou wast a stranger in his land."

The bishop's reply from Deuteronomy.

With regard to the gloss which gave to the words "far off," the signification "of a different religion," the bishop did not contend that this was a wrong reading, but he argued that the words did not mean that upon that account alone, namely difference of religion, war might be made upon distant nations by the Jews. The words "far off" served to distinguish other Gentiles from the seven tribes who occupied the Land of Promise, and to whom no terms of peace were to be offered. With them it was to be a war of extermination; but there was nothing to show that a war with other Gentiles could be lawfully undertaken, solely on account of their idolatry. Finally, the bishop urged this general argument, that the examples from the Old Testament, as regarded those cruel chastisements, were given us " to marvel at and not to imitate," for which assertion he alleged the authority of certain decretals.

Upon the second reason, the rudeness of the Indian nature, Las Casas, with his extensive knowledge of Indian life, was easily triumphant; and, upon the third reason, namely the extension of the true faith, Las Casas could appeal to his own successes, and those of his brother Dominicans, in " the land of war."

With regard to Doctor Sepulveda's fourth reason, Las Casas alleged the general rule, "Of

Answer of Las Casas

to Sepulveda's fourth reason. two evils, choose the least." Human sacrifices were a less evil than indiscriminate warfare. " Thou shalt not kill," is a more positive command than Thou shalt defend the innocent. Moreover, by these wars the true faith was defamed, and had fallen into odium with the natives. Then Las Casas boldly urged what defence can be urged for human sacrifices—namely, that to the barbarous and Gentile apprehension, they were an offering up to God of the best that the worshippers possessed. He reminded his hearers of the sacrifice that Abraham was ready to make. The bishop also brought forward instances of great nations, such as the Romans and the Carthaginians, who had not been free from the guilt of human sacrifice; and he quoted Plutarch to show that when the Romans themselves became more humane and civilized in this respect, and, in their march of conquest, came upon barbarous nations who were addicted to human sacrifices, they did not punish them for this cause, but simply prohibited the commission of such offences for the future.

This controversy was conducted throughout with much skill and learning upon both sides, and with constant danger to Las Casas of bringing upon himself the wrath of the higher ecclesiastical and civil authorities. As, for instance, in opposing Sepulveda on the ground that force should not be employed to promote the faith, he was obliged to use great tact; for what was to be said about the past doings of many emperors and popes? Indeed, in the course of his long career of controversy, it is a matter for surprise that he did not come within the grasp of the Inquisition.

At the conclusion of his address to the junta, Las Casas made a fierce onslaught upon Doctor Sepulveda's mode of maintaining the rights of the kings of Spain. The following is the substance of what the bishop said upon this important branch of the controversy. "The doctor founds these rights upon our superiority in arms, and upon our having more bodily strength than the Indians. This is simply to place our kings in the position of tyrants. The right of those kings rests upon their extension of the Gospel in the New World, and their good government of the Indian nations. These duties they would be bound to fulfil even at their own expense; much more so considering the treasures they have re-

The bishop's view of the jurisdiction of the kings of Spain in the Indies.

ceived from the Indies. To deny this doctrine is to flatter and deceive our monarchs, and to put their salvation in peril. The doctor perverts the natural order of things, making the means the end, and what is accessory the principal. The accessory is temporal advantage: the principal, the preaching of the true faith. He who is ignorant of this, small is his knowledge; and he who denies it, is no more of a Christian than Mahomet was."

Then, after a not unbecoming allusion to his own prolonged labours, the bishop says:—" To this end [that is, to prevent the total perdition of the Indies], I direct all my efforts: not, as the doctor would make out, to shut the gates of justification, and disannul the sovereignty of the kings of Castille; but I shut the gates upon false claims made on their behalf, of no reality, altogether vain; and I open the gates to those claims of sovereignty which are founded upon law, which are solid, strong, truly catholic, and truly Christian."

Result of the controversy.

Thus the controversy ended. The result seems to have been, substantially, a drawn battle. At first, according to Sepulveda, the jurists had to give way to the theologians. But a timely reinforcement came to Sepulveda's aid, in the person of a learned Franciscan monk, named Bernardino Arevalo. At the beginning of the controversy he had been unable, from illness, to attend the junta; but, afterwards recovering, he brought such weight to Sepulveda's side of the argument, that the junta ultimately pronounced a sentence (one theologian alone protesting against it), concurring with the opinions expressed in Sepulveda's treatise *De Justis Belli Causis*. His victory, however, was a fruitless one. The government must have been convinced the other way, or at least must have thought that the promulgation of Sepulveda's views would be dangerous; for Prince Philip, then governing in the name of his father, gave directions that Sepulveda's work should not be allowed to enter the Indies. In royal orders, dated from Valladolid, in October and November of that same year, 1550, the Prince commanded the Viceroy of Mexico, and the Governor of Terra-firma, to seize upon any copy they could find of Sepulveda's work, and to send it back to Spain.

The junta pronounces in favour of Sepulveda.

Sepulveda's treatise not allowed to enter the Indies.

Sepulveda seems to have felt that Las Casas had conducted the cause with exceeding vigour, and had proved himself a terrible opponent; for, in a private letter describing the controversy, Sepulveda speaks of him as "most subtile, most vigilant, and most fluent, compared with whom the Ulysses of Homer was inert and stuttering." Las Casas, at the time of the controversy, was seventy-six years of age.

CHAPTER XII.

Las Casas appeals to Philip II. through Carranza—He writes a Treatise on Peru—His Death—Review of his Life.

THE controversy with Sepulveda was but one of the many labours of Las Casas, and he continued to exercise his self-imposed functions of Protector to the Indians with his accustomed zeal. He resided in the Dominican college of St. Gregory at Valladolid, with his faithful friend and spiritual brother, Ladrada, who seems to have spurred him to exertion in behalf of the Indians, as may be gathered from the following anecdote. Ladrada, being deaf, was in the habit of speaking loudly; and the collegiate fathers could hear him, when he was confessing Las Casas, exclaim, " Bishop, beware lest you go to hell if you do not labour for a remedy for those poor Indians, as you are

Las Casas resides in the Dominican college at Valladolid.

Admonition of Ladrada to Las Casas.

in duty bound to do." But this was more an admonition than a correction, as Remesal observes, for never was there known in Las Casas the slightest carelessness in this respect, especially in those days.

In the year 1555 there arose a great occasion for all the efforts that Las Casas could make on behalf of the Indians. Philip the Second had succeeded to the throne of Spain. He ruled over immense possessions, such as might well make him a terror to the European family of nations. But his finances were in a most deplorable state, and any project for improving them must have been very welcome to the king and his councillors.

Financial condition of Philip II.

Now there was one easy mode by which, with a few strokes of the pen, Philip could raise a very large sum of money. All the Spanish colonists in the New World held their possessions upon a most uncertain tenure. Philip had only to give up the claims of the crown to the reversion of the *encomiendas,* and he would be sure to receive an ample and immediate recompense. Neither had the monarch to begin the negotiation. There was already in England, attending

The reversion of the encomiendas saleable.

Philip's Court, "a sinner," as Las Casas calls him, from Peru, who was urging some such measure on the monarch.* Never was the fate of the Indians in greater peril. There were, however, two persons, both of whom had laid down their high offices, and had retired into monasteries, who were towers of strength to the poor Indians. These were Charles the Fifth and Las Casas. The latter had shown great boldness on many occasions of his life, but on this his daring verged upon audacity. His appeal to Philip was made through the king's confessor, Bartolomé Carranza de Miranda. Through him he dares to tell the monarch that any conclusion he may come to in England will be rash, because he is surrounded by few advisers, and those having no especial knowledge of the New World, and not being in communication with the Council of the Indies. If the king commits an error on this great occasion, can he allege the pretext of invincible ignorance? Las Casas boldly tells Carranza, that in England and Flanders our sovereigns seem to have forgotten that they have

<small>Las Casas appeals to Philip II. through Carranza.</small>

<small>Letter of Las Casas to Carranza.</small>

---

* Don Antonio de Ribera by name.

a kingdom of Spain to govern. What right have they to impose upon the miserable Indians tributes of money, watered with tears, to pay the debts of their crown? How repugnant to all just ideas, and what an atrocity it is, to wish to promote the interests of the king, without thinking even of God! If such a system is persisted in, will they in England and Flanders look with a favourable eye at this maxim, that the means may become the end, and the end the means? As to the *encomenderos* possessing any claim, they have not merited a single *maravedi*. " On the contrary I maintain," adds Las Casas, " that the king will be rigorously punished for not having chastised these assassins as they have deserved.* The kings of Castille owe a great debt to him who discovered the New World. They are also under obligation to those who have restored the royal authority in Peru. But they are not, on that account, to deliver up the wretched inhabitants as one gives up to the butcher the

---

* " Je dirai, au contraire, que le roi sera rigoureusement puni pour n'avoir pas châtié ces assassins comme ils l'ont mérité."—LLORENTE, *Œuvres de Don Barthélemi de las Casas*, tom. ii. p. 135. Paris, 1822.

most stupid animals to be slaughtered. If your paternity thinks it right to read this clause to his highness, or indeed the whole of my memorial, I beg you to believe that I shall feel the greatest satisfaction."

Las Casas wishes the letter to be read to Philip II.

To show that he was not the only person entirely opposed to the sale of the reversions of the *encomiendas*, Las Casas, in the course of this letter, makes the following statement:—" It is about fifteen days ago that a member of the Council of the Indies, horrified at what is now known of the situation of America, and at the proposition which is now mooted, made me fear the judgments of God, reproaching me with not doing half my duty in that I did not summon, twenty times a day, the whole earth to my aid, and that I did not go, with a stick in my hand and a beggar's wallet on my back, even into England, to protest against these tyrants; for it was to me that God had entrusted this charitable and difficult undertaking. What would he have said if he had seen all that I have seen for the last sixty years?"

A member of the council urges Las Casas to further exertions.

It is impossible to tell what effect this letter had upon Carranza, and upon Philip; but it is probable that it was considerable; and all the more so, in that he had not intruded his advice upon them, for it is evident, in the course of the letter, that they had first written to consult Las Casas upon the subject.*

Charles V. disapproves of the sale of encomiendas.

Charles the Fifth was as decided as Las Casas upon the point at issue. If we may trust the report of the Venetian ambassador, Soriano, this was almost the only public matter that Charles had influenced, up to that time, since his retirement into the monastery of Yuste.† The dying emperor supported the views of his old friend Las Casas; and the weight of two such authorities on Indian affairs was such that the scheme

The project is abandoned.

of selling the reversion of the *encomiendas*, which would have led to the total slavery of the Indians, was abandoned.

Las Casas continued to occupy himself in the affairs of the Indies, corresponding with persons

---

* " Je répondrai un peu plus loin à ce qu'elle" (son Altesse) "a dit de la nécessité de pourvoir à l'entretien des Espagnols qui sont employés dans les Indes."—LLORENTE, *Œuvres de Don Barthélemi de las Casas*, tom. ii. p. 135.

† See Ranke, Fürsten und Volker von Sud Europa, &c

in America, and being referred to for advice and information by the council at home.

He also continued to labour at his greatest literary work, the *History of the Indies.* This work is said to have been commenced in 1527, when he first became a Dominican monk; but it is clear from the last sentence but one in this History, that he was still engaged upon it in the year 1561, the eighty-seventh year of his own age.*

In 1564 he had reached his ninetieth year, and in that year he wrote a treatise on the subject of Peru, which is, perhaps, one of the best that his fertile pen ever produced. As if he were aware that whatever he should do now must be done speedily, this paper is composed with more brevity, though not with less force, than almost any of his productions. In it there is a statement which the student may look for in vain

A treatise of Las Casas on Peru.

---

* " Pero esta ignorancia y cequedad del Consejo del Rey tubo su origen primero, lo qual fué causa de proveer que se hiciesen aquellos requerimientos, y plega á Dios que hoy, que es elaño que pasa de sesenta y uno, el consejo esté libre della."—LAS CASAS, *Hist. de las Indias*, MS. lib. iii. cap. 166.

amongst the most elaborate histories that were written at that period, or have been written since, of the Spanish Conquest in America. It is constantly mentioned that the tribute to be raised from *encomiendas*, in this or that district, was settled by this or that governor or royal auditor; but no accurate account is given of what the tribute was. In this treatise of Las Casas is set forth the tribute to be paid annually by five hundred Indian families in Arequipa. They are to furnish, (1), 180 Peruvian sheep. An additional hardship was, that these sheep could not be procured in that district, but had to be sought for in a neighbouring province. (2), 300 pieces of cotton goods, each sufficient for the dress of an Indian; (3), 1000 bushels of maize; (4), 850 bushels of wheat; (5), 1000 fowls; (6), 1000 sacks, with cords to them; (7), 60 baskets of *coca*; (8), 100 cotton napkins; (9), 30 swine; (10), 50 *arrobas* of *camaron** (a kind of fish); (11), 500 *arrobas* of another kind of fish; (12), 5 *arrobas* of wool; (13), 40 skins of sea-

An annual tribute in a certain encomienda.

---

* An arroba was twenty-five pounds in weight, each pound consisting of sixteen ounces.

wolves, dressed, and 40 others undressed; (14), 2 *arrobas* of cord; (15), 3 tents; (16), 8 tablecloths; (17), 2000 baskets of pepper; (18), 2 *arrobas* of balls of cotton; (19), 9 house cloths; (20), 3 *arrobas* of fat, to make candles; (21), 15 Indians for the domestic service of the Spanish *encomendero*; (22), 8 Indians for the cultivation of his garden; (23), 8 others, to have charge of his flocks and cattle.

This monstrous tribute might well call forth indignation, even from a man uninterested in the subject. Upon such a tribute Las Casas rests his assertion that the Indians are deprived of their goods and of their liberty, and that it is impossible not to apply the epithet of tyrannical to the government under which they live; for, according to Aristotle, every government of a free people ought to have for its object the temporal and the spiritual good of the members of the body politic. Such was the intrepid writing, skilfully interwoven with the most important facts, which Las Casas had the energy to produce at this advanced period of his life.

Of all that is done in any great transaction, so small a part can be told, that the historian is often most unwillingly compelled to commit an act of seeming injustice, when he carefully commemorates the deeds of the chief of a party, to the exclusion of those of many of his associates. Las Casas was but one, though immeasurably the first, of a numerous body of men who may rightly be called the Protectors of the Indians. Amongst these protectors was an ex-auditor of the *Audiencias* of Guatemala and Mexico, named Zurita. He also informed the Emperor of the excessive nature of the imposts levied upon the Indians, and declared that it was one of the causes which led to the depopulation of the New World. Another cause of the destruction of the Indians, according to Zurita, was their being compelled to work at the great edifices erected in the Spanish towns. They were forced, he says, to labour from the point of day until late in the evening. "I have seen," he adds, "after the *Angelus*, a great number of Indians cruelly conducted from their work by a very powerful personage. They bore along an enormous piece of wood, as large as a royal pine-tree, and when they stopped to rest, a negro who followed them, armed with a whip, forced them to continue their march, striking them

[Marginal notes: Many other Protectors besides Las Casas. Evidence of the Auditor Zurita. The Indians at work.]

with this whip, from the first man to the last, not that they should gain time, and undertake other labours, for the day's work was finished, but to prevent them from resting, and to keep up the bad habit, so common, of beating them incessantly, and maltreating them. As they were all naked, except that they wore a piece of linen round their loins, and as the negro struck as hard as he could, all the strokes of the whip had their full effect. Not one of the Indians said a word, or turned his head, for they were all broken down by misery. It is the custom to urge them constantly in their work, not to allow them to take any rest, and to chastise them if they attempt to do so. This ill-treatment of the Indians is the cause of my having, with the permission of your majesty, resigned my place of auditor." Such testimony as the above, confirmed by the resignation of office on the part of the witness, is most important in support of the statements and the conduct of Las Casas, the chief Protector of the Indians.

The memorial on Peru, written by Las Casas in his ninetieth year, appears to have been the last effort of his fertile pen. Two years later, however, in 1566, he came forward, not to write, but to act on behalf of his Indians. In that year a grievance that was suffered by the province of Guatemala was made known to him. The Guatemalans had been deprived of their *audiencia*. The Dominicans in that province wrote to Las Casas, telling him that the country suffered very much for want of an *audiencia*. The natives had no chance of justice, as they had to make a journey to Mexico, in order to prosecute any appeal. Las Casas well knew the importance of this matter. He accordingly left his collegiate monastery at Valladolid, and went to Madrid. There he put the case of the Guatemalans so strongly, to the King and to the Council of the Indies, that the *audiencia* was restored to Guatemala. This was the last work of Las Casas. He fell ill at Madrid, and, after a short illness, died there in July, 1566, being ninety-two years of age. His obsequies were attended by a large concourse of the inhabitants of that city; and he was buried with all due solemnity in the convent chapel of " Our Lady of Atocha."

In parting from Las Casas, it must be felt that all ordinary eulogies would be feeble and inadequate. His was one of those few lives that are beyond biography, and require a history to be written in order to illustrate them. His career affords, perhaps, a solitary instance of a man who, being neither a conqueror, a discoverer, nor an inventor, has, by the pure force of benevolence, become so notable a figure, that large portions of history cannot be written, or at least cannot be understood, without the narrative of his deeds and efforts being made one of the principal threads upon which the history is strung. In early American history Las Casas is, undoubtedly, the principal figure. His extraordinary longevity has something to do with this pre-eminence. Very few men can be named who have taken so active a part in public affairs over such an extended period as nearly seventy years. He was an important person in reference to all that concerned the Indies, during the reigns of Ferdinand the Catholic, of Philip the Handsome, of his son Charles the Fifth, and of Philip the Second.

Other men have undertaken great projects of benevolence, and have partially succeeded in them; but there is not any man whose success or failure, in such endeavours, has led to the great

The life of Las Casas a portion of history.

civil and military events which ensued upon the successes and failures of Las Casas. Take away all he said, and did, and preached, and wrote, and preserved (for the early historians of the New World owe the records of many of their most valuable facts to him); and the history of the conquest would lose a considerable portion of its most precious materials.

It may be fearlessly asserted, that Las Casas had a greater number of bitter enemies than any man who lived in his time; and many were the accusations they brought against him. But these were, for the most part frivolous in the extreme, or were pointed at such failings as are manifest to every reader of his life. There is nothing unexpected in them. That he was hasty, vehement, uncompromising, and occasionally, though rarely, indiscreet, must be very clear to everyone. But such a man was needed. It was for others to suggest expedients and compromises. During his lifetime there was always one person to maintain that strict justice should be done to the Indians, and to uphold the great principle that monarchs were set to rule for the benefit of their subjects. Without him the cause of the native would at once have

The accusations of his enemies.

descended into a lower level. Then, though vehement, he was eminently persuasive; and few who came near him escaped the influence of his powerful and attractive mind. The one event of his life which his enemies fastened upon for censure, and as regards which their accusations are certainly not frivolous, was his unfortunate attempt at colonization on the coast of Cumaná. To do those enemies justice, it must be admitted that they did not know the motives which had actuated him in obtaining that territory, nor how little blame could be attributed to him for the failure of that romantic enterprise. They could only ridicule his labourers, adorned with crosses, as they said, like the knights of Calatrava; and declare that, as a colonist, he had made a signal failure. These accusers were not aware that, but for the rapacity of conquerors like themselves, who had previously infuriated the natives, Las Casas might have succeeded in converting and civilizing the inhabitants of the Pearl Coast, as he afterwards succeeded in peaceably reducing the inhabitants of the "Land of War."

<small>His failure as a colonist.</small>

The event in his life which his contemporaries did not notice, but which has since been much deplored, and greatly magnified, was his being concerned in the introduction of negroes into the New World. For this he has himself made a touching and most contrite apology, expressing at the same time a fear lest his small share in the transaction might never be forgiven to him. In the cause of the Indians, whether he upheld it in speech, in writing, or in action, he appears never for one moment to have swerved from the exact path of equity. He has been justly called "The Great Apostle of the Indies."

His contrite apology respecting the first importation of negroes.

THE END.

CHISWICK PRESS:—C. WHITTINGHAM AND CO., TOOKS COURT, CHANCERY LANE.

AN

ALPHABETICAL LIST

OF BOOKS CONTAINED IN

BOHN'S LIBRARIES.

Detailed Catalogue, arranged according to the various Libraries, will be sent on application.

ADDISON'S Works. With the Notes of Bishop Hurd, Portrait, and 8 Plates of Medals and Coins. Edited by H. G. Bohn. 6 vols. '3s. 6d. each.

ÆSCHYLUS, The Dramas of. Translated into English Verse by Anna Swanwick. 4th Edition, revised. 5s.

—— The Tragedies of. Newly translated from a revised text by Walter Headlam, Litt.D., and C. E. S. Headlam, M.A. 5s.

—— The Tragedies of. Translated into Prose by T. A. Buckley, B.A. 3s. 6d.

ALLEN'S (Joseph, R. N.) Battles of the British Navy. Revised Edition, with 57 Steel Engravings. 2 vols. 5s. each.

AMMIANUS MARCELLINUS. History of Rome during the Reigns of Constantius, Julian, Jovianus, Valentinian, and Valens. Translated by Prof. C. D. Yonge, M.A. 7s. 6d.

ANDERSEN'S Danish Legends and Fairy Tales. Translated by Caroline Peachey. With 120 Wood Engravings. 5s.

ANTONINUS (M. Aurelius), The Thoughts of. Trans. literally, with Notes and Introduction by George Long, M.A. 3s. 6d.

APOLLONIUS RHODIUS. 'The Argonautica.' Translated by E. P. Coleridge, B.A. 5s.

APPIAN'S Roman History. Translated by Horace White, M.A., LL.D. With Maps and Illustrations. 2 vols. 6s. each.

APULEIUS, The Works of. Comprising the Golden Ass, God of Socrates, Florida, and Discourse of Magic. 5s.

ARIOSTO'S Orlando Furioso. Translated into English Verse by W. S. Rose. With Portrait, and 24 Steel Engravings. 2 vols. 5s. each.

ARISTOPHANES' Comedies. Translated by W. J. Hickie. 2 vols. 5s. each.

ARISTOTLE'S Nicomachean Ethics. Translated, with Introduction and Notes, by the Venerable Archdeacon Browne. 5s.

—— **Politics and Economics.** Translated by E. Walford, M.A., with Introduction by Dr. Gillies. 5s.

—— **Metaphysics.** Translated by the Rev. John H. M'Mahon, M.A. 5s.

—— **History of Animals.** Trans. by Richard Cresswell, M.A. 5s.

—— **Organon**; or, Logical Treatises, and the Introduction of Porphyry. Translated by the Rev. O. F. Owen, M.A. 2 vols. 3s. 6d. each.

—— **Rhetoric and Poetics.** Trans. by T. Buckley, B.A. 5s.

ARRIAN'S Anabasis of Alexander, together with the Indica. Translated by E. J. Chinnock, M.A., LL.D. With Maps and Plans. 5s.

ATHENÆUS. The Deipnosophists; or, the Banquet of the Learned. Trans. by Prof. C. D. Yonge, M.A. 3 vols. 5s. each.

BACON'S Moral and Historical Works, including the Essays, Apophthegms, Wisdom of the Ancients, New Atlantis, Henry VII., Henry VIII., Elizabeth, Henry Prince of Wales, History of Great Britain, Julius Cæsar, and Augustus Cæsar. Edited by J. Devey, M.A. 3s. 6d.

—— **Novum Organum** and Advancement of Learning. Edited by J. Devey, M.A. 5s.

BASS'S Lexicon to the Greek Testament. 2s.

BAX'S Manual of the History of Philosophy, for the use of Students. By E. Belfort Bax. 5s.

BEAUMONT and FLETCHER, their finest Scenes, Lyrics, and other Beauties, selected from the whole of their works, and edited by Leigh Hunt. 3s. 6d.

BECHSTEIN'S Cage and Chamber Birds, their Natural History, Habits, Food, Diseases, and Modes of Capture. Translated, with considerable additions on Structure, Migration, and Economy, by H. G. Adams. Together with SWEET BRITISH WARBLERS. With 43 coloured Plates and Woodcut Illustrations. 5s.

BEDE'S (Venerable) Ecclesiastical History of England. Together with the ANGLO-SAXON CHRONICLE. Edited by J. A. Giles, D.C.L. With Map. 5s.

BELL (Sir Charles). The Anatomy and Philosophy of Expression, as connected with the Fine Arts. By Sir Charles Bell, K.H. 7th edition, revised. 5s.

BERKELEY (George), Bishop of Cloyne, The Works of. Edited by George Sampson. With Biographical Introduction by the Right Hon. A. J. Balfour, M.P. 3 vols. 5s. each.

BION. See THEOCRITUS.

BJÖRNSON'S Arne and the Fisher Lassie. Translated by W. H. Low, M.A. 3s. 6d.

BLAIR'S Chronological Tables Revised and Enlarged. Comprehending the Chronology and History of the World, from the Earliest Times to the Russian Treaty of Peace, April 1856. By J. Willoughby Rosse. Double vol. 10s.

BLEEK, Introduction to the Old Testament. By Friedrich Bleek. Edited by Johann Bleek and Adolf Kamphausen. Translated by G. H. Venables, under the supervision of the Rev. Canon Venables. 2 vols. 5s. each.

BOETHIUS'S Consolation of Philosophy. King Alfred's Anglo-Saxon Version of. With a literal English Translation on opposite pages, Notes, Introduction, and Glossary, by Rev. S. Fox, M.A. 5s.

BOHN'S Dictionary of Poetical Quotations. 4th edition. 6s.

BOHN'S Handbooks of Games. New edition. In 2 vols., with numerous Illustrations 3s. 6d. each.
 Vol. I.—TABLE GAMES:—Billiards, Chess, Draughts, Backgammon, Dominoes, Solitaire, Reversi, Go-Bang, Rouge et Noir, Roulette, E.O., Hazard, Faro.
 Vol. II. — CARD GAMES: — Whist, Solo Whist, Poker, Piquet, Ecarté, Euchre, Bézique, Cribbage, Loo, Vingt-et-un, Napoleon, Newmarket, Pope Joan, Speculation, &c., &c.

BOND'S A Handy Book of Rules and Tables for verifying Dates with the Christian Era, &c. Giving an account of the Chief Eras and Systems used by various Nations; with the easy Methods for determining the Corresponding Dates. By J. J. Bond. 5s.

BONOMI'S Nineveh and its Palaces. 7 Plates and 294 Woodcut Illustrations. 5s.

BOSWELL'S Life of Johnson, with the TOUR IN THE HEBRIDES and JOHNSONIANA. Edited by the Rev. A. Napier, M.A. With Frontispiece to each vol. 6 vols. 3s. 6d. each.

BRAND'S Popular Antiquities of England, Scotland, and Ireland. Arranged, revised, and greatly enlarged, by Sir Henry Ellis, K.H., F.R.S., &c., &c. 3 vols. 5s. each.

BREMER'S (Frederika) Works. Translated by Mary Howitt. 4 vols. 3s. 6d. each.

BRIDGWATER TREATISES.
Bell (Sir Charles) on the Hand. With numerous Woodcuts. 5s.

Kirby on the History, Habits, and Instincts of Animals. Edited by T. Rymer Jones. With upwards of 100 Woodcuts. 2 vols. 5s. each.

Kidd on the Adaptation of External Nature to the Physical Condition of Man. 3s. 6d.

Chalmers on the Adaptation of External Nature to the Moral and Intellectual Constitution of Man. 5s.

BRINK (B. ten) Early English Literature. By Bernhard ten Brink. Vol. I. To Wyclif. Translated by Horace M. Kennedy. 3s. 6d.

Vol. II. Wyclif, Chaucer, Earliest Drama Renaissance. Translated by W. Clarke Robinson, Ph.D. 3s. 6d.

Vol. III. From the Fourteenth Century to the Death of Surrey. Edited by Dr. Alois Brandl. Trans. by L. Dora Schmitz. 3s. 6d.

—— Five Lectures on Shakspeare. Trans. by Julia Franklin. 3s. 6d.

BROWNE'S (Sir Thomas) Works Edited by Simon Wilkin. 3 vols. 3s. 6d. each.

BURKE'S Works. 8 vols. 3s. 6d. each.

I.—Vindication of Natural Society—Essay on the Sublime and Beautiful, and various Political Miscellanies.

II.—Reflections on the French Revolution — Letters relating to the Bristol Election— Speech on Fox's East India Bill, &c.

III.—Appeal from the New to the Old Whigs—On the Nabob of Arcot's Debts— The Catholic Claims, &c.

IV.—Report on the Affairs of India, and Articles of Charge against Warren Hastings.

V.—Conclusion of the Articles of Charge against Warren Hastings—Political Letters on the American War, on a Regicide Peace, to the Empress of Russia.

VI.—Miscellaneous Speeches— Letters and Fragments— Abridgments of English History, &c. With a General Index.

VII. & VIII.—Speeches on the Impeachment of Warren Hastings; and Letters. With Index. 2 vols. 3s. 6d. each.

——— **Life.** By Sir J. Prior. 3s. 6d.

BURNEY. The Early Diary of Fanny Burney (Madame D'Arblay), 1768-1778. With a selection from her Correspondence and from the Journals of her sisters, Susan and Charlotte Burney. Edited by Annie Raine Ellis. 2 vols. 3s. 6d. each.

——— **Evelina.** By Frances Burney (Mme. D'Arblay). With an Introduction and Notes by A. R. Ellis. 3s. 6d.

BURNEY'S Cecilia. With an Introduction and Notes by A. R. Ellis. 2 vols. 3s. 6d. each.

BURN (R.) Ancient Rome and its Neighbourhood. An Illustrated Handbook to the Ruins in the City and the Campagna, for the use of Travellers. By Robert Burn, M.A. With numerous Illustrations, Maps, and Plans. 7s. 6d.

BURNS (Robert), Life of. By J. G. Lockhart, D.C.L. A new and enlarged Edition. Revised by William Scott Douglas. 3s. 6d.

BURTON'S (Robert) Anatomy of Melancholy. Edited by the Rev. A. R. Shilleto, M.A. With Introduction by A. H. Bullen, and full Index. 3 vols. 3s. 6d. each.

BURTON (Sir R. F.) Personal Narrative of a Pilgrimage to Al-Madinah and Meccah. By Captain Sir Richard F. Burton, K.C.M.G. With an Introduction by Stanley Lane-Poole, and all the original Illustrations. 2 vols. 3s. 6d. each.

*** This is the copyright edition, containing the author's latest notes.

BUTLER'S (Bishop) Analogy of Religion, Natural and Revealed, to the Constitution and Course of Nature; together with two Dissertations on Personal Identity and on the Nature of Virtue, and Fifteen Sermons. 3s. 6d.

BUTLER'S (Samuel) Hudibras. With Varioum Notes, a Biography, Portrait, and 28 Illustrations. 5s.

——— or, further Illustrated with 60 Outline Portraits. 2 vols. 5s. each.

CÆSAR. Commentaries on the Gallic and Civil Wars, Translated by W. A. McDevitte, B.A. 5s.

CAMOENS' Lusiad; or, the Discovery of India. An Epic Poem. Translated by W. J. Mickle. 5th Edition, revised by E. R. Hodges, M.C.P. 3s. 6d.

CARAFAS (The) of Maddaloni. Naples under Spanish Dominion. Translated from the German of Alfred de Reumont. 3s. 6d.

CARLYLE'S French Revolution. Edited by J. Holland Rose, Litt.D. Illus. 3 vols. 5s. each.

—— Sartor Resartus. With 75 Illustrations by Edmund J. Sullivan. 5s.

CARPENTER'S (Dr. W. B.) Zoology. Revised Edition, by W. S. Dallas, F.L.S. With very numerous Woodcuts. Vol. I. 6s. [*Vol. II. out of print.*]

CARPENTER'S Mechanical Philosophy, Astronomy, and Horology. 181 Woodcuts. 5s.

—— Vegetable Physiology and Systematic Botany. Revised Edition, by E. Lankester, M.D., &c. With very numerous Woodcuts. 6s.

—— Animal Physiology. Revised Edition. With upwards of 300 Woodcuts. 6s.

CASTLE (E.) Schools and Masters of Fence, from the Middle Ages to the End of the Eighteenth Century. By Egerton Castle, M.A., F.S.A. With a Complete Bibliography. Illustrated with 140 Reproductions of Old Engravings and 6 Plates of Swords, showing 114 Examples. 6s.

CATTERMOLE'S Evenings at Haddon Hall. With 24 Engravings on Steel from designs by Cattermole, the Letterpress by the Baroness de Carabella. 5s.

CATULLUS, Tibullus, and the Vigil of Venus. A Literal Prose Translation. 5s.

CELLINI (Benvenuto). Memoirs of, written by Himself. Translated by Thomas Roscoe. 3s. 6d.

CERVANTES' Don Quixote de la Mancha. Motteaux's Translation revised. 2 vols. 3s. 6d. each.

—— Galatea. A Pastoral Romance. Translated by G. W. J. Gyll. 3s. 6d.

—— Exemplary Novels. Translated by Walter K. Kelly. 3s. 6d.

CHAUCER'S Poetical Works. Edited by Robert Bell. Revised Edition, with a Preliminary Essay by Prof. W. W. Skeat, M.A. 4 vols. 3s. 6d. each.

CHESS CONGRESS of 1862. A Collection of the Games played. Edited by J. Löwenthal. 5s.

CHEVREUL on Colour. Translated from the French by Charles Martel. Third Edition, with Plates, 5s.; or with an additional series of 16 Plates in Colours, 7s. 6d.

CHINA, Pictorial, Descriptive, and Historical. With Map and nearly 100 Illustrations. 5s.

CHRONICLES OF THE CRUSADES. Contemporary Narratives of the Crusade of Richard Cœur de Lion, by Richard of Devizes and Geoffrey de Vinsauf; and of the Crusade at St. Louis, by Lord John de Joinville. 5s.

CICERO'S Orations. Translated by Prof. C. D. Yonge, M.A. 4 vols. 5s. each.

—— Letters. Translated by Evelyn S. Shuckburgh. 4 vols. 5s. each.

—— On Oratory and Orators. With Letters to Quintus and Brutus. Translated by the Rev. J. S. Watson, M.A. 5s.

—— On the Nature of the Gods, Divination, Fate, Laws, a Republic, Consulship. Translated by Prof. C. D. Yonge, M.A., and Francis Barham. 5s.

—— Academics, De Finibus, and Tusculan Questions. By Prof. C. D. Yonge, M.A. 5s.

—— Offices; or, Moral Duties. Cato Major, an Essay on Old Age; Lælius, an Essay on Friendship; Scipio's Dream; Paradoxes; Letter to Quintus on Magistrates. Translated by C. R. Edmonds. 3s. 6d.

CORNELIUS NEPOS.—See JUSTIN.

CLARK'S (Hugh) Introduction to Heraldry. 18th Edition, Revised and Enlarged by J. R. Planché, Rouge Croix. With nearly 1000 Illustrations. 5s. Or with the Illustrations Coloured, 15s.

CLASSIC TALES, containing Rasselas, Vicar of Wakefield, Gulliver's Travels, and The Sentimental Journey. 3s. 6d.

COLERIDGE'S (S. T.) Friend. A Series of Essays on Morals, Politics, and Religion. 3s. 6d.

—— Aids to Reflection, and the CONFESSIONS OF AN INQUIRING SPIRIT, to which are added the ESSAYS ON FAITH and the BOOK OF COMMON PRAYER. 3s. 6d.

COLERIDGE'S Lectures and Notes on Shakespeare and other English Poets. Edited by T. Ashe. 3s. 6d.

—— Biographia Literaria; together with Two Lay Sermons. 3s. 6d.

—— Table-Talk and Omniana. Edited by T. Ashe, B.A. 3s. 6d.

—— Miscellanies, Æsthetic and Literary; to which is added, THE THEORY OF LIFE. Collected and arranged by T. Ashe, B.A. 3s. 6d.

COMTE'S Positive Philosophy. Translated and condensed by Harriet Martineau. With Introduction by Frederic Harrison. 3 vols. 5s. each.

COMTE'S Philosophy of the Sciences, being an Exposition of the Principles of the *Cours de Philosophie Positive*. By G. H. Lewes. 5s.

CONDÉ'S History of the Dominion of the Arabs in Spain. Translated by Mrs. Foster. 3 vols. 3s. 6d. each.

COOPER'S Biographical Dictionary. Containing Concise Notices (upwards of 15,000) of Eminent Persons of all Ages and Countries. By Thompson Cooper, F.S.A. With a Supplement, bringing the work down to 1883. 2 vols. 5s. each.

COXE'S Memoirs of the Duke of Marlborough. With his original Correspondence. By W. Coxe, M.A., F.R.S. Revised edition by John Wade. 3 vols. 3s. 6d. each.

—— History of the House of Austria (1218-1792). With a Continuation from the Accession of Francis I. to the Revolution of 1848. 4 vols. 3s. 6d. each.

CRAIK'S (G. L.) Pursuit of Knowledge under Difficulties. Illustrated by Anecdotes and Memoirs. Revised edition, with numerous Woodcut Portraits and Plates. 5s.

CUNNINGHAM'S Lives of the Most Eminent British Painters. A New Edition, with Notes and Sixteen fresh Lives. By Mrs. Heaton. 3 vols. 3s. 6d. each.

DANTE. Divine Comedy. Translated by the Rev. H. F. Cary, M.A. 3s. 6d.

—— Translated into English Verse by I. C. Wright, M.A. 3rd Edition, revised. With Portrait, and 34 Illustrations on Steel, after Flaxman.

DANTE. The Inferno. A Literal Prose Translation, with the Text of the Original printed on the same page. By John A. Carlyle, M.D. 5s.

DE COMMINES (Philip), Memoirs of. Containing the Histories of Louis XI. and Charles VIII., Kings of France, and Charles the Bold, Duke of Burgundy. Together with the Scandalous Chronicle, or Secret History of Louis XI., by Jean de Troyes. Translated by Andrew R. Scoble. With Portraits. 2 vols. 3s. 6d. each.

DEFOE'S Novels and Miscellaneous Works. With Prefaces and Notes, including those attributed to Sir W. Scott. 7 vols. 3s. 6d. each.

    I.—Captain Singleton, and Colonel Jack.

    II.—Memoirs of a Cavalier, Captain Carleton, Dickory Cronke, &c.

    III.—Moll Flanders, and the History of the Devil.

DEFOE'S NOVELS AND MISCELLANEOUS WORKS—*continued*.

    IV.—Roxana, and Life of Mrs. Christian Davies.

    V.—History of the Great Plague of London, 1665; The Storm (1703); and the True-born Englishman.

    VI.—Duncan Campbell, New Voyage round the World, and Political Tracts.

    VII.—Robinson Crusoe.

DEMMIN'S History of Arms and Armour, from the Earliest Period. By Auguste Demmin. Translated by C. C. Black, M.A. With nearly 2000 Illustrations. 7s. 6d.

DEMOSTHENES' Orations. Translated by C. Rann Kennedy. 5 vols. Vol. I., 3s. 6d.; Vols. II.-V., 5s. each.

DE STAËL'S Corinne or Italy. By Madame de Staël. Translated by Emily Baldwin and Paulina Driver. 3s. 6d.

DICTIONARY of Latin and Greek Quotations; including Proverbs, Maxims, Mottoes, Law Terms and Phrases. With all the Quantities marked, and English Translations. With Index Verborum (622 pages). 5s.

DICTIONARY of Obsolete and Provincial English. Compiled by Thomas Wright, M.A., F.S.A., &c. 2 vols. 5s. each.

DIDRON'S Christian Iconography: a History of Christian Art in the Middle Ages. Translated by E. J. Millington and completed by Margaret Stokes. With 240 Illustrations. 2 vols. 5s. each.

DIOGENES LAERTIUS. Lives and Opinions of the Ancient Philosophers. Translated by Prof. C. D. Yonge, M.A. 5s.

DOBRÉE'S Adversaria. Edited by the late Prof. Wagner. 2 vols. 5s. each.

DODD'S Epigrammatists. A Selection from the Epigrammatic Literature of Ancient, Mediæval, and Modern Times. By the Rev. Henry Philip Dodd, M.A. Oxford. 2nd Edition, revised and enlarged. 6s.

DONALDSON'S The Theatre of the Greeks. A Treatise on the History and Exhibition of the Greek Drama. With numerous Illustrations and 3 Plans. By John William Donaldson, D.D. 5s.

DRAPER'S History of the Intellectual Development of Europe. By John William Draper, M.D., LL.D. 2 vols. 5s. each.

DUNLOP'S History of Fiction. A new Edition. Revised by Henry Wilson. 2 vols. 5s. each.

DYER'S History of Modern Europe, from the Fall of Constantinople. 3rd edition, revised and continued to the end of the Nineteenth Century. By Arthur Hassall, M.A. 6 vols. 3s. 6d each.

DYER'S (Dr. T. H.) Pompeii : its Buildings and Antiquities. By T. H. Dyer, LL.D. With nearly 300 Wood Engravings, a large Map, and a Plan of the Forum. 7s. 6d.

DYER (T. F. T.) British Popular Customs, Present and Past. An Account of the various Games and Customs associated with Different Days of the Year in the British Isles, arranged according to the Calendar. By the Rev. T. F. Thiselton Dyer, M.A. 5s.

EBERS' Egyptian Princess. An Historical Novel. By George Ebers. Translated by E. S. Buchheim. 3s. 6d.

EDGEWORTH'S Stories for Children. With 8 Illustrations by L. Speed. 3s. 6d.

ELZE'S William Shakespeare. —See SHAKESPEARE.

EMERSON'S Works. 5 vols. 3s. 6d. each.
I.—Essays and Representative Men.
II.—English Traits, Nature, and Conduct of Life.
III.—Society and Solitude—Letters and Social Aims — Addresses.
VI.—Miscellaneous Pieces.
V.—Poems.

EPICTETUS, The Discourses of. With the ENCHEIRIDION and Fragments. Translated by George Long, M.A. 5s.

EURIPIDES. A New Literal Translation in Prose. By E P. Coleridge, M.A. 2 vols. 5s. each.

EUTROPIUS.—See JUSTIN.

EUSEBIUS PAMPHILUS, Ecclesiastical History of. Translated by Rev. C. F. Cruse, M.A. 5s.

EVELYN'S Diary and Correspondendence. Edited from the Original MSS. by W. Bray, F.A.S. With 45 engravings. 4 vols. 5s. each.

FAIRHOLT'S Costume in England. A History of Dress to the end of the Eighteenth Century. 3rd Edition, revised, by Viscount Dillon, V.P.S.A. Illustrated with above 700 Engravings. 2 vols. 5s. each.

Contained in Bohn's Libraries.

FIELDING'S Adventures of Joseph Andrews and his Friend Mr. Abraham Adams. With Cruikshank's Illustrations. 3s. 6d.

—— **History of Tom Jones, a Foundling.** With Cruikshank's Illustrations. 2 vols. 3s. 6d. each.

—— **Amelia.** With Cruikshank's Illustrations. 5s.

FLAXMAN'S Lectures on Sculpture. By John Flaxman, R.A. With Portrait and 53 Plates. 6s.

FOSTER'S (John) Essays: on Decision of Character; on a Man's writing Memoirs of Himself; on the epithet Romantic; on the aversion of Men of Taste to Evangelical Religion. 3s. 6d.

—— **Essays** on the Evils of Popular Ignorance; to which is added, a Discourse on the Propagation of Christianity in India. 3s. 6d.

—— **Essays** on the Improvement of Time. With NOTES OF SERMONS and other Pieces. 3s. 6d.

GASPARY'S History of Italian Literature. Translated by Herman Oelsner, M.A., Ph.D. Vol. I. 3s. 6d.

GEOFFREY OF MONMOUTH, Chronicle of.—*See Old English Chronicles.*

GESTA ROMANORUM, or Entertaining Moral Stories invented by the Monks. Translated by the Rev. Charles Swan. Revised Edition, by Wynnard Hooper, B.A. 5s.

GILDAS, Chronicles of.—*See Old English Chronicles.*

GIBBON'S Decline and Fall of the Roman Empire. Complete and Unabridged, with Variorum Notes. Edited by an English Churchman. With 2 Maps and Portrait. 7 vols. 3s. 6d. each.

GILBART'S History, Principles, and Practice of Banking. By the late J. W. Gilbart, F.R.S. New Edition (1907), revised by Ernest Sykes. 2 vols. 10s.

GIL BLAS, The Adventures of. Translated from the French of Lesage by Smollett. With 24 Engravings on Steel, after Smirke, and 10 Etchings by George Cruikshank. 6s.

GIRALDUS CAMBRENSIS' Historical Works. Translated by Th. Forester, M.A., and Sir R. Colt Hoare. Revised Edition, Edited by Thomas Wright, M.A., F.S.A. 5s.

GOETHE'S Faust. Part I. German Text with Hayward's Prose Translation and Notes. Revised by C. A. Buchheim, Ph.D. 5s.

GOETHE'S Works. Translated into English by various hands. 14 vols. 3s. 6d. each.

   I. and II.—Poetry and Truth from My Own Life. New and revised edition.

   III.—Faust. Two Parts, complete. (Swanwick.)

   IV.—Novels and Tales.

   V.—Wilhelm Meister's Apprenticeship.

   VI.—Conversations with Eckermann and Soret.

   VIII.—Dramatic Works.

   IX.—Wilhelm Meister's Travels.

   X.—Tour in Italy, and Second Residence in Rome.

   XI.—Miscellaneous Travels.

   XII.—Early and Miscellaneous Letters.

   XIV.—Reineke Fox, West-Eastern Divan and Achilleid.

GOLDSMITH'S Works. A new Edition, by J. W. M. Gibbs. 5 vols. 3s. 6d. each.

GRAMMONT'S Memoirs of the Court of Charles II. Edited by Sir Walter Scott. Together with the BOSCOBEL TRACTS, including two not before published, &c. New Edition. 5s.

GRAY'S Letters. Including the Correspondence of Gray and Mason. Edited by the Rev. D. C. Tovey, M.A. Vols. I. and II. 3s. 6d. each.

GREEK ANTHOLOGY. Translated by George Burges, M.A. 5s.

GREEK ROMANCES of Heliodorus, Longus, and Achilles Tatius—viz., The Adventures of Theagenes & Chariclea; Amours of Daphnis and Chloe; and Loves of Clitopho and Leucippe. Translated by Rev. R. Smith, M.A. 5s.

GREGORY'S Letters on the Evidences, Doctrines, & Duties of the Christian Religion. By Dr. Olinthus Gregory. 3s. 6d.

GREENE, MARLOWE, and BEN JONSON. Poems of. Edited by Robert Bell. 3s. 6d.

GRIMM'S TALES. With the Notes of the Original. Translated by Mrs. A. Hunt. With Introduction by Andrew Lang, M.A. 2 vols. 3s. 6d. each.

—— **Gammer Grethel**; or, German Fairy Tales and Popular Stories. Containing 42 Fairy Tales. Trans. by Edgar Taylor. With numerous Woodcuts after George Cruikshank and Ludwig Grimm. 3s. 6d.

GROSSI'S Marco Visconti. Translated by A. F. D. The Ballads rendered into English Verse by C. M. P. 3s. 6d.

GUIZOT'S History of the English Revolution of 1640. From the Accession of Charles I. to his Death. Translated by William Hazlitt. 3s. 6d.

—— **History of Civilisation**, from the Fall of the Roman Empire to the French Revolution. Translated by William Hazlitt. 3 vols. 3s. 6d. each.

HALL'S (Rev. Robert) Miscellaneous Works and Remains. 3s. 6d.

HAMPTON COURT: A Short History of the Manor and Palace. By Ernest Law, B.A. With numerous Illustrations. 5s.

HARDWICK'S History of the Articles of Religion. By the late C. Hardwick. Revised by the Rev. Francis Procter, M.A. 5s.

HAUFF'S Tales. The Caravan—The Sheik of Alexandria—The Inn in the Spessart. Trans. from the German by S. Mendel. 3s. 6d.

HAWTHORNE'S Tales. 4 vols. 3s. 6d. each.

  I.—Twice-told Tales, and the Snow Image.

  II.—Scarlet Letter, and the House with the Seven Gables.

  III.—Transformation [The Marble Faun], and Blithedale Romance.

  IV.—Mosses from an Old Manse.

HAZLITT'S Table-talk. Essays on Men and Manners. By W. Hazlitt. 3s. 6d.

HAZLITT'S Lectures on the Literature of the Age of Elizabeth and on Characters of Shakespeare's Plays. 3s. 6d.

—— Lectures on the English Poets, and on the English Comic Writers. 3s. 6d.

—— The Plain Speaker. Opinions on Books, Men, and Things. 3s. 6d.

—— Round Table. 3s. 6d.

—— Sketches and Essays. 3s. 6d.

—— The Spirit of the Age; or, Contemporary Portraits. Edited by W. Carew Hazlitt. 3s. 6d.

—— View of the English Stage. Edited by W. Spencer Jackson. 3s. 6d.

HEATON'S Concise History of Painting. New Edition, revised by Cosmo Monkhouse. 5s.

HEGEL'S Lectures on the Philosophy of History. Translated by J. Sibree, M.A.

HEINE'S Poems, Complete Translated by Edgar A. Bowring, C.B. 3s. 6d.

—— Travel-Pictures, including the Tour in the Harz, Norderney, and Book of Ideas, together with the Romantic School. Translated by Francis Storr. A New Edition, revised throughout. With Appendices and Maps. 3s. 6d.

HELP'S Life of Christopher Columbus, the Discoverer of America. By Sir Arthur Helps, K.C.B. 3s. 6d.

—— Life of Hernando Cortes, and the Conquest of Mexico. 2 vols. 3s. 6d. each.

—— Life of Pizarro. 3s. 6d.

—— Life of Las Casas the Apostle of the Indies. 3s. 6d.

HENDERSON (E.) Select Historical Documents of the Middle Ages, including the most famous Charters relating to England, the Empire, the Church, &c., from the 6th to the 14th Centuries. Translated from the Latin and edited by Ernest F. Henderson, A.B., A.M., Ph.D. 5s.

HENFREY'S Guide to English Coins, from the Conquest to the present time. New and revised Edition by C. F. Keary, M.A., F.S.A. 6s.

HENRY OF HUNTINGDON'S History of the English. Translated by T. Forester, M.A. 5s.

HENRY'S (Matthew) Exposition of the Book of the Psalms. 5s.

HELIODORUS. Theagenes and Chariclea. — See GREEK ROMANCES.

HERODOTUS. Translated by the Rev. Henry Cary, M.A. 3s. 6d.

—— Analysis and Summary of By J. T. Wheeler. 5s.

HESIOD, CALLIMACHUS, and THEOGNIS. Translated by the Rev. J. Banks, M.A. 5s.

HOFFMANN'S (E. T. W.) The Serapion Brethren. Translated from the German by Lt.-Col. Alex. Ewing. 2 vols. 3s. 6d. each.

HOLBEIN'S Dance of Death and Bible Cuts. Upwards of 150 Subjects, engraved in facsimile, with Introduction and Descriptions by Francis Douce and Dr. Thomas Frognall Dibden. 5s.

HOMER'S Iliad. A new translation by E. H. Blakeney, M.A. Vol. I. containing Books I.-XII. 5s.

—— Translated into English Prose by T. A. Buckley, B.A. 5s.

HOMER'S Odyssey. Hymns, Epigrams, and Battle of the Frogs and Mice. Translated into English Prose by T. A. Buckley, B.A. 5s.

—— See also POPE.

HOOPER'S (G.) Waterloo: The Downfall of the First Napoleon: a History of the Campaign of 1815. By George Hooper. With Maps and Plans. 3s. 6d.

—— **The Campaign of Sedan:** The Downfall of the Second Empire, August–September, 1870. With General Map and Six Plans of Battle. 3s. 6d.

HORACE. A new literal Prose translation, by A. Hamilton Bryce, LL.D. 3s. 6d.

HUGO'S (Victor) Dramatic Works. Hernani—Ruy Blas—The King's Diversion. Translated by Mrs. Newton Crosland and F. L. Slous. 3s. 6d.

—— Poems, chiefly Lyrical. Translated by various Writers, now first collected by J. H. L. Williams. 3s. 6d.

HUMBOLDT'S Cosmos. Translated by E. C. Otté, B. H. Paul, and W. S. Dallas, F.L.S. 5 vols. 3s. 6d. each, excepting Vol. V. 5s.

—— **Personal Narrative of his Travels to the Equinoctial Regions of America** during the years 1799–1804. Translated by T. Ross. 3 vols. 5s. each.

—— **Views of Nature.** Translated by E. C. Otté and H. G. Bohn. 5s.

HUMPHREYS' Coin Collector's Manual. By H. N. Humphreys. with upwards of 140 Illustrations on Wood and Steel. 2 vols. 5s. each.

HUNGARY: its History and Revolution, together with a copious Memoir of Kossuth. 3s. 6d.

HUTCHINSON (Colonel). Memoirs of the Life of. By his Widow, Lucy: together with her Autobiography, and an Account of the Siege of Lathom House. 3s. 6d.

HUNT'S Poetry of Science. By Richard Hunt. 3rd Edition, revised and enlarged. 5s.

INGULPH'S Chronicles of the Abbey of Croyland, with the CONTINUATION by Peter of Blois and other Writers. Translated by H. T. Riley, M.A. 5s.

IRVING'S (Washington) Complete Works. 15 vols. With Portraits, &c. 3s. 6d. each.

I.—Salmagundi, Knickerbocker's History of New York.

II.—The Sketch-Book, and the Life of Oliver Goldsmith.

III.—Bracebridge Hall, Abbotsford and Newstead Abbey.

IV.—The Alhambra, Tales of a Traveller.

V.—Chronicle of the Conquest of Granada, Legends of the Conquest of Spain.

VI. & VII.—Life and Voyages of Columbus, together with the Voyages of his Companions.

VIII.—Astoria, A Tour on the Prairies.

IX.—Life of Mahomet, Lives of the Successors of Mahomet.

X.—Adventures of Captain Bonneville, U.S.A., Wolfert's Roost.

XI.—Biographies and Miscellaneous Papers.

XII.–XV.—Life of George Washington. 4 vols.

IRVING'S (Washington) Life and Letters. By his Nephew, Pierre E. Irving. 2 vols. 3s. 6d. each.

ISOCRATES, The Orations of. Translated by J. H. Freese, M.A. Vol. I. 5s.

JAMES'S (G. P. R.) Life of Richard Cœur de Lion. 2 vols. 3s. 6d. each.

JAMESON'S (Mrs.) Shakespeare's Heroines. Characteristics of Women: Moral, Poetical, and Historical. By Mrs. Jameson. 3s. 6d.

JESSE'S (E.) Anecdotes of Dogs. With 40 Woodcuts and 34 Steel Engravings. 5s.

JESSE'S (J. H.) Memoirs of the Court of England during the Reign of the Stuarts, including the Protectorate. 3 vols. With 42 Portraits. 5s. each.

—— Memoirs of the Pretenders and their Adherents. With 6 Portraits. 5s.

JOHNSON'S Lives of the Poets. Edited by Mrs. Alexander Napier, with Introduction by Professor Hales. 3 vols. 3s. 6d. each.

JOSEPHUS (Flavius), The Works of. Whiston's Translation, revised by Rev. A. R. Shilleto, M.A. With Topographical and Geographical Notes by Colonel Sir C. W. Wilson, K.C.B. 5 vols. 3s. 6d. each.

JULIAN, the Emperor. Containing Gregory Nazianzen's Two Invectives and Libanus' Monody, with Julian's extant Theosophical Works. Translated by C. W. King, M.A. 5s.

JUNIUS'S Letters. With all the Notes of Woodfall's Edition, and important Additions. 2 vols. 3s. 6d. each.

JUSTIN, CORNELIUS NEPOS, and EUTROPIUS. Translated by the Rev. J. S. Watson, M.A. 5s.

JUVENAL, PERSIUS, SULPICIA and LUCILIUS. Translated by L. Evans, M.A. 5s.

KANT'S Critique of Pure Reason. Translated by J. M. D. Meiklejohn. 5s.

—— Prolegomena and Metaphysical Foundations of Natural Science. Translated by E. Belfort Bax. 5s.

KEIGHTLEY'S (Thomas) Mythology of Ancient Greece and Italy. 4th Edition, revised by Leonard Schmitz, Ph.D., LL.D. With 12 Plates from the Antique. 5s.

KEIGHTLEY'S Fairy Mythology, illustrative of the Romance and Superstition of Various Countries. Revised Edition, with Frontispiece by Cruikshank. 5s.

LA FONTAINE'S Fables. Translated into English Verse by Elizur Wright. New Edition, with Notes by J. W. M. Gibbs. 3s. 6d.

LAMARTINE'S History of the Girondists. Translated by H. T. Ryde. 3 vols. 3s. 6d. each.

—— History of the Restoration of Monarchy in France (a Sequel to the History of the Girondists). 4 vols. 3s. 6d. each.

—— History of the French Revolution of 1848. 3s. 6d.

LAMB'S (Charles) Essays of Elia and Eliana. Complete Edition. 3s. 6d.

LAMB'S (Charles) Specimens of English Dramatic Poets of the Time of Elizabeth. 3s. 6d.

—— **Memorials and Letters of Charles Lamb.** By Serjeant Talfourd. New Edition, revised, by W. Carew Hazlitt. 2 vols. 3s. 6d. each.

—— **Tales from Shakespeare.** With Illustrations by Byam Shaw. 3s. 6d.

LANE'S Arabian Nights' Entertainments. Edited by Stanley Lane-Poole, M.A., Litt.D. 4 vols. 3s. 6d. each.

LAPPENBERG'S History of England under the Anglo-Saxon Kings. Translated by B. Thorpe, F.S.A. New edition, revised by E. C. Otté. 2 vols. 3s. 6d. each.

LEONARDO DA VINCI'S Treatise on Painting. Translated by J. F. Rigaud, R.A., With a Life of Leonardo by John William Brown. With numerous Plates. 5s.

LEPSIUS'S Letters from Egypt, Ethiopia, and the Peninsula of Sinai. Translated by L. and J. B. Horner. With Maps. 5s.

LESSING'S Dramatic Works, Complete. Edited by Ernest Bell, M.A. With Memoir of Lessing by Helen Zimmern. 2 vols. 3s. 6d. each.

—— **Laokoon, Dramatic Notes, and the Representation of Death by the Ancients.** Translated by E. C. Beasley and Helen Zimmern. Edited by Edward Bell, M.A. With a Frontispiece of the Laokoon group. 3s. 6d.

LILLY'S Introduction to Astrology. With a GRAMMAR OF ASTROLOGY and Tables for Calculating Nativities, by Zadkiel. 5s.

LIVY'S History of Rome. Translated by Dr. Spillan, C. Edmonds, and others. 4 vols. 5s. each.

LOCKE'S Philosophical Works. Edited by J. A. St. John. 2 vols. 3s. 6d. each.

LOCKHART (J. G.)—*See* BURNS.

LODGE'S Portraits of Illustrious Personages of Great Britain, with Biographical and Historical Memoirs. 240 Portraits engraved on Steel, with the respective Biographies unabridged. 8 vols. 5s. each.

[*Vols. IV. and VII. out of print.*]

LOUDON'S (Mrs.) Natural History. Revised edition, by W. S. Dallas, F.L.S. With numerous Woodcut Illus. 5s.

LOWNDES' Bibliographer's Manual of English Literature. Enlarged Edition. By H. G. Bohn. 6 vols. cloth, 5s. each. Or 4 vols. half morocco, 2l. 2s.

LONGUS. Daphnis and Chloe. —*See* GREEK ROMANCES.

LUCAN'S Pharsalia. Translated by H. T. Riley, M.A. 5s.

LUCIAN'S Dialogues of the Gods, of the Sea Gods, and of the Dead. Translated by Howard Williams, M.A. 5s.

LUCRETIUS. A Prose Translation. By H. A. J. Munro. Reprinted from the Final (4th) Edition. With an Introduction by J. D. Duff, M.A. 5s.

LUTHER'S Table-Talk. Translated and Edited by William Hazlitt. 3s. 6d.

—— **Autobiography.** — *See* MICHELET.

Contained in Bohn's Libraries. 15

MACHIAVELLI'S History of Florence, together with the Prince, Savonarola, various Historical Tracts, and a Memoir of Machiavelli. 3s. 6d.

MALLET'S Northern Antiquities, or an Historical Account of the Manners, Customs, Religions and Laws, Maritime Expeditions and Discoveries, Language and Literature, of the Ancient Scandinavians. Translated by Bishop Percy. Revised and Enlarged Edition, with a Translation of the PROSE EDDA, by J. A. Blackwell. 5s.

MANZONI. The Betrothed: being a Translation of 'I Promessi Sposi.' By Alessandro Manzoni. With numerous Woodcuts. 5s.

MARCO POLO'S Travels; the Translation of Marsden revised by T. Wright, M.A., F.S.A. 5s.

MARRYAT'S (Capt. R.N.) Masterman Ready. With 93 Woodcuts. 3s. 6d.

—— **Mission;** or, Scenes in Africa. Illustrated by Gilbert and Dalziel. 3s. 6d.

—— **Pirate and Three Cutters.** With 8 Steel Engravings, from Drawings by Clarkson Stanfield, R.A. 3s. 6d.

—— **Privateersman.** 8 Engravings on Steel. 3s. 6a

—— **Settlers in Canada.** 10 Engravings by Gilbert and Dalziel. 3s. 6d.

—— **Poor Jack.** With 16 Illustrations after Clarkson Stansfield, R.A. 3s. 6d.

—— **Peter Simple.** With 8 full-page Illustrations. 3s. 6d.

MARTIAL'S Epigrams, complete. Translated into Prose, each accompanied by one or more Verse Translations selected from the Works of English Poets, and other sources. 7s. 6d.

MARTINEAU'S (Harriet) History of England, from 1800–1815. 3s. 6d.

—— **History of the Thirty Years' Peace,** A.D. 1815-46. 4 vols. 3s. 6d. each.

—— *See Comte's Positive Philosophy.*

MATTHEW OF WESTMINSTER'S Flowers of History, from the beginning of the World to A.D. 1307. Translated by C. D. Yonge, M.A. 2 vols. 5s. each.

MAXWELL'S Victories of Wellington and the British Armies. Frontispiece and 5 Portraits. 5s.

MENZEL'S History of Germany, from the Earliest Period to 1842. 3 vols. 3s. 6d. each.

MICHAEL ANGELO AND RAPHAEL, their Lives and Works. By Duppa aud Quatremere de Quincy. With Portraits, and Engravings on Steel. 5s.

MICHELET'S Luther's Autobiography. Trans. by William Hazlitt. With an Appendix (110 pages) of Notes. 3s. 6d.

—— **History of the French Revolution** from its earliest indications to the flight of the King in 1791. 3s. 6d.

MIGNET'S History of the French Revolution, from 1789 to 1814. 3s. 6d. New edition reset.

MILL (J. S.). Early Essays by John Stuart Mill. Collected from various sources by J. W. M. Gibbs. 3s. 6d.

MILLER (Professor). History Philosophically Illustrated,from the Fall of the Roman Empire to the French Revolution. 4 vols. 3s. 6d. each.

MILTON'S Prose Works. Edited by J. A. St. John. 5 vols. 3s. 6d. each.

—— **Poetical Works,** with a Memoir and Critical Remarks by James Montgomery, an Index to Paradise Lost, Todd's Verbal Index to all the Poems, and a Selection of Explanatory Notes by Henry G. Bohn. Illustrated with 120 Wood Engravings from Drawings by W. Harvey. 2 vols. 3s. 6d. each.

MITFORD'S (Miss) Our Village Sketches of Rural Character and Scenery. With 2 Engravings on Steel. 2 vols. 3s. 6d. each.

MOLIÈRE'S Dramatic Works. A new Translation in English Prose, by C. H. Wall. 3 vols. 3s. 6d. each.

MONTAGU. The Letters and Works of Lady Mary Wortley Montagu. Edited by her great-grandson, Lord Wharncliffe's Edition, and revised by W. Moy Thomas. New Edition, revised, with 5 Portraits. 2 vols. 5s. each.

MONTAIGNE'S Essays. Cotton's Translation, revised by W. C. Hazlitt. New Edition. 3 vols. 3s. 6d. each.

MONTESQUIEU'S Spirit of Laws. New Edition, revised and corrected. By J. V. Pritchard, A.M. 2 vols. 3s. 6d. each.

MORE'S Utopia. Robinson's translation, with Roper's 'Life of Sir Thomas More,' and More's Letters to Margaret Roper and others. Edited, with Introduction and Notes, by George Sampson. 5s.

MORPHY'S Games of Chess. Being the Matches and best Games played by the American Champion, with Explanatory and Analytical Notes by J. Löwenthal. 5s.

MOTLEY (J. L.). The Rise of the Dutch Republic. A History. By John Lothrop Motley. New Edition, with Biographical Introduction by Moncure D. Conway. 3 vols. 3s. 6d. each.

MUDIE'S British Birds; or, History of the Feathered Tribes of the British Islands. Revised by W. C. L. Martin. With 52 Figures of Birds and 7 Coloured Plates of Eggs. 2 vols.

NEANDER (Dr. A.). History of the Christian Religion and Church. Trans. from the German by J. Torrey. 10 vols. 3s. 6d. each. [*Vols. VI. and X. out of print.*

—— **Life of Jesus Christ.** Translated by J. McClintock and C. Blumenthal. 3s. 6d.

—— **History of the Planting and Training of the Christian Church by the Apostles.** Translated by J. E. Ryland. 2 vols. 3s. 6d. each.

—— **Memorials of Christian Life in the Early and Middle Ages;** including Light in Dark Places. Trans. by J. E. Ryland. 3s. 6d.

NIBELUNGEN LIED. The Lay of the Nibelungs, metrically translated from the old German text by Alice Horton, and edited by Edward Bell, M.A. To which is prefixed the Essay on the Nibelungen Lied by Thomas Carlyle. 5s.

NEW TESTAMENT (The) in Greek. Griesbach's Text, with various Readings at the foot of the page and Parallel References in the margin; also a Critical

Introduction and Chronological Tables. By an eminent Scholar, with a Greek and English Lexicon. 3rd Edition, revised and corrected. Two Facsimiles of Greek Manuscripts. 900 pages. 5s.
The Lexicon may be had separately, price 2s.

NICOLINI'S History of the Jesuits: their Origin, Progress, Doctrines, and Designs. With 8 Portraits. 5s.

NORTH (R.) Lives of the Right Hon. Francis North, Baron Guildford, the Hon. Sir Dudley North, and the Hon. and Rev. Dr. John North. By the Hon. Roger North. Together with the Autobiography of the Author. Edited by Augustus Jessopp, D.D. 3 vols. 3s. 6d. each.

NUGENT'S (Lord) Memorials of Hampden, his Party and Times. With a Memoir of the Author, an Autograph Letter, and Portrait. 5s.

OLD ENGLISH CHRONICLES, including Ethelwerd's Chronicle, Asser's Life of Alfred, Geoffrey of Monmouth's British History, Gildas, Nennius, and the spurious chronicle of Richard of Cirencester. Edited by J. A. Giles, D.C.L. 5s.

OMAN (J. C.) The Great Indian Epics: the Stories of the RAMAYANA and the MAHABHARATA. By John Campbell Oman, Principal of Khalsa College, Amritsar. With Notes, Appendices, and Illustrations. 3s. 6d.

ORDERICUS VITALIS' Ecclesiastical History of England and Normandy. Translated by T. Forester, M.A. To which is added the CHRONICLE OF ST. EVROULT. 4 vols. 5s. each.
[Vols. II. and IV. out of print.

OVID'S Works, complete. Literally translated into Prose. 3 vols. 5s. each.

PASCAL'S Thoughts. Translated from the Text of M. Auguste Molinier by C. Kegan Paul. 3rd Edition. 3s. 6d.

PAULI'S (Dr. R.) Life of Alfred the Great. Translated from the German. To which is appended Alfred's ANGLO-SAXON VERSION OF OROSIUS. With a literal Translation interpaged, Notes, and an ANGLO-SAXON GRAMMAR and GLOSSARY, by B. Thorpe. 5s.

PAUSANIAS' Description of Greece. Newly translated by A. R. Shilleto, M.A. 2 vols. 5s. each.

PEARSON'S Exposition of the Creed. Edited by E. Walford, M.A. 5s.

PEPYS' Diary and Correspondence. Deciphered by the Rev. J. Smith, M.A., from the original Shorthand MS. in the Pepysian Library. Edited by Lord Braybrooke. 4 vols. With 31 Engravings. 5s. each.

PERCY'S Reliques of Ancient English Poetry. With an Essay on Ancient Minstrels and a Glossary. Edited by J. V. Pritchard, A.M. 2 vols. 3s. 6d. each.

PERSIUS.—See JUVENAL.

PETRARCH'S Sonnets, Triumphs, and other Poems. Translated into English Verse by various Hands. With a Life of the Poet by Thomas Campbell. With Portrait and 15 Steel Engravings. 5s.

PICKERING'S History of the Races of Man, and their Geographical Distribution. With AN

ANALYTICAL SYNOPSIS OF THE NATURAL HISTORY OF MAN by Dr. Hall. With a Map of the World and 12 coloured Plates. 5s.

PINDAR. Translated into Prose by Dawson W. Turner. To which is added the Metrical Version by Abraham Moore. 5s.

PLANCHÉ. History of British Costume, from the Earliest Time to the Close of the Eighteenth Century. By J. R. Planché, Somerset Herald. With upwards of 400 Illustrations. 5s.

PLATO'S Works. Literally translated, with Introduction and Notes. 6 vols. 5s. each.
 I.—The Apology of Socrates, Crito, Phædo, Gorgias, Protagoras, Phædrus, Theætetus, Euthyphron, Lysis. Translated by the Rev. H. Carey.
 II.—The Republic, Timæus, and Critias. Translated by Henry Davis.
 III.—Meno, Euthydemus, The Sophist, Statesman, Cratylus, Parmenides, and the Banquet. Translated by G. Burges.
 IV.—Philebus, Charmides, Laches, Menexenus, Hippias, Ion, The Two Alcibiades, Theages, Rivals, Hipparchus, Minos, Clitopho, Epistles. Translated by G. Burges.
 V.—The Laws. Translated by G. Burges.
 VI.—The Doubtful Works. Translated by G. Burges.

—— Summary and Analysis of the Dialogues. With Analytical Index. By A. Day, LL.D. 5s.

PLAUTUS'S Comedies. Translated by H. T. Riley, M.A. 2 vols. 5s. each.

PLINY. The Letters of Pliny the Younger. Melmoth's translation, revised by the Rev. F. C. T. Bosanquet, M.A. 5s.

PLOTINUS, Select Works of. Translated by Thomas Taylor. With an Introduction containing the substance of Porphyry's Plotinus. Edited by G. R. S. Mead, B.A., M.R.A.S. 5s.

PLUTARCH'S Lives. Translated by A. Stewart, M.A., and George Long, M.A. 4 vols. 3s. 6d. each.

—— Morals. Theosophical Essays. Translated by C. W. King, M.A. 5s.

—— Morals. Ethical Essays. Translated by the Rev. A. R. Shilleto, M.A. 5s.

POETRY OF AMERICA. Selections from One Hundred American Poets, from 1776 to 1876. By W. J. Linton. 3s. 6d.

POLITICAL CYCLOPÆDIA. A Dictionary of Political, Constitutional, Statistical, and Forensic Knowledge; forming a Work of Reference on subjects of Civil Administration, Political Economy, Finance, Commerce, Laws, and Social Relations. 4 vols. 3s. 6d. each.
[Vol. I. out of print.]

POPE'S Poetical Works. Edited, with copious Notes, by Robert Carruthers. With numerous Illustrations. 2 vols. 5s. each.
[Vol. I. out of print.]

—— Homer's Iliad. Edited by the Rev. J. S. Watson, M.A. Illustrated by the entire Series of Flaxman's Designs. 5s.

—— Homer's Odyssey, with the Battle of Frogs and Mice, Hymns, &c., by other translators. Edited by the Rev. J. S. Watson, M.A. With the entire Series of Flaxman's Designs. 5s.

—— Life, including many of his Letters. By Robert Carruthers. With numerous Illustrations. 5s.

POUSHKIN'S Prose Tales: The Captain's Daughter—Doubrovsky — The Queen of Spades — An Amateur Peasant Girl—The Shot —The Snow Storm—The Postmaster — The Coffin Maker — Kirdjali—The Egyptian Nights—Peter the Great's Negro. Translated by T. Keane. 3s. 6d.

PRESCOTT'S Conquest of Mexico. Copyright edition, with the notes by John Foster Kirk, and an introduction by G. P. Winship. 3 vols. 3s. 6d. each.

—— Conquest of Peru. Copyright edition, with the notes of John Foster Kirk. 2 vols. 3s. 6d. each.

—— Reign of Ferdinand and Isabella. Copyright edition, with the notes of John Foster Kirk. 3 vols. 3s. 6d. each.

PROPERTIUS. Translated by Rev. P. J. F. Gantillon, M.A., and accompanied by Poetical Versions, from various sources. 3s. 6d.

PROVERBS, Handbook of. Containing an entire Republication of Ray's Collection of English Proverbs, with his additions from Foreign Languages and a complete Alphabetical Index; in which are introduced large additions as well of Proverbs as of Sayings, Sentences, Maxims, and Phrases, collected by H. G. Bohn. 5s.

POTTERY AND PORCELAIN, and other Objects of Vertu. Comprising an Illustrated Catalogue of the Bernal Collection of Works of Art, with the prices at which they were sold by auction, and names of the possessors. To which are added, an Introductory Lecture on Pottery and Porcelain, and an Engraved List of all the known Marks and Monograms. By Henry G. Bohn. With numerous Wood Engravings, 5s.; or with Coloured Illustrations, 10s. 6d.

PROUT'S (Father) Reliques. Collected and arranged by Rev. F. Mahony. New issue, with 21 Etchings by D. Maclise, R.A. Nearly 600 pages. 5s.

QUINTILIAN'S Institutes of Oratory, or Education of an Orator. Translated by the Rev. J. S. Watson, M.A. 2 vols. 5s.

RACINE'S (Jean) Dramatic Works. A metrical English Version. By R. Bruce Boswell, M.A. Oxon. 2 vols. 3s. 6d. each.

RANKE'S History of the Popes, during the Last Four Centuries. Translated by E. Foster. Mrs. Foster's translation revised, with considerable additions, by G. R. Dennis, B.A. 3 vols. 3s. 6d. each.

—— History of Servia and the Servian Revolution. With an Account of the Insurrection in Bosnia. Translated by Mrs. Kerr. 3s. 6d.

RECREATIONS in SHOOTING. By 'Craven.' With 62 Engravings on Wood after Harvey, and 9 Engravings on Steel, chiefly after A. Cooper, R.A. 5s.

RENNIE'S Insect Architecture. Revised and enlarged by Rev. J. G. Wood, M.A. With 186 Woodcut Illustrations. 5s.

REYNOLDS' (Sir J.) Literary Works. Edited by H. W. Beechy. 2 vols. 3s. 6d. each.

RICARDO on the Principles of Political Economy and Taxation. Edited by E. C. K. Gonner, M.A. 5s.

RICHTER (Jean Paul Friedrich). Levana, a Treatise on Education: together with the Autobiography (a Fragment), and a short Prefatory Memoir. 3s. 6d.

RICHTER (Jean Paul Friedrich). Flower, Fruit, and Thorn Pieces, or the Wedded Life, Death, and Marriage of Firmian Stanislaus Siebenkaes, Parish Advocate in the Parish of Kuhschnapptel. Newly translated by Lt.-Col. Alex. Ewing. 3s. 6d.

ROGER DE HOVEDEN'S Annals of English History, comprising the History of England and of other Countries of Europe from A.D. 732 to A.D. 1201. Translated by H. T. Riley, M.A. 2 vols. 5s. each.

ROGER OF WENDOVER'S Flowers of History, comprising the History of England from the Descent of the Saxons to A.D. 1235, formerly ascribed to Matthew Paris. Translated by J. A. Giles, D.C.L. 2 vols. 5s. each.
[*Vol. II. out of print.*

ROME in the NINETEENTH CENTURY. Containing a complete Account of the Ruins of the Ancient City, the Remains of the Middle Ages, and the Monuments of Modern Times. By C. A. Eaton. With 34 Steel Engravings. 2 vols. 5s. each.

—— *See* BURN.

ROSCOE'S (W.) Life and Pontificate of Leo X. Final edition, revised by Thomas Roscoe. 2 vols. 3s. 6d. each.

—— Life of Lorenzo de' Medici, called 'the Magnificent.' With his poems, letters, &c. 10th Edition, revised, with Memoir of Roscoe by his Son. 3s. 6d.

RUSSIA. History of, from the earliest Period, compiled from the most authentic sources by Walter K. Kelly. With Portraits. 2 vols. 3s. 6d. each.

SALLUST, FLORUS, and VELLEIUS PATERCULUS. Trans. by J. S. Watson, M.A. 5s.

SCHILLER'S Works. Translated by various hands. 7 vols. 3s. 6d. each :—

I.—History of the Thirty Years' War.

II.—History of the Revolt in the Netherlands, the Trials of Counts Egmont and Horn, the Siege of Antwerp, and the Disturbances in France preceding the Reign of Henry IV.

III.—Don Carlos, Mary Stuart, Maid of Orleans, Bride of Messina, together with the Use of the Chorus in Tragedy (a short Essay).
These Dramas are all translated in metre.

IV.—Robbers (with Schiller's original Preface), Fiesco, Love and Intrigue, Demetrius, Ghost Seer, Sport of Divinity.
The Dramas in this volume are translated into Prose.

V.—Poems.

VI.—Essays, Æsthetical and Philosophical.

VII.—Wallenstein's Camp, Piccolomini and Death of Wallenstein, William Tell.

SCHILLER and GOETHE. Correspondence between, from A.D. 1794–1805. Translated by L. Dora Schmitz. 2 vols. 3s. 6d. each.

SCHLEGEL'S (F.) Lectures on the Philosophy of Life and the Philosophy of Language. Translated by the Rev. A. J. W. Morrison, M.A. 3s. 6d.

—— Lectures on the History of Literature, Ancient and Modern. Translated from the German. 3s. 6d.

—— Lectures on the Philosophy of History. Translated by J. B. Robertson. 3s. 6d.

SCHLEGEL'S Lectures on Modern History, together with the Lectures entitled Cæsar and Alexander, and The Beginning of our History. Translated by L. Purcell and R. H. Whitetock. 3s. 6d.

—— Æsthetic and Miscellaneous Works. Translated by E. J. Millington. 3s. 6d.

SCHLEGEL'S (A. W.) Lectures on Dramatic Art and Literature. Translated by J. Black. Revised Edition, by the Rev. A. J. W. Morrison, M.A. 3s. 6d.

SCHOPENHAUER on the Fourfold Root of the Principle of Sufficient Reason, and On the Will in Nature. Translated by Madame Hillebrand. 5s.

—— Essays. Selected and Translated. With a Biographical Introduction and Sketch of his Philosophy, by E. Belfort Bax. 5s.

SCHOUW'S Earth, Plants, and Man. Translated by A. Henfrey. With coloured Map of the Geography of Plants. 5s.

SCHUMANN (Robert). His Life and Works, by August Reissmann. Translated by A. L. Alger. 3s. 6d.

—— Early Letters. Originally published by his Wife. Translated by May Herbert. With a Preface by Sir George Grove, D.C.L. 3s. 6d.

SENECA on Benefits. Newly translated by A. Stewart, M.A. 3s. 6d.

—— Minor Essays and On Clemency. Translated by A. Stewart, M.A. 5s.

SHAKESPEARE DOCUMENTS. Arranged by D. H. Lambert, B.A. 3s. 6d.

SHAKESPEARE'S Dramatic Art. The History and Character of Shakespeare's Plays. By Dr. Hermann Ulrici. Translated by L. Dora Schmitz. 2 vols. 3s. 6d. each.

SHAKESPEARE (William). A Literary Biography by Karl Elze, Ph.D., LL.D. Translated by L. Dora Schmitz. 5s.

SHARPE (S.) The History of Egypt, from the Earliest Times till the Conquest by the Arabs, A.D. 640. By Samuel Sharpe. 2 Maps and upwards of 400 Illustrative Woodcuts. 2 vols. 5s. each.

SHERIDAN'S Dramatic Works, Complete. With Life by G. G. S. 3s. 6d.

SISMONDI'S History of the Literature of the South of Europe. Translated by Thomas Roscoe. 2 vols. 3s. 6d. each.

SMITH'S Synonyms and Antonyms, or Kindred Words and their Opposites. Revised Edition. 5s.

—— Synonyms Discriminated. A Dictionary of Synonymous Words in the English Language, showing the Accurate signification of words of similar meaning. Edited by the Rev. H. Percy Smith, M.A. 6s.

SMITH'S (Adam) The Wealth of Nations. Edited by E. Belfort Bax. 2 vols. 3s. 6d. each.

—— Theory of Moral Sentiments. With a Memoir of the Author by Dugald Stewart. 3s. 6d.

SMYTH'S (Professor) Lectures on Modern History. 2 vols. 3s. 6d. each.

—— Lectures on the French Revolution. 2 vols. 3s. 6d. each. [*Vol. I. out of print.*

SMITH'S (Pye) Geology and Scripture. 2nd Edition. 5s.

SMOLLETT'S Adventures of Roderick Random. With short Memoir and Bibliography, and Cruikshank's Illustrations. 3s. 6d.

—— Adventures of Peregrine Pickle. With Bibliography and Cruikshank's Illustrations. 2 vols. 3s. 6d. each.

—— The Expedition of Humphry Clinker. With Bibliography and Cruikshank's Illustrations. 3s. 6d.

SOCRATES (surnamed 'Scholasticus'). The Ecclesiastical History of (A.D. 305-445). Translated from the Greek. 5s.

SOPHOCLES, The Tragedies of. A New Prose Translation, with Memoir, Notes, &c., by E. P. Coleridge, M.A. 5s.

SOUTHEY'S Life of Nelson. With Portraits, Plans, and upwards of 50 Engravings on Steel and Wood. 5s.

—— Life of Wesley, and the Rise and Progress of Methodism. 5s.

—— Robert Southey. The Story of his Life written in his Letters. Edited by John Dennis. 3s. 6d.

SOZOMEN'S Ecclesiastical History. Translated from the Greek. Together with the ECCLESIASTICAL HISTORY OF PHILOSTORGIUS, as epitomised by Photius. Translated by Rev. E. Walford, M.A. 5s.

SPINOZA'S Chief Works. Translated, with Introduction, by R. H. M. Elwes. 2 vols. 5s. each.

STANLEY'S Classified Synopsis of the Principal Painters of the Dutch and Flemish Schools. By George Stanley. 5s.

STAUNTON'S Chess-Player's Handbook. 5s.

—— Chess Praxis. A Supplement to the Chess-player's Handbook. 5s.

—— Chess-player's Companion. Comprising a Treatise on Odds, Collection of Match Games, and a Selection of Original Problems. 5s.

—— Chess Tournament of 1851. With Introduction and Notes. 5s.

STOCKHARDT'S Experimental Chemistry. Edited by C. W. Heaton, F.C.S. 5s.

STOWE (Mrs. H. B.) Uncle Tom's Cabin. Illustrated. 3s. 6d.

STRABO'S Geography. Translated by W. Falconer, M.A., and H. C. Hamilton. 3 vols. 5s. each.

STRICKLAND'S (Agnes) Lives of the Queens of England, from the Norman Conquest. Revised Edition. With 6 Portraits. 6 vols. 5s. each.

—— Life of Mary Queen of Scots. 2 vols. 5s. each.

—— Lives of the Tudor and Stuart Princesses. With Portraits. 5s.

STUART and REVETT'S Antiquities of Athens, and other Monuments of Greece. With 71 Plates engraved on Steel, and numerous Woodcut Capitals. 5s.

SUETONIUS' Lives of the Twelve Cæsars and Lives of the Grammarians. Thomson's translation, revised by T. Forester. 5s.

SWIFT'S Prose Works. Edited by Temple Scott. With a Biographical Introduction by the Right Hon. W. E. H. Lecky, M.P.

With Portraits and Facsimiles. 12 vols. 5s. each.
  I.—A Tale of a Tub, The Battle of the Books, and other early works. Edited by Temple Scott. With a Biographical Introduction by W. E. H. Lecky.
  II.—The Journal to Stella. Edited by Frederick Ryland, M.A. With 2 Portraits and Facsimile.
  III. & IV.—Writings on Religion and the Church.
  V.—Historical and Political Tracts (English).
  VI.—The Drapier's Letters. With facsimiles of Wood's Coinage, &c.
  VII.—Historical and Political Tracts (Irish).
  VIII.—Gulliver's Travels. Edited by G. R. Dennis, B.A. With Portrait and Maps.
  IX.—Contributions to Periodicals.
  X.—Historical Writings.
  XI.—Literary Essays.
  XII.—Full Index and Bibliography, with Essays on the Portraits of Swift by Sir Frederick Falkiner, and on the Relations beween Swift and Stella by the Very Rev. Dean Bernard.

TACITUS. The Works of. Literally translated. 2 vols. 5s. each.

TASSO'S Jerusalem Delivered. Translated into English Spenserian Verse by J. H. Wiffen. With 8 Engravings on Steel and 24 Woodcuts by Thurston. 5s.

TAYLOR'S (Bishop Jeremy) Holy Living and Dying. 3s. 6d.

TEN BRINK.—See BRINK.

TERENCE and PHÆDRUS. Literally translated by H. T. Riley, M.A. To which is added, Smart's Metrical Version of Phædrus. 5s.

THEOCRITUS, BION, MOSCHUS, and TYRTÆUS. Literally translated by the Rev. J. Banks, M.A. To which are appended the Metrical Versions of Chapman. 5s.

THEODORET and EVAGRIUS. Histories of the Church from A.D. 332 to A.D. 427; and from A.D. 431 to A.D. 544. Translated. 5s.

THIERRY'S History of the Conquest of England by the Normans. Translated by William Hazlitt. 2 vols. 3s. 6d. each.

THUCYDIDES. The Peloponnesian War. Literally translated by the Rev. H. Dale. 2 vols. 3s. 6d. each.

—— **An Analysis and Summary of.** By J. T. Wheeler. 5s.

THUDICHUM (J. L. W.) A Treatise on Wines. Illustrated. 5s.

URE'S (Dr. A.) Cotton Manufacture of Great Britain. Edited by P. L. Simmonds. 2 vols. 5s. each.

—— **Philosophy of Manufactures.** Edited by P. L. Simmonds. 7s. 6d.

VASARI'S Lives of the most Eminent Painters, Sculptors, and Architects. Translated by Mrs. J. Foster, with a Commentary by J. P. Richter, Ph.D. 6 vols. 3s. 6d. each.

VIRGIL. A Literal Prose Translation by A. Hamilton Bryce, LL.D. With Portrait. 3s. 6d.

VOLTAIRE'S Tales. Translated by R. B. Boswell. Containing Bebouc, Memnon, Candide, L'Ingénu, and other Tales. 3s. 6d.

WALTON'S Complete Angler. Edited by Edward Jesse. With Portrait and 203 Engravings on Wood and 26 Engravings on Steel. 5s.

WALTON'S Lives of Donne, Hooker, &c. New Edition revised by A. H. Bullen, with a Memoir of Izaak Walton by Wm. Dowling. With numerous Illustrations. 5s.

WELLINGTON, Life of. By 'An Old Soldier.' From the materials of Maxwell. With Index and 18 Steel Engravings. 5s.

—— Victories of. *See* MAXWELL.

WERNER'S Templars in Cyprus. Translated by E. A. M. Lewis. 3s. 6d.

WESTROPP (H. M.) A Handbook of Archæology, Egyptian, Greek, Etruscan, Roman. Illustrated. 5s.

WHEATLEY'S A Rational Illustration of the Book of Common Prayer. 3s. 6d.

WHITE'S Natural History of Selborne. With Notes by Sir William Jardine. Edited by Edward Jesse. With 40 Portraits and coloured Plates. 5s.

WIESELER'S Chronological Synopsis of the Four Gospels. Translated by the Rev. Canon Venables. 3s. 6d.

WILLIAM of MALMESBURY'S Chronicle of the Kings of England. Translated by the Rev. J. Sharpe. Edited by J. A. Giles, D.C.L. 5s.

XENOPHON'S Works. Translated by the Rev. J. S. Watson, M.A., and the Rev. H. Dale. In 3 vols. 5s. each.

YOUNG (Arthur). Travels in France during the years 1787, 1788, and 1789. Edited by M. Betham Edwards. 3s. 6d.

—— Tour in Ireland, with General Observations on the state of the country during the years 1776–79. Edited by A. W. Hutton. With Complete Bibliography by J. P. Anderson, and Map. 2 vols. 3s. 6d. each.

YULE-TIDE STORIES. A Collection of Scandinavian and North-German Popular Tales and Traditions. Edited by B. Thorpe. 5s.

BOHN'S LIBRARIES.

A SPECIAL OFFER.

MESSRS. BELL have made arrangements to supply selections of 100 or 50 volumes from these famous Libraries, for £11 11s. or £6 6s. net respectively. The volumes may be selected without any restriction from the full List of the Libraries, now numbering nearly 800 volumes.

WRITE FOR FULL PARTICULARS.

THE YORK LIBRARY
A NEW SERIES OF REPRINTS ON THIN PAPER.

With specially designed title-pages, binding, and end-papers.

Fcap. 8vo. in cloth, 2s. net;
In leather, 3s. net.

'The York Library is noticeable by reason of the wisdom and intelligence displayed in the choice of unhackneyed classics. . . . A most attractive series of reprints. . . . The size and style of the volumes are exactly what they should be.'—*Bookman.*

The following volumes are now ready:

CHARLOTTE BRONTË'S JANE EYRE.

BURNEY'S EVELINA. Edited, with an Introduction and Notes, by ANNIE RAINE ELLIS.

BURNEY'S CECILIA. Edited by ANNIE RAINE ELLIS. 2 vols.

BURTON'S ANATOMY OF MELANCHOLY. Edited by the Rev. A. R. SHILLETO, M.A., with Introduction by A. H. BULLEN. 3 vols.

BURTON'S (SIR RICHARD) PILGRIMAGE TO AL-MADINAH AND MECCAH. With Introduction by STANLEY LANE-POOLE. 2 vols.

CALVERLEY. THE IDYLLS OF THEOCRITUS, with the Eclogues of Virgil. Translated into English Verse by C. S. CALVERLEY. With an Introduction by R. Y. TYRRELL, Litt.D.

CERVANTES' DON QUIXOTE. MOTTEUX'S Translation, revised. With LOCKHART'S Life and Notes. 2 vols.

CLASSIC TALES: JOHNSON'S RASSELAS, GOLDSMITH'S VICAR OF WAKEFIELD, STERNE'S SENTIMENTAL JOURNEY, WALPOLE'S CASTLE OF OTRANTO. With Introduction by C. S. FEARENSIDE, M.A.

COLERIDGE'S AIDS TO REFLECTION, and the Confessions of an Inquiring Spirit.

COLERIDGE'S FRIEND. A series of Essays on Morals, Politics, and Religion.

COLERIDGE'S TABLE TALK AND OMNIANA. Arranged and Edited by T. ASHE, B.A.

COLERIDGE'S LECTURES AND NOTES ON SHAKE-SPEARE, and other English Poets. Edited by T. ASHE, B.A.

DRAPER'S HISTORY OF THE INTELLECTUAL DEVELOPMENT OF EUROPE. 2 vols.

EBERS' AN EGYPTIAN PRINCESS. Translated by E. S. BUCHHEIM.

GEORGE ELIOT'S ADAM BEDE.

EMERSON'S WORKS. A new edition in 5 volumes, with the Text edited and collated by GEORGE SAMPSON.

FIELDING'S TOM JONES (2 vols.), AMELIA (1 vol.), JOSEPH ANDREWS (1 vol.).

GASKELL'S SYLVIA'S LOVERS.

THE YORK LIBRARY—*continued.*

GESTA ROMANORUM, or Entertaining Moral Stories invented by the Monks. Translated from the Latin by the Rev. CHARLES SWAN. Revised edition, by WYNNARD HOOPER, M.A.

GOETHE'S FAUST. Translated by ANNA SWANWICK, LL.D. Revised edition, with an Introduction and Bibliography by KARL BREUL, Litt.D., Ph.D.

GOETHE'S POETRY AND TRUTH FROM MY OWN LIFE. Translated by M. STEELE-SMITH, with Introduction and Bibliography by KARL BREUL, Litt.D.

HAWTHORNE'S TRANSFORMATION (THE MARBLE FAUN).

HOOPER'S WATERLOO: THE DOWNFALL OF THE FIRST NAPOLEON. With Maps and Plans.

IRVING'S SKETCH BOOK.

IRVING'S BRACEBRIDGE HALL, OR THE HUMOURISTS.

JAMESON'S SHAKESPEARE'S HEROINES.

LAMB'S ESSAYS. Including the Essays of Elia, Last Essays of Elia, and Eliana.

MARCUS AURELIUS ANTONINUS, THE THOUGHTS OF. Translated by GEORGE LONG, M.A. With an Essay on Marcus Aurelius by MATTHEW ARNOLD.

MARRYAT'S MR. MIDSHIPMAN EASY. With 8 Illustrations. 1 vol. PETER SIMPLE. With 8 Illustrations. 1 vol.

MIGNET'S HISTORY OF THE FRENCH REVOLUTION, from 1789 to 1814.

MONTAIGNE'S ESSAYS. Cotton's translation. Revised by W. C. HAZLITT. 3 vols.

MOTLEY'S RISE OF THE DUTCH REPUBLIC. With a Biographical Introduction by MONCURE D. CONWAY. 3 vols.

PASCAL'S THOUGHTS. Translated from the Text of M. AUGUSTE MOLINIER by C. KEGAN PAUL. Third edition.

PLUTARCH'S LIVES. Translated, with Notes and a Life by AUBREY STEWART, M.A., and GEORGE LONG, M.A. 4 vols.

RANKE'S HISTORY OF THE POPES, during the Last Four Centuries. Mrs. Foster's translation. Revised by G. R. DENNIS. 3 vols.

SWIFT'S GULLIVER'S TRAVELS. Edited, with Introduction and Notes, by G. R. DENNIS, with facsimiles of the original illustrations.

SWIFT'S JOURNAL TO STELLA. Edited, with Introduction and Notes, by F. RYLAND, M.A.

TROLLOPE'S BARSETSHIRE NOVELS.—THE WARDEN (1 vol.), BARCHESTER TOWERS (1 vol.), DR. THORNE (1 vol.), FRAMLEY PARSONAGE (1 vol.), SMALL HOUSE AT ALLINGTON (2 vols.), LAST CHRONICLE OF BARSET (2 vols.).

VOLTAIRE'S ZADIG AND OTHER TALES. Translated by R. BRUCE BOSWELL.

ARTHUR YOUNG'S TRAVELS IN FRANCE, during the years 1787, 1788, and 1789. Edited with Introduction and Notes, by M. BETHAM EDWARDS.

Other Volumes are in Preparation.

MASTERS OF LITERATURE

Crown 8vo. 3s. 6d. net.

THIS Series aims at giving in a handy volume the finest passages from the writings of the greatest authors. Each volume is edited by a well-known scholar, and contains representative selections connected by editorial comments. The Editor also contributes a lengthy Introduction, biographical and literary. A Portrait will be included in each volume.

First List of Volumes:

SCOTT. By Professor A. J. GRANT.

THACKERAY. By G. K. CHESTERTON.

FIELDING. By Professor SAINTSBURY.

CARLYLE. By the Rev. A. W. EVANS.

DEFOE. By JOHN MASEFIELD.

DICKENS. By THOMAS SECCOMBE.

DE QUINCEY. By SIDNEY LOW.

EMERSON. By G. H. PERRIS.

HAZLITT. By E. V. LUCAS.

STERNE. By Dr. SIDNEY LEE.

BELL'S HANDBOOKS
OF
THE GREAT MASTERS
IN PAINTING AND SCULPTURE.

EDITED BY G. C. WILLIAMSON, LITT.D.

NEW AND CHEAPER REISSUE.

Post 8vo. With 40 Illustrations and Photogravure Frontispiece. 3s. 6d. net each.

The following Volumes have been issued:

BOTTICELLI. By A. STREETER. 2nd Edition.
BRUNELLESCHI. By LEADER SCOTT.
CORREGGIO. By SELWYN BRINTON, M.A. 2nd Edition.
CARLO CRIVELLI. By G. MCNEIL RUSHFORTH, M.A.
DELLA ROBBIA. By the MARCHESA BURLAMACCHI. 2nd Edition.
ANDREA DEL SARTO. By H. GUINNESS. 2nd Edition.
DONATELLO. By HOPE REA. 2nd Edition.
GERARD DOU. By Dr. W. MARTIN. Translated by Clara Bell.
GAUDENZIO FERRARI. By ETHEL HALSEY.
FRANCIA. By GEORGE C. WILLIAMSON, Litt.D.
GIORGIONE. By HERBERT COOK, M.A.
GIOTTO. By F. MASON PERKINS.
FRANS HALS. By GERALD S. DAVIES, M.A.
BERNARDINO LUINI. By GEORGE C. WILLIAMSON, Litt.D. 3rd Edition.
LEONARDO DA VINCI. By EDWARD MCCURDY, M.A.
MANTEGNA. By MAUD CRUTTWELL.
MEMLINC. By W. H. JAMES WEALE.
MICHEL ANGELO. By Lord RONALD SUTHERLAND GOWER, M.A., F.S.A.
PERUGINO. By G. C. WILLIAMSON, Litt.D. 2nd Edition.
PIERO DELLA FRANCESCA. By W. G. WATERS, M.A.
PINTORICCHIO. By EVELYN MARCH PHILLIPPS.
RAPHAEL. By H. STRACHEY. 2nd Edition.
REMBRANDT. By MALCOLM BELL. 2nd Edition.
RUBENS. By HOPE REA.
LUCA SIGNORELLI. By MAUD CRUTTWELL. 2nd Edition.
SODOMA. By the CONTESSA LORENZO PRIULI-BON.
TINTORETTO. By J. B. STOUGHTON HOLBORN, M.A.
VAN DYCK. By LIONEL CUST, M.V.O., F.S.A.
VELASQUEZ. By R. A. M. STEVENSON. 3rd Edition.
WATTEAU. By EDGCUMBE STALEY, B.A.
WILKIE. By Lord RONALD SUTHERLAND GOWER, M.A., F.S.A.

Write for Illustrated Prospectus.

New Editions, fcap. 8vo. 2s. 6d. each net.

THE ALDINE EDITION

OF THE

BRITISH POETS.

'This excellent edition of the English classics, with their complete texts and scholarly introductions, are something very different from the cheap volumes of extracts which are just now so much too common.'—*St. James's Gazette.*

'An excellent series. Small, handy, and complete.'—*Saturday Review.*

Blake. Edited by W. M. Rossetti.

Burns. Edited by G. A. Aitken. 3 vols.

Butler. Edited by R. B. Johnson. 2 vols.

Campbell. Edited by His Son-in-law, the Rev. A. W. Hill. With Memoir by W. Allingham.

Chatterton. Edited by the Rev. W. W. Skeat, M.A. 2 vols.

Chaucer. Edited by Dr. R. Morris, with Memoir by Sir H. Nicolas. 6 vols.

Churchill. Edited by Jas. Hannay. 2 vols.

Coleridge. Edited by T. Ashe, B.A. 2 vols.

Collins. Edited by W. Moy Thomas.

Cowper. Edited by John Bruce, F.S.A. 3 vols.

Dryden. Edited by the Rev. R. Hooper, M.A. 5 vols.

Goldsmith. Revised Edition by Austin Dobson. With Portrait.

Gray. Edited by J. Bradshaw, LL.D.

Herbert. Edited by the Rev. A. B. Grosart.

Herrick. Edited by George Saintsbury. 2 vols.

Keats. Edited by the late Lord Houghton.

Kirke White. Edited, with a Memoir, by Sir H. Nicolas.

Milton. Edited by Dr. Bradshaw. 2 vols.

Parnell. Edited by G. A. Aitken.

Pope. Edited by G. R. Dennis. With Memoir by John Dennis. 3 vols.

Prior. Edited by R. B. Johnson. 2 vols.

Raleigh and Wotton. With Selections from the Writings of other COURTLY POETS from 1540 to 1650. Edited by Ven. Archdeacon Hannah, D.C.L.

Rogers. Edited by Edward Bell, M.A.

Scott. Edited by John Dennis. 5 vols.

Shakespeare's Poems. Edited by Rev. A. Dyce.

Shelley. Edited by H. Buxton Forman. 5 vols.

Spenser. Edited by J. Payne Collier. 5 vols.

Surrey. Edited by J. Yeowell.

Swift. Edited by the Rev. J. Mitford. 3 vols.

Thomson. Edited by the Rev. D. C. Tovey. 2 vols.

Vaughan. Sacred Poems and Pious Ejaculations. Edited by the Rev. H. Lyte.

Wordsworth. Edited by Prof. Dowden. 7 vols.

Wyatt. Edited by J. Yeowell.

Young. 2 vols. Edited by the Rev. J. Mitford.

THE ALL-ENGLAND SERIES.
HANDBOOKS OF ATHLETIC GAMES.

'The best instruction on games and sports by the best authorities, at the lowest prices.'—*Oxford Magazine.*

Small 8vo. cloth, Illustrated. Price 1s. each.

Cricket. By FRED C. HOLLAND.
Cricket. By the Hon. and Rev. E. LYTTELTON.
Croquet. By Lieut.-Col. the Hon. H. C. NEEDHAM.
Lawn Tennis. By H. W. W. WILBERFORCE. With a Chapter for Ladies, by Mrs. HILLYARD.
Squash Tennis. By EUSTACE H. MILES. Double vol. 2s.
Tennis and Rackets and Fives. By JULIAN MARSHALL, Major J. SPENS, and Rev. J. A. ARNAN TAIT.
Golf. By H. S. C. EVERARD. Double vol. 2s.
Rowing and Sculling. By GUY RIXON.
Rowing and Sculling. By W. B. WOODGATE.
Sailing. By E. F. KNIGHT, dbl. vol. 2s.
Swimming. By MARTIN and J. RACSTER COBBETT.
Camping out. By A. A. MACDONELL. Double vol. 2s.
Canoeing. By Dr. J. D. HAYWARD. Double vol. 2s.
Mountaineering. By Dr. CLAUDE WILSON. Double vol. 2s.
Athletics. By H. H. GRIFFIN.
Riding. By W. A. KERR, V.C. Double vol. 2s.
Ladies' Riding. By W. A. KERR, V.C.
Boxing. By R. G. ALLANSON-WINN. With Prefatory Note by Bat Mullins.

Fencing. By H. A. COLMORE DUNN.
Cycling. By H. H. GRIFFIN, L.A.C., N.C.U., O.T.C. With a Chapter for Ladies, by Miss AGNES WOOD. Double vol. 2s.
Wrestling. By WALTER ARMSTRONG. New Edition.
Broadsword and Singlestick. By R. G. ALLANSON-WINN and C. PHILLIPPS-WOLLEY.
Gymnastics. By A. F. JENKIN. Double vol. 2s.
Gymnastic Competition and Display Exercises. Compiled by F. GRAF.
Indian Clubs. By G. T. B. COBBETT and A. F. JENKIN.
Dumb-bells. By F. GRAF.
Football — Rugby Game. By HARRY VASSALL.
Football — Association Game. By C. W. ALCOCK. Revised Edition.
Hockey. By F. S. CRESWELL. New Edition.
Skating. By DOUGLAS ADAMS. With a Chapter for Ladies, by Miss L. CHEETHAM, and a Chapter on Speed Skating, by a Fen Skater. Dbl. vol. 2s.
Baseball. By NEWTON CRANE.
Rounders, Fieldball, Bowls, Quoits, Curling, Skittles, &c. By J. M. WALKER and C. C. MOTT.
Dancing. By EDWARD SCOTT. Double vol. 2s.

THE CLUB SERIES OF CARD AND TABLE GAMES.

'No well-regulated club or country house should be without this useful series of books.'—*Globe.* Small 8vo. cloth, Illustrated. Price 1s. each.

Bridge. By 'TEMPLAR.'
Whist. By Dr. WM. POLE, F.R.S.
Solo Whist. By ROBERT F. GREEN.
Billiards. By Major-Gen. A. W. DRAYSON, F.R.A.S. With a Preface by W. J. Peall.
Hints on Billiards. By J. P. BUCHANAN. Double vol. 2s.
Chess. By ROBERT F. GREEN.
The Two-Move Chess Problem. By B. G. LAWS.
Chess Openings. By I GUNSBERG.
Draughts and Backgammon. By 'BERKELEY.'
Reversi and Go Bang. By 'BERKELEY.'

Dominoes and Solitaire. By 'BERKELEY.'
Bézique and Cribbage. By 'BERKELEY.'
Écarté and Euchre. By 'BERKELEY.'
Piquet and Rubicon Piquet. By 'BERKELEY.'
Skat. By LOUIS DIEHL.
*** A Skat Scoring-book. 1s.
Round Games, including Poker, Napoleon, Loo, Vingt-et-un, &c. By BAXTER-WRAY.
Parlour and Playground Games. By Mrs. LAURENCE GOMME.

www.ingramcontent.com/pod-product-compliance
Lightning Source LLC
Chambersburg PA
CBHW021158230426
43667CB00006B/458